Organizational Change, Leadership and Ethics

Given recent financial crises and scandals, the rise of corporate social responsibility and the challenge of environmental, socio-cultural and economic sustainability, few would disagree that the role of ethics has taken centre stage in the management of organizations. In reality, however, organizations have found it extremely difficult to promote successful, ethical behaviour as this rarely results in short-term gains that can be appraised and rewarded.

By and Burnes bring together leading international scholars in the fields of organizational change and leadership to explore and understand the context, theory and successful promotion of ethical behaviour in organizations. By focusing on real-world examples, contributors analyse the issues and challenges that hinder the ethical change leadership required to lead sustainable organizations.

This unique volume brings together the worlds of organizational change, leadership, business ethics and corporate social responsibility, resulting in a book that will be valuable reading in all four fields. With contributions from leading scholars, including David Boje, Dexter Dunphy, Suzanne Benn and Carl Rhodes, *Organizational Change, Leadership and Ethics* is a must-read.

Rune Todnem By is Academic Group Leader (Organizational Behaviour, Leadership and Change) at Staffordshire University Business School, UK. He is editor-in-chief of the *Journal of Change Management* and co-editor of *Managing Organizational Change in Public Services* (2009, Routledge). His research interests span organizational behaviour, organizational change, leadership, ethics and public services management.

Bernard Burnes is Professor of Organizational Change at the Manchester Business School at the University of Manchester, UK. His teaching and research cover organizational change in its broadest sense. This includes the history, development and current state of organizational change, organizational and inter-organizational behaviour, leadership, strategy and culture. He is co-editor of *The Routledge Companion to Organizational Change* (2011).

Understanding Organizational Change

Series editor:
Professor Bernard Burnes

The management of change is now acknowledged as being one of the most important issues facing management today. By focusing on particular perspectives and approaches to change, particular change situations, and particular types of organization, this series provides a comprehensive overview and an in-depth understanding of the field of organizational change.

Organizational Change, Leadership and Ethics

Leading organizations towards sustainability

Edited by
Rune Todnem By and Bernard Burnes

Routledge
Taylor & Francis Group

LONDON AND NEW YORK

First published 2013
by Routledge
2 Park Square, Milton Park, Abingdon, Oxon OX14 4RN

Simultaneously published in the USA and Canada
by Routledge
711 Third Avenue, New York, NY 10017

Routledge is an imprint of the Taylor & Francis Group, an informa business

British Library Cataloguing in Publication Data
A catalogue record for this book is available from the British Library

Library of Congress Cataloging in Publication Data
  Organizational change, leadership and ethics :
  leading organizations toward sustainability /
  edited by Rune Todnem By and Bernard Burnes.
  p. cm.—(Understanding organizational change)
  Includes bibliographical references and index.
  1. Organizational change—Moral and ethical aspects.
  2. Leadership—Moral and ethical aspects.
  3. Social responsibility of business. 4. Business ethics.
  I. By, Rune Todnem. II. Burnes, Bernard, 1953–
  HD58.8.O7295 2012
  658.4'092—dc23
  2012003293

ISBN: 978–0–415–59244–4 (hbk)
ISBN: 978–0–203–10601–3 (ebk)

Typeset in Times New Roman
by Swales & Willis Ltd, Exeter, Devon

Contents

Tables and figures

Tables

Figures

The authors

Suzanne Benn is Professor of Sustainable Enterprise at the UTS Business School, University of Technology, Sydney, Australia. Suzanne has a background in the sciences and the social sciences. Her current research interests range across corporate sustainability and corporate social responsibility, business education for sustainability and organizational change and development for sustainability. Her interdisciplinary academic publications include four books and more than 90 refereed journal articles, book chapters and refereed conference papers. Email: suzanne.benn@uts.edu.au

David M. Boje is a Bill Daniels Ethics Fellow and Professor in Business Administration in the Management Department at New Mexico State University, USA. His main research is the interplay of storytelling, ontology and complexity. He has published 130 articles and 17 books. Email: dboje@nmsu.edu

Bernard Burnes is Professor of Organizational Change at the Manchester Business School at the University of Manchester, UK. His teaching and research cover organizational change in its broadest sense. This includes the history, development and current state of organizational change, organizational and inter-organizational behaviour, leadership, strategy and culture. He is co-editor of *The Routledge Companion to Organizational Change* (2011).

Rune Todnem By is Academic Group Leader (Organizational Behaviour, Leadership and Change) at Staffordshire University Business School, UK, and Editor-in-Chief of Routledge's *Journal of Change Management*. His primary research interests are change management in society and organizations, leadership and organizational ethics. Email: r.t.by@staffs.ac.uk

Judith A. Clair is an Associate Professor of Organization Studies
at Boston College, USA. Judith received her PhD in organizational
behaviour from the University of Southern California. Her research
interests are social identities at work and impacts of critical events, such
as crises and downsizing, on individuals and organizations. Judith's work
has appeared in *Academy of Management Review, Human Relations,
Organizational Dynamics, Academy of Management Executive,
SAM Advanced Management Journal, Research in Corporate Social
Performance and Policy, Industrial and Environmental Crisis Quarterly,
Technological Forecasting and Social Change* and *Advances in
Qualitative Organizational Research.* Email: judith.clair@bc.edu

Thomas Diefenbach is Associate Professor of Business Ethics at
Ritsumeikan Asia Pacific University (APU), Japan. In his research,
Thomas investigates primarily the problematic existence and relationships
of individuals within all types of organizations and societies, different
forms of organizations, and the fundamental principles of past, present
and future societies. He reasons about these phenomena mainly from
socio-philosophical, organization-theoretical and critical perspectives.
Thomas is particularly interested in identifying, investigating and
developing non-hierarchical structures and processes as well as alternative
and innovative forms of management, organizations and societies. He is
an editorial board member of the *Journal of Change Management* and the
author of *Management and the Dominance of Managers* (2009). Thomas'
work has been published in *Organization Studies, Public Administration*
and the *Journal of Organizational Change Management.* Email:
tdiefenb@apu.ac.jp

Ronald L. Dufresne is an Assistant Professor of Leadership at Saint
Joseph's University in Philadelphia, USA. His research interests include
the roles of integrity, hypocrisy and vulnerability in authentic leadership;
the leadership processes that promote individual, team and organization
learning from critical incidents; and organizational factors and practices
that enable the development of ethical leaders. He has published 15
journal articles and book chapters in outlets including the *Journal of
Business Ethics, Human Relations, Human Resource Management* and the
Journal of Management Inquiry. Email: ron.dufresne@sju.edu

Dexter Dunphy is Emeritus Professor and Senior Associate, Centre
for Corporate Governance in the Faculty of Business, University of
Technology, Sydney, Australia. He has an international reputation
for thought leadership, research and consulting on the management
of organizational change and corporate sustainability, and has held

visiting professorships at major international universities. He has written or edited 24 books and over 90 journal articles and chapters. Dexter is a member of the Westpac Community Consultative Council and was Foundation Director of the Centre for Corporate Change at the Australian Graduate School of Management. Dexter has consulted widely on large-scale corporate change and actively supports and documents sustainability initiatives in leading companies. Email: dexter. dunphy@gmail.com

Henrika Franck is a post doc researcher at the Hanken School of Economics in Helsinki. Henrika's research focuses on strategies used by organizations and individuals in the management of change, with a particular emphasis on the construction and interpretation of ethical issues. Email: henrika.franck@hanken.fi

Malcolm Higgs is Professor of Organisational Behaviour and HR Management at the University of Southampton School of Management, UK. He is involved in researching, teaching and consulting in the field of organizational change with an emphasis on the role of leaders in change implementation. Malcolm has authored over 60 journal papers and book chapters and seven books as well as being the co-developer of two psychometric instruments. His current research focus is on understanding the antecedents and consequences of narcissistic leadership behaviours. Email: Malcolm.higgs@soton.ac.uk

Saku Mantere is Professor of Management and Organization, Hanken School of Economics and Business Administration, Helsinki, Finland. His research is focused on what makes organizations strategic and how strategic management affects organizations. He is particularly interested in strategic change, middle management agency and strategy discourse. His work has been published in such journals as the *Academy of Management Review*, *Academy of Management Journal*, *Organization Science*, *Journal of Management Studies* and *Strategic Organization*. Saku is Associate Editor of the *Scandinavian Journal of Management* and was co-editor of the *Journal of Management Studies'* special issue on 'Strategy as Discourse'. Email: saku.mantere@hanken.fi

Rebecca Newton is a business psychologist and an expert in leadership development and change leadership, with a PhD from the London School of Economics and Political Science. She is a Visiting Fellow in the Department of Management at the London School of Economics, UK, where she lectures in Leadership, is part of the global faculty team for Duke Corporate Education, and was formerly a Visiting Fellow at

Harvard University. Her research interests span a wide range of leadership development and change management issues. She is published in the *Journal of Change Management* where she now serves on the editorial board. Rebecca runs her own London-based consulting practice and has acted as a special advisor, facilitator and coach to senior executives and professionals from some of the world's leading organizations over more than ten years, working internationally in the private and public sectors. Email: r.l.newton@lse.ac.uk

Moritz Patzer holds a PhD in Business Studies from the University of Zurich, Switzerland. He is a research fellow at the Institute of Business Administration (IBW) at the Chair of Prof. Scherer. His research is focused on leadership ethics, business ethics, theories of the firm and the philosophy of science, about which he has edited and published several books and articles. Email: moritz.patzer@patzerverlag.de

Carl Rhodes is Professor of Management at the University of Leicester, UK. His research focuses on critically interrogating the narration and representation of organizational experience in practice and popular culture, with a particular concern with the possibilities for organizational ethics and responsibility. Carl's most recent books are *Organizations and Popular Culture* (Routledge, 2012, co-edited with Simon Lilley), *Bits of Organization* (Liber, 2009, co-edited with Alison Pullen) and *Critical Representations of Work and Organization in Popular Culture* (Routledge, 2008, co-authored with Robert Westwood). Email: c.rhodes@le.ac.uk

Rohny Saylors is a Ph.D. student at New Mexico State University, USA. His work with practical pragmatism adds to the conversation started by Jörgen Sandburg and Haridimous Tsoukas regarding practical rationality, and the conversation started by Karl Weick regarding the value of pragmatism. Practical pragmatism combines the existential ontology of Heidegger with the pragmatic functionalist psychology and sociology of James, Dewey and Mead. Email: rsaylors@gmail.com

Aaron C.T. Smith is Professor and Deputy Pro-Vice Chancellor at the Royal Melbourne Institute of Technology (RMIT University), Australia. He has research interests in the management of psychological, organizational and policy change in business, sport and health. Aaron also has an extensive background in organizational consulting, having worked in the Asia-Pacific, Europe, North America and the Middle East for clients in a diverse range of sectors and industries, including multinational corporations, professional sporting clubs, national and state sport associations, media companies, sport and entertainment facilities, government and not-for-profit organizations. Email: aaron.smith@rmit.edu.au

Fiona Sutherland is a Senior Lecturer in the Graduate School of Management at La Trobe University in Melbourne, Australia. Her principal areas of research are in organizational studies, and organizational analysis and change. Fiona's journal article publications focus in particular on organizational dualities and changing forms of organization. She is also co-author with Professor Aaron Smith (RMIT University) of a 2011 research book titled *Philosophies of Organizational Change*. Fiona serves on the editorial board of the *Journal of Change Management*. Email: fiona.sutherland@latrobe.edu.au

Christian Voegtlin holds a PhD in Business Administration from the University of Zurich, Switzerland. He works as a senior researcher and lecturer for the Institute of Business Administration (IBW) at the Chair of Prof. Scherer. He has recently published his PhD thesis and articles in the *Journal of Business Ethics* on responsible leadership. His main research interests are in responsible and ethical leadership, business ethics and corporate social responsibility, and work motivation. Email: christian.voegtlin@uzh.ch

Series editor's preface

The belief that organizations should be run on an ethical basis has a long history. From the earliest days of the Industrial Revolution onwards, far-sighted industrialists, like Robert Owen and Titus Salt in textiles, and George Cadbury and Joseph Rowntree in confectionery, tried to run their businesses on ethical lines. In the 1930s and 1940s, both business leaders, such as Chester Barnard, and influential academics, such as Kurt Lewin, promoted ethical approaches to leading and changing organisations. In the last two decades, this process has been encouraged by international bodies, national governments and NGOs through such initiatives as Corporate Social Responsibility and the Fairtrade movement. Despite this, as the 2008 global financial crisis and other business scandals have revealed, unethical and criminal behaviour appears to have mushroomed out of control in many organisations, and many business leaders seem to have adopted as their motto Gordon Gekko's infamous slogan: 'greed is good'.

Therefore, a book which addresses the relationship between ethics, leadership and change is both timely and welcome. Though ethical behaviour and values lie at the core of the OD approach to change, from the 1980s other approaches have emerged which have a far more ambiguous relationship with ethics. In an era where rapid and often brutal change became the order of the day, OD was criticised as too slow and too piecemeal. Instead, a plethora of approaches began to emerge which, whilst not easy to classify, might be described as anti-OD. These newer approaches to change were less wary than OD of embracing and using power and politics to promote organizational change. Unfortunately, as political behaviour became more 'respectable', ethical behaviour was sidelined. However, in recent years, there has been a resurgence of interest in the work of Kurt Lewin, and with that an increasing recognition of the need for leadership and change to be based on an ethical foundation. This book will play an important role in promoting this resurgence. After all, as Franklin D. Roosevelt commented on the causes of the Great Depression of the 1930s:

> We have always known that heedless self-interest was bad morals; we know now that it is bad economics. Out of the collapse of a prosperity whose builders boasted their practicality has come the conviction that in the long run economic morality pays.

However, this 'economic morality' will only prevail if all organizational stakeholders are able and prepared to ensure that ethical rather than unethical behaviour is pursued by leaders, and this can only be achieved if those of us in the field play our part to promote ethical approaches to leadership and change.

Bernard Burnes
Professor of Organisational Change
Manchester Business School
The University of Manchester

Acknowledgements

We would like to take the opportunity to thank everyone who made this book possible. In particular, we would like to send a big thank you to all contributing authors and the team at Routledge and Swales & Willis Ltd. We would also like to thank our students, colleagues, families and friends for all being part of our lives.

Introduction
Ethical Change Leadership

Rune Todnem By and Bernard Burnes

Barker (2001: 491) proposes that 'leadership is all about change'.
And he doesn't stop there. He goes on stating that leadership is 'a
process of transformative change where the ethics of individuals are
integrated into the mores of a community as a means of evolutionary
social development' (Barker, 2001:491). Hence, the title of this book
could have been so much shorter, as 'Leadership' encompasses both
elements of change and ethics. However, for the purpose of this book
it is essential to acknowledge that there is no one right approach to
changes, leadership or ethics. These are all complex issues which are
highly context-dependent, and none of them are value-free (Macleod
and By, 2009; Burnes and Jackson, 2011). All three are matters of
subjectivity and although there may be some universal agreement on
elements of ethics, there is no rule book. Although ethics is all about
attempting to differentiate right from wrong and good from bad, about
increasing positive consequences and decreasing negative consequences
(see Burnes and By, 2011), there is no right or wrong approach and
we should not be subscribing to the TINA (There Is No Alternative)
principle (Diefenbach, 2007).

The purpose of this latest addition to the series Understanding
Organizational Change is not to shout *eureka* and claim some new, earth-
shattering contribution to the field. The purpose is simply to address an
issue as old as civilization itself by re-establishing a focus on what for so
many operating, wheeling and dealing, living, developing, surviving and
breathing within organizations seem to be uncomfortable with: ethics,
change and leadership (ECL). All interconnected, they form the basis
for sustainable organizations. As with many soft issues they are rarely
seriously addressed beyond being a tick-the-box exercise because they
don't offer short-term gains for which to appraise and reward management

performance and political ambition. ECL is not in any serious way dealt with through yet another quick-fix restructuring process or yet another business plan or policy. Successful and sustainable ECL takes serious and considerable amounts of effort and is a medium- to long-term investment focusing on securing a fit between culture and organizational purpose and values. As such, it is not secured through leaders looking for short-term gains which we foolishly, and perhaps out of human nature, are so eager to reward.

As a society we seem to suffer from serious organizational short-term memory loss (see for example Buchanan, 2011). We seem to stubbornly refuse to learn from past experience and time and again allow senior/ executive managers to get away with implementing just another off-the-shelf change initiative for the sake of it. For the purpose of what? To the benefit of whom? These are questions we rarely ask. There are only so many times one should be allowed to restructure any organization without being held accountable for the resources required/wasted, opportunity costs and the lack of any real improvement. It is all getting a bit predictable and repetitive, and one shouldn't really claim any value for money with regards to the 'leaders' appointed to put these highly cyclical change 'initiatives' into motion.

Many leaders are arguably no more than very well-paid followers. Where is their courage, integrity, compassion, vision, contribution and ethical stance? Attending the same executive courses, utilizing the same executive mentors, networking during the same executive lunches they seem to become more and more alike – less and less leaders – all speaking the same language of very often outdated management and leadership blah blah. Many are scared of causing any upset or standing out from the crowd, as there is no guarantee that breaking with the mould will have a positive impact on career progression. Therefore, let's do what is safe. Let's do what has proved successful for the career in the past. However, leadership is not about conforming or repeating the past, nor is it about playing it safe. It is about having the courage, values and beliefs to do what is right. What is right not just for the individual but for the majority of the stakeholders affected.

Having said that, there is no us and them in situations of ECL. To blame unethical decision making, failure of change and the lack of vision and leadership on our leaders is simply too naïve a reaction. As always, it's safe and comfortable projecting guilt and blame onto others. It's like peeing in your pants on a cold winter's night: warm and comfortable to start with, but then it freezes up and leaves you worse off as a consequence! We all need to appreciate that the situation is somewhat more complex than what can be resolved through blaming others. We all have a role to play and responsibility to take when these decisions of ECL are to be made. To really deal with ECL will be uncomfortable and challenging to us all – leaders and followers alike.

With this book, consisting of five parts, we are barely scratching the surface of what are essential questions to be asked and debated, and the intention is to provide more questions than answers in order to hopefully add some fuel to this important discussion. In Part I, three chapters are providing us with some context and theory. In Chapter 1, *Moritz Patzer* and *Christian Voegtlin* provide an introduction and overview to leadership ethics, which still very much remains an underdeveloped field. They set out to outline the challenges of leadership ethics and change, and the need to retain moral integrity in the light of ethical pluralism in the context of globalization. In Chapter 2, *Rebecca Newton* sets out to explore how ethical leadership is practically observed and categorized during organizational change. She considers whether ethical change leadership can be developed before providing research-led suggestions for how leaders can promote ethical leadership within their ever-changing organizations. In Chapter 3, *Carl Rhodes* explores the relationship between justice and leadership – a relationship where justice is not perceived as a goal that can be achieved through specific and measurable leadership or change management practices, but rather as an ongoing condition of which the response defines the ethical quality of leadership.

In Part II we explore some specific issues and challenges of ethical change leadership. In Chapter 4, *David Boje*, *Matt Elmore* and *Rohny Saylors* introduce 'social materiality' as an alternative approach to ethics, change and leadership. They argue this new approach deals with the intra-play of materiality and storytelling, which social construction theory would render as virtuality. Moreover, they suggest that the current plight of ethical leadership and change may in fact lie in the limitations of social constructionism philosophy. In Chapter 5, *Ronald Dufresne* and *Judith Clair* explore the relationship between integrity and hypocrisy in leadership. Their central premise is that all leaders engage to some degree in hypocrisy, and that effective and ethical leaders are those that are aware of their own hypocrisy and seek to close these hypocrisy gaps in order to gain integrity. Forming part of this exploration is a discussion about how the monitoring and remedying of hypocrisy gaps relates to effective and ethical leadership. In Chapter 6, *Henrika Franck* and *Saku Mantere* examine how moral agency is enacted in a process of strategic change. They explore how moral agency is inherent in human behaviour but restricted, and in some cases impossible, in strategic discourse. Irony is then introduced as a possible coping mechanism.

In Part III we set out to have a further look at factors of success and failure with regards to change leadership and ethics. *Thomas Diefenbach*, in Chapter 7, critically interrogates whether individual leaders' and managers' poor leadership performance and organizational misbehaviour can perhaps be explained either by their incompetence or immorality. Looking at the failures and shortcomings of organizational managers and leaders he focuses his discussion on two aspects: managerial abuse of other employees, or petty tyranny, as a potential result of managerial incompetence; and the (im)morality of actual leadership behaviour and its manifestation. In Chapter 8, *Malcolm Higgs* follows up on the previous chapter by focusing on leadership derailment. He sets out to provide answers to two essential questions: what are the causes of damaging and/ or unethical leadership behaviours; and how can the consequences of such 'bad' leadership be avoided or mitigated.

Part IV provides a focus on ethical change leadership and organizational sustainability. In Chapter 9, *Dexter Dunphy* and *Suzanne Benn* investigate the challenges that achieving corporate sustainability poses for the nature of organizational leadership and for the selection and development of leaders. They argue that due to current and ongoing environmental challenges a 'New Wave' leadership is required, which will encompass major transformations at the enterprise level and new values and skills for the individual leader. In Chapter 10, *Fiona Sutherland* and *Aaron Smith* argue that the change–continuity continuum defines organizations. They propose that sustainable leadership for change demands accepting a worldview where either/or choices are no longer valid, and that change and continuity do not exist as opposite sides of the leadership see-saw, but rather co-exist as dualities that sit side by side without compromising one another.

Finally, in Part V, Chapter 11, *Bernard Burnes* provides a conclusion to the book which reminds us that we have already accrued much knowledge about ethics, change and leadership. He points to the work of Kurt Lewin and argues that in order to move forward in creating sustainable organizations, we need to look backwards and fully take on board the knowledge and experience already available to us.

References

Barker, R. A. (2001). The nature of leadership. *Human Relations,* 54(4), 469–494.

Buchanan, D. A. (2011). Reflections: Good practice, not rocket science – understanding failures to change after extreme events. *Journal of Change Management,* 11(3), 273–288.

Burnes, B. and By, R. T. (2011). Leadership and change: The case for greater ethical clarity. *Journal of Business Ethics* (published online 2 November 2011, DOI 10.1007/s10551-011-1088-2).

Burnes, B. and Jackson, P. (2011). Success and failure in organisational change: An exploration of the role of values. *Journal of Change Management*, 11(2), 133–162.

Diefenbach, T. (2007). The managerialistic ideology of organizational change management. *Journal of Organizational Change,* 20(1), 126–144.

Macleod, C. and By, R. T. (2009). Organizational change management in public services: Key findings and emerging themes. In: R. T. By and C. Macleod (eds), *Managing Organizational Change in Public Services: International Issues, Challenges and Cases.* Milton Park: Routledge.

Part I
Context and theory

1 Leadership ethics and organizational change

Sketching the field

Moritz Patzer and Christian Voegtlin

Introduction

Some ten years ago UN Secretary-General Kofi Annan called upon global business leaders to join the fight against human rights violations, inhumane working conditions, the rising threat of pollution and the spreading problem of corruption. He proposed the Global Compact Initiative as a means to foster sustainable and socially responsible business practices. Since then the world has witnessed scandals like Enron, WorldCom, Siemens and many other high-profile cases of leadership failure and managerial misconduct. These developments reached a climax in the financial sub-prime crises starting in 2007 and the 'Euro-crisis' of 2010, events which have by now permeated public discourse and put regulators, as well as private actors, on the spot to find answers to the new challenges of global business.

Yet, as politicians and practitioners look towards theory for answers to the rising call for socially responsible leadership, hopes for quick fixes or even adequate support are being disappointed. Leadership ethics – being the overarching label for questions on ethics, fairness, legitimacy and sustainability in the context of leadership – still remains an underdeveloped field (Ciulla, 1995; Ciulla, 2005b; Doh and Stumpf, 2005b; Rost, 1995). Within it we find a variety of competing and partly contradictory efforts that focus on different research foci of leadership's new challenges, ranging from aspects of globalization (Bartlett and Ghoshal, 2003; Danon-Leva, 2005; Mendenhall *et al.*, 2008), to moral responsibility (Brown *et al.*, 2005; Brown and Trevino, 2006; Doh and Stumpf, 2005a; Johnson, 2009; Maak and Pless, 2006a; Maak and Pless, 2006b; Sharma and Bhal, 2004) and to political theory (Cradden, 2005; Patzer, 2009).

While these hallmarks indicate a dramatic change in the perception of what 'good leadership' at the onset of the twenty-first century is, research is still struggling to address the multitude of new challenges of globally responsible leadership (Bennis, 2007; Waldman and Siegel, 2008). It is the aim of this chapter to address this situation.

We do this with regard to the underlying causes for and characteristics of the new leadership challenges, as well as the conceptual state of leadership ethics as a research field. First, we argue that the former must be analysed in the context of globalization. Understood as the processes of socio-economic transformation (Beck, 1992; Beck, 2000), globalization has led to regulatory deficits on the level of the nation state (Habermas, 2001b) that redefine the societal role of private actors in a globalizing society (Matten and Crane, 2005; Moon *et al.*, 2005; Scherer *et al.*, 2006). This sets the stage for new concepts of responsible global leadership that acknowledge the economic needs for effective leadership and the need to retain moral integrity in the light of ethical pluralism.

Second, globalization, new societal roles and ethical pluralism pose substantial challenges for a new understanding of leadership, especially in change processes. Furthermore, researchers and practitioners are faced with a research field that is characterized by a pluralism of different labels, research foci and research methodologies. The divide between positivist and post-positivist approaches inhibits efforts for a comprehensive perception of what good leadership means for present and future business.

By sketching these challenges of leadership ethics we hope to foster some understanding of the characteristics of responsible global leadership and to improve the dialogue between existing research strands within this new field. The chapter is structured as follows. First, we highlight the new challenges leaders are facing in a globalizing world. We start with the globalization process and its implications for organizations and subsequently, for leadership. Leadership is then connected to the ethical challenges of change. In the second part, we sketch the field of leadership ethics along its conceptual challenges and potentials and portray the thoughts on transformational leadership, ethical leadership, servant leadership, and responsible leadership as an introduction into different concepts of good leadership. We will conclude with a summary of our findings.

Global challenges for global leaders

An ongoing globalization process puts organizations in the need for continuous change and the adaption to new challenges in unstable environments. As Graetz (2000:550) acknowledges, 'against a backdrop of increasing globalization, deregulation, the rapid pace of technological innovation, a growing knowledge workforce, and shifting social and demographic trends, few would dispute that the primary task for management today is the leadership of organizational change.'

However, globalization not only increases the pressure for organizational change but also the ethical challenges leaders face. In the following we will illustrate these challenges which are due to the globalization process and due to what Habermas (2001b) calls an emerging 'postnational constellation', before we turn to the ethical challenges of change.

The globalization process

Globalization can be understood as the process of intensifying social and economic transactions (Scherer *et al.*, 2009a:327). It is accompanied by a dissolving relevance of territorially-bound social, economic and political activities, and a stronger worldwide interconnection of important social actors (Beck, 2000; Crane and Matten, 2007:17; Scherer, 2003:59ff).

It is still an ongoing process that is triggered by several factors. First, technological developments in the field of communication, media and logistics enable a worldwide interconnection and make global trade economically profitable. Second, political decisions and events, like the breakup of territorial power blocks (e.g. the Soviet Union), the reduction of trade and tariff barriers, or the establishment of free trade areas (the EU) accelerate the process. A third factor is socio-cultural processes that comprise e.g. an increasingly mobile workforce and the export of cultural goods[1]. It also includes the emergence of pluralistic societies: these are a result of the dissolution of traditional social structures, such as the family, the local community (Habermas, 1991; Horkheimer and Adorno, 1988) and civic solidarity (Habermas, 2001b), as well as an ongoing individualization of personal lifestyles (Scherer *et al.*, 2009a:327; Sennet, 1998). Finally, the awareness of global risks such as environmental hazards, global warming, worldwide diseases and epidemics, nuclear threats, and also economic risks like the Global Financial Crisis (GFC), fosters cross-border coordination of nation-state activities and the incorporation of non-state actors like NGOs and multinational corporations into the decision-making processes (in relation to the factors of globalization, see Beck, 2000; Scherer *et al.*, 2009a; Scherer and Palazzo, 2008).

These processes, which, due to their interdependent nature, cannot always be clearly separated, have direct effects on the regulatory power of the nation state to control global business (Habermas, 2001b). Habermas holds that these effects on the nation state lead to the emergence of a postnational constellation. Global problems, such as global warming or environmental pollution, can no longer be solved within national boundaries. These problems have spillover effects across territorial demarcations (e.g. CO_2 emissions), which leads to a discrepancy between those parties that cause an effect and those that are affected by the outcomes. The growing mobility of corporations allowing them to move to countries with cheap labour or favourable tax opportunities puts states in competition with regard to fiscal revenues and employment. This leads in part to a race-to-the-bottom, in which states underbid each other with tax-saving opportunities to attract multinational corporations (Scherer and Smid, 2000).

Western societies especially are becoming pluralistic and multicultural societies consisting of individualists, a phenomenon which also relates to the workforce of organizations. It becomes more difficult for organizations to build and sustain a common culture and to bring together the very different beliefs and attitudes of its members. Additionally, the room for nation states to control the activities of multinational organizations across open (trade) borders through means of law is becoming narrower (Habermas, 2001a; Habermas, 2001b).

Thus, the nation state is losing its regulatory power over corporations (Beck, 2000; Habermas, 2001b), while at the same time, governance gaps emerge on the global level. There is no equivalent to the nation state as regulatory authority on the global level that could regulate markets to either prohibit externalities of business conduct or to internalize unwanted outcomes (Kobrin, 2001; Kobrin, 2008). This in turn increases the responsibility of multinational firms to control their business conduct (Young, 2004) and increases the awareness on the part of external stakeholder groups who put pressure on the corporations to act socially responsibly.

Implications for organizations

These developments have implications for the corporation and, subsequently, for their main actors, the leaders. In the neo-classical theory of the firm, the state provides the regulatory framework, within which the sole responsibility of economic actors is to maximize profits (Friedman, 1970). All externalities should be controlled by legal rules and organizations are free to act as long as they comply with those rules.

If the nation state can no longer guarantee those rules, the responsibility falls (partially) back to the organization (Matten and Crane, 2005; Moon *et al.*, 2005; Scherer and Palazzo, 2007). This has implications for their operations. Firms conduct business within the emerging global governance gaps, where they either exploit the regulatory free space consequently to their own advantage, or where they act as quasi-political actors in providing standards and helping to close those gaps (Scherer *et al.*, 2009a). The political activity is reflected in the participation in global initiatives or self-regulating standards such as the UN Global Compact, the Global Reporting Initiative, the Forest Stewardship Council or the Social Accounting 8000 standard (Scherer *et al.*, 2006; Scherer *et al.*, 2009a).

Coinciding with the new responsibilities for organizations, is the process of an increasingly interconnected global society that is becoming more sensitive to social and environmental violations as well as the growth of non-governmental organizations that gather and reinforce particular interests (Den Hond and De Bakker, 2007; Mitchell *et al.*, 1997).

As a consequence, organizations are monitored more closely by a diverse group of stakeholders, who increase the pressure to legitimize organizational conduct (Palazzo and Scherer, 2006). Stakeholder management becomes a vital aspect of the strategic agenda (Freeman, 1984; Post *et al.*, 2002b).

These developments challenge the corporation and its organizational change process in two ways. While organizations are faced, on the one hand, with an ongoing adaption process to the changing environment of global competition, they are, on the other hand, increasingly confronted by diverse stakeholder groups that demand an enhanced awareness for corporate social responsibility (CSR). If organizations disregard such stakeholder demands, it can have severe effects on their reputation and their license to operate.

Within this setting, a whole research stream has evolved around the terms CSR (Crane *et al.*, 2008; Scherer and Palazzo, 2008) and stakeholder management (Donaldson and Preston, 1995; Freeman, 1984; Laplume *et al.*, 2008). In relation to the aforementioned problems, scholars call for a role of firms as corporate citizens or as political actors (Matten and Crane, 2005; Scherer and Palazzo, 2007) that engage in proactive stakeholder management to secure their legitimacy and their license to operate in a global society.

Implications for leaders

For organizational leaders this means that they face two important challenges they have to cope with. First, there is the economic challenge of a worldwide interconnected business. Second, there are the ethical challenges in partially unregulated markets due to an emerging postnational constellation.

The economic imperatives demand of leaders to gain and sustain competitive advantage and to increase profits while facing global competition. They must constantly adapt to new business challenges and thus maintain a continuous change process (By, 2005).

The ethical challenges are caused by the extension of responsibility due to the globalization process (Patzer and Scherer, 2010; Young, 2004). Leaders have to consider the wider consequences of their business conduct, such as environmental pollution, global warming, creating and securing employment, safety at work and labour standards, in order to encounter the growing demands of external constituencies.

Additionally, leaders are faced with the diversity challenge of cultural heterogeneous contexts as they have to motivate and coordinate the activities of employees from diverse backgrounds.

At the same time, they are confronted with the absence of consistent regulatory rules and moral norms. In the course of global economic activities they have to cope with an increase in ethical dilemmas that call for legitimate solutions, while they have no ethical orientation on which they can rely. This problem is enhanced by the increasing necessity to address the demands of internal and external stakeholder groups (Maak and Pless, 2006c; Post *et al.*, 2002a; Schneider, 2002).

The pressure exerted by the stakeholders requires leaders to extend the internal view of the traditional leader–follower interaction to incorporate stakeholders into the decision making process. This transcends the traditional understanding of leadership as an influence process. Therein the leader–follower relation usually is characterized by a hierarchical or positional power difference. In an extended view of the leader–follower interaction the influence process increasingly takes the form of a balancing of different interests in dialogue. The stakeholder dialogue serves as a process to secure the legitimacy of business conduct and to build and retain the license to operate for firms (Palazzo and Scherer, 2006; Post *et al.*, 2002b; Suchman, 1995).

To guarantee the social acceptance of organizational conduct, leaders have to make legitimate decisions that can be accepted by all affected. This makes it necessary to weigh and balance the different stakeholder interests and puts CSR on the strategic agenda. Leaders are increasingly confronted with the need to bring together social and economic imperatives without neglecting the interests of the organization.

The economic as well as the ethical challenges can no longer be addressed by organizational solutions alone. The constantly changing business environment cannot be countered solely by institutionalized procedures, as it requires the flexibility to address unforeseen events. Leaders are the focal persons in organizations. They have the positional power and the discretion, first, to act in a timely maner to new situations and challenges, second, to engage in an active stakeholder dialogue and third, to implement (legitimate) solutions within the organization and finally, to take responsibility and to justify their conduct in the case of all possible accusations (Patzer, 2009).

Leadership and change

These developments affect the role of leaders in the organizational change process. Change management has been defined as 'the process of continually renewing an organization's direction, structure, and capabilities to serve the ever-changing needs of external and internal customers' (Moran and Brightman, 2001:111). What the interconnected business world of a global society is now transcending is the sole focus on the *customer* as reflected in the definition. It broadens the focus towards recognizing the need of a wider stakeholder society. Leaders have to estimate consequences for stakeholders that may be affected and to look for legitimate solutions in organizational restructuring. Further, the continuous restructuring and renewing of organizational directions enhances the constant need to motivate a heterogeneous workforce with many different interests and abilities. It is becoming more difficult to secure employee commitment to a common (ethical) culture of an organization and to the pursuit of shared organizational goals. Finally, change has to be directed towards satisfying the need of many different constituencies and towards combining social and economic imperatives.

Hence leaders can act as social entrepreneurs. Social entrepreneurship can be understood as pursuing ventures that bring together a social mission, an emphasis on innovation and a market orientation (Nicholls and Cho, 2006:115). Social entrepreneurs thereby play the role of change agents. By engaging in stakeholder dialogues, the different constituencies can contribute their knowledge and expertise to solve problems and foster social innovation that can assist firms to combine social and economic imperatives and help them realize mutually beneficial solutions.

Lewin (1951) divided change processes originally into three phases: unfreezing, changing, and refreezing. Unfreezing is the awareness that change is required (e.g. triggered by a crisis or unforeseen events). The changing phase encompasses looking for new ways of doing things, or solutions to overcome a crisis. Refreezing refers to implementing and establishing the new solutions or approaches. If we relate the new demands of globalization to the role of leaders in organizational change processes, the ethical challenges of leading responsible change in an interconnected business world start with reflecting about the legitimacy of the change process and the consequences for possibly affected stakeholders (unfreezing phase). They further include developing an appropriate vision that fosters economic profits and that is ethically sensitive, as well as being capable of building relationships of trust with the affected parties (Yukl, 2006:284ff; Maak and Ulrich, 2007:316ff). During the process of change, leaders face the challenge of engaging in dialogue with the relevant stakeholders and coordinating the different interests while searching for consensual solutions. Once new solutions have been implemented leaders face the task of defending and explaining the accomplished change efforts against possible reproaches. Finally, there remains the task of continuous improvement and learning. This implies, for example, (ethically sensitive) cultural adaption and encouraging moral organizational learning (Yukl, 2006:284ff; Maak and Ulrich, 2007:316ff).

Taken together, the new challenges of the globalization process imply a new conceptualization of organizational leadership. If leaders are to be able to react adequately to the diverse demands of multiple stakeholder groups, the internal view of leadership as leader–follower interaction needs to be extended to an understanding of leadership as leader–stakeholder interaction (Maak and Pless, 2006b). Further, leadership needs a theoretical foundation that can guide leaders and provide ethical orientation in dealing with heterogeneous cultural backgrounds or complex moral dilemmas. It should enable them to produce ethical decisions, satisfying a majority of stakeholders involved.

We will now turn to leadership ethics and discuss the literature on the intersection between leadership and ethics in light of the new challenges identified.

Leadership ethics as a research field in the making

So far we have delineated the new challenges for leaders and their organizations that arise from the processes of globalization in its broadest sense. The implications from heterogeneous legal frameworks, the decreasing regulative capabilities of the nation state, the increasing importance of soft law as well as societal and environmental issues form the context wherein business takes place. Consequently this contextual multitude has increasingly been addressed by researchers acknowledging the need for an enlarged understanding of the role of business in a globalizing society (Crane *et al.*, 2008; Scherer and Palazzo, 2008). On a *macro level* the relationship of business and society are discussed with regard to the increased political involvement of corporations. Alternative theories such as 'Corporate Citizenship' (Matten and Crane, 2005; Moon *et al.*, 2005; Pies *et al.*, 2009; Waddock, 2008) or 'political CSR' (Scherer and Palazzo, 2007) are discussed to take these phenomena into account. On an organizational *meso level*, research focuses on the implications of an enlarged societal role of the corporations for the organizational policies, structures and processes. These discussions focus on topics such as standardized ethics initiatives (Gilbert and Rasche, 2008), organizational legitimacy (Palazzo and Scherer, 2006), organizational ethics programs (Stansbury and Barry, 2007), organizational communication (Scherer and Baumann, 2007), corporate governance (Thompson, 2008) and HR policies (Preuss *et al.*, 2009).

In contrast to the extensive body of literature that exists on the macro and meso level, the implications of globalization for the *micro level* of analysis, that is, for individual behaviour, have only recently started to attract the attention of researchers (Bies *et al.*, 2007; Scherer *et al.*, 2009b). It is here where we see the principal domain of *leadership ethics* as an evolving field that is dedicated to the analysis of the implications of global change processes for leadership and the impact of leaders on responsible organizational behaviour, organizational legitimacy and organizational change.

Leadership ethics: Framing the question for 'good leadership'

Ciulla (1995) introduced the term 'leadership ethics' back in the mid-nineties, following the call for a stronger integration of ethics and leadership (Smith, 1995; Rost, 1991; Rost, 1995). Mapping out the territory of leadership studies as the starting point to explore the relevance of ethics in leadership research she stressed the importance of the question for '*good leadership*' (Ciulla, 1995). Since then Ciulla has repeatedly emphasized the need to put 'ethics at the heart of leadership' (Ciulla, 2004b; Ciulla, 2004a; Ciulla, 2005a). Yet ten years after the original publication she admits that taking into account the small body of literature one might consider leadership ethics rather a topic than a field (Ciulla, 2005b).

In contrast to earlier attempts the discussion on what good leadership is has gathered significant momentum in recent years (Doh and Stumpf, 2005a; Johnson, 2009; Maak and Pless, 2006a). At the bottom of this renaissance lie the aforementioned fundamental change processes that have altered the reality of business as a whole as well as the increased public interest in the conduct of their leaders. Yet, although 'bad leadership' appears to be easily identified and has become the interest of different studies (Kellerman, 2004; Lipman-Blumen, 2005), it still remains unclear what 'good leadership' is. This state can be attributed to three fundamental characteristics of leadership ethics: first, the definitional endeavours related to the concept of leadership; second, the notion of 'good'; and third, the paradigmatic divide between different concepts of good leadership. We will take a closer look at each of these.

Problems with the concept of leadership

The concept of leadership, if there is *one* such thing, lacks rigor. Regardless of decades of intensive research, leadership theory remains a highly fragmented field (Bennis and Nanus, 1997; Calas and Smircich, 1988; Hunt *et al.*, 1988; Rost, 1991). Leadership is coevally ubiquitous and unknown. Its popularity as a cross-cultural social phenomenon in scientific as well as practice-oriented publications has led to an undifferentiated use of the terms *leadership* and *leader*. They are often used in a sense rather resembling *management* and *manager*. Whereas the latter pair can be understood as representing an objectives-driven conduct, which makes use of bureaucratic and organizational means to fulfil contractual obligations, the former can be characterized as representing a purpose- and change-driven conduct that is based on values and visions (Antonakis *et al.*, 2004a; 2005b).

Looking for an ontology of leadership, Bennis proposes that it should be seen as grounded in a relationship: 'In its simplest form, it is a tripod – a leader or leaders, followers, and the common goal they want to achieve' (Bennis, 2007:3f; Drath *et al.*, 2008). Within this relationship intentional influence and guidance is provided by the leaders who, together with their followers, intend real changes reflecting their shared purposes (Rost, 1995; Yukl, 2006). Yet, beyond such a broad sketch research has traditionally centred around foci like 'traits', 'styles', 'contingencies' or 'charisma' with each theory highlighting different aspects of leaders and their actions without providing a comprehensive grasp of the nature of leadership. So while standard overview texts choose to recapitulate the multitude of approaches (Bass, 1990; Antonakis *et al.*, 2004b; Yukl, 2006) the search for leadership's Rosetta stone that enables us to break the code still goes on (Calas and Smircich, 1988; Ciulla, 2006). As this deficit of a shared understanding continues to burden the study of leadership, it also applies to the question for 'good leadership'.

The notion of 'good'

To differentiate the good from the bad, the desirable from the unwanted, we need judgements on values. Hence we have to state our ethical orientations. Obviously this is no easy task. Practical philosophers have weighted these orientations for centuries and we as business ethicists would do good to learn our lessons from their work. Yet in the light of a multitude of existing ethical theories manoeuvring in this terrain easily becomes a tedious task. In search for an overview one commonly finds the differentiation between teleological and deontological concepts of ethics. *Teleological concepts of ethics* stress the importance of the ends of actions. Hence the moral rightness of an action is determined by its outcomes and their contribution to a greater good. Most prominent among these theories are variants of Utilitarianism in the tradition of Bentham and Mill. In contrast to this, *deontological concepts of ethics* do not make consequences but intentions the primary criteria to evaluate the moral quality of actions. The intentions itself are derived from the perception of one's duty (derived from the Greek word *déon*) that relates to an intrinsic understanding of good actions. Among these concepts the work of Kant, Contractualism, the writing of Rawls, and discourse ethics as forwarded by Apel and Habermas are the most influential.

At this point instead of just 'choosing' among these different notions of good, thereby inheriting the myriad assumptions made in each concept, it can be helpful to focus on the three justification problems that are characteristic for business and leadership ethics: first, the philosophical, second, the economical and lastly the practical.

Philosophical justification poses the question of the possibility to reasonably justify moral principles and to show whether some norms are more valid or universally applicable than others. The principal possibility as well as the different modes of such a justification are controversial. All efforts to justify actions, norms of moral principles are prone to the trilemma associated with the work of the German philosopher Hans Albert (1985) that sees justification as either circular, with arguments resting on prior arguments; regressive, with each argument needing another argument for justification; or axiomatic/dogmatic, proposing a 'firm' starting point for the argumentation. This justificational struggle and the resulting critique apply to religious as well as secular, to teleological as well as deontological approaches. The question resulting hereof is whether modern leaders refer to a reasonable (if not justifiable) moral premise that acknowledges the challenges explained in section one of this chapter. Different cultures, religious backgrounds and notions of capitalism burden the search for good leadership.

Economical justification refers to the relation of moral and economic rationalities. With regard to leadership this is often seen as the ethics/effectiveness continuum (Ciulla, 2006), leadership effectiveness being the 'extent to which the leader's organizational unit performs its task successfully and attains its goals' (Yukl, 2006). In this context, research has to address central issues of good leadership: Can effective leaders be ethical? Does ethics precede effectiveness? Is effectiveness ethical?

We deem it important not to reduce this continuum to an antagonistic relationship. Instead we see ethical reflections as a requirement of effective leadership under the condition of globalization. Such an understanding distances itself from the traditional scholarly understanding of a value-free economic rationality (Friedman, 1970; Jensen, 2002; Sundaram and Inkpen, 2004). Economic choices and preferences are not ethically neutral. As economic theory itself suggests an idea of 'good', leaders cannot blindly rely on, for example, profit-maximization calculations but have to situationally mediate between conflicting ethical interests.

This is closely linked to the third justificational problem, that of practical justification. It represents the challenges leaders face with regard to the question of incorporating ethics in their own and others' conduct. Abstract moral principles are limited in their direct use. It is rather necessary to develop an ethical vision supported through codes of conduct, educational programmes and examples of good leadership to foster personal and organizational change. How can we lead by example? What does good leadership ultimately mean in the course of daily business?

These three justificational problems sketch the challenges for any comprehensive concept of good leadership and hence the extent of leadership ethics as a field. After the definitional confusion they pose the second hurdle for researchers working in a field in the making.

Caught in the middle: The paradigmatic divide in the field

The third hurdle that inhibits progress in leadership ethics research is the latent struggle of different research paradigms that has accompanied business ethics since its beginnings.

A paradigm as the notion of alternative explanations of social science phenomena provides the answer to the two basic questions of research: what is the purpose of research?; and by what means and methods can this purpose be achieved? (Burrell and Morgan, 1979; Scherer and Patzer, 2008). Hence a paradigm is characterized by its specific research interests and its employed methods as well as its underlying assumptions about the examined object (ontology) (Habermas, 1986; Kuhn, 1962; Pfeffer, 1993). Elsewhere we have suggested to differentiate between positivist (1) and post-positivist (2) approaches to leadership ethics (Patzer, 2009, 2008; Patzer and Scherer, 2010; Scherer and Palazzo, 2007):

(1) A positivist research paradigm stands in the tradition of classical leadership theory with its strong quantitative bias (Bryman, 1996:280). It approaches social phenomena through the use of the empirical methods of a naturalistic model of explanation, thereby aiming 'to explain observable phenomena through general or statistical laws and situational conditions' (Scherer and Palazzo, 2007:1098; Donaldson, 1996; Hempel, 1998). As it pursues a technical research interest (Habermas, 1986) it is focussed on the explanation of existing functional mechanisms for stabilizing the status quo of a social system. Within leadership ethics, concepts like 'transforming leadership' (Burns, 1978; Burns, 2003;

Bass and Avolio, 1990) – now often referred to as 'transformational leadership' – 'ethical leadership' (Brown *et al.*, 2005; Brown, 2007; Brown and Trevino, 2006) and 'authentic leadership' (Avolio and Gardner, 2005; Walumbwa *et al.*, 2008) exhibit a positivist layout. We will explore some of these in the next section.

(2) The methods of the post-positivist research paradigm resemble those of philosophy rather than those of social science. The evaluation of the behaviour of social actors and entities in terms of right or wrong are of central importance (Trevino and Weaver, 1994; Weaver and Trevino, 1994). Based on a pluralistic methodology that is united in its acknowledgement of the 'good argument' (Weaver and Trevino, 1998), it pursues an emancipatory research interest (Habermas, 1986) that is concerned with the critical reflection of the social processes, structures and power relationships. Within leadership ethics 'responsible leadership' (Maak and Pless, 2006a; Maak and Pless, 2006b; Patzer, 2009) but also 'servant leadership' (Greenleaf, 1977) have post-positivist characteristics.

At present, both paradigms are being developed separately from each other. This disconnectedness is unfortunate for two reasons: first, as both streams of literature provide important insights into the notion of good leadership the lack of mutual acknowledgment obscures the potential of a comprehensive dialogue on the future of leadership under the conditions of globalization; second, it lures research ventures into statements that are beyond their methodological repertoire. Positivist research has a strong descriptive lens to uncover the key metrics of good leadership prevalent in present leadership practice. Yet, when it comes to normative evaluation of leadership behaviour and prescriptions for future leaders, post-positivist research is better suited to provide an understanding of the underlying value judgments that make leadership 'good'.

Concepts of good leadership

Among the different publications and approaches that we have mentioned we will explain only the following four. *Transformational* and *ethical* leadership both stand for a positivist approach. Additionally we will look at *servant* and *responsible* leadership as exponents of a post-positivist perspective. Whereas transformational and servant leadership have some history in leadership studies, ethical and responsible leadership are fairly new concepts that have arisen out of the recent call for new leadership ethics.

Transformational leadership

Transformational leadership is one of the earlier and more prominent leadership approaches, with a strong emphasis on morale and good leadership. Burns (1978) introduced the term in his historical analysis of political leaders. Bass and Avolio (Avolio, 1999; Bass, 1985; Bass and Avolio, 2004) built upon Burns' work and related transformational leadership to the business environment.

Transformational leadership is a process whereby leaders encourage their followers to live up to their standards. Transformational leadership is morally good leadership in the sense that such leadership is based on strong values and in that transformational leaders try to raise their followers to higher standards of morality and motivation (Burns, 1978). Burns contrasts transformational leadership with transactional leadership. While transformational leadership is based on end-values like justice and equality (Rokeach, 1973), which leaders try to instill into their followers, transactional leadership is characterized by an exchange relationship and is based on modal values that are concerned with the means of the act (fairness) (Ciulla, 1995).

The transformational leadership approach is difficult to classify according to its ethical background. It is comparable to a virtue ethics approach. Yet, it is based predominantly on moral or ethical psychology research that explains the (moral) relationship between leader and follower (Ciulla, 1995:15). The research on transformational leadership in business and management studies shifted the focus away from the normative component towards a more descriptive and prescriptive empirical approach with an emphasis on the charismatic aspect of transformational leadership (Ciulla, 1995). More recently, the discussion about the *authentic* transformational leader (Bass and Steidlmeier, 1999) has gained momentum (the research on authentic leadership Avolio and Gardner, 2005; Walumbwa *et al.*, 2008).

Ethical leadership

Brown, Trevino and colleagues propose a more recent leadership concept which they explicitly refer to as ethical leadership (Brown *et al.*, 2005; Brown and Trevino, 2006; Trevino *et al.*, 2000; Trevino *et al.*, 2003.) Trevino *et al.* (2003) followed a descriptive, inductive approach and developed their concept using qualitative research. They interviewed senior managers and ethics officers, asking them what ethical leadership is. The patterns that emerged throughout the interviews were used to bring forth an empirical scale.

What they discovered were two dimensions of ethical leadership (Trevino *et al.*, 2000). The first dimension is the leader as a moral person who embraces positive characteristics and values, such as being honest and trustworthy, a fair decision-maker and someone who cares about people. The second dimension of ethical leadership is characterized by the leader as a moral manager. This dimension emphasizes the role of an ethical leader as a positive role model who fosters ethical conduct among followers and disciplines them for unethical behaviour (Brown and Trevino, 2006). Brown and colleagues thereby draw on Bandura's (1986) social learning theory for the theoretical underpinning. They define ethical leadership as 'the demonstration of normatively appropriate conduct through personal actions and interpersonal relationships, and the promotion of such conduct to followers through two-way communication, reinforcement, and decision-making' (Brown *et al.*, 2005:120).

Ethical leadership is a descriptive and predictive approach that tries to explain and examine the influence process between leader and followers, with a special focus on ethical behaviour, for example, through a positive effect of ethical leadership on follower ethical decision making or pro-social behaviour. The approach is thereby based on (implicit) underlying virtues like, for example, trustworthiness, honesty and fairness.

Servant leadership

Another concept that strongly carries the notion of good leadership is 'servant leadership'. The term was coined by Greenleaf who proposed the idea of a reversed relationship of leaders and their followers, with the former serving the latter (Greenleaf, 1977; Graham, 1991). It becomes the duty of the leader to assist his followers and to foster personal responsibility. Servant leadership is best illustrated by the fictional character of the servant Leo from Hermann Hesse's 'Journey to the East' (Hesse, 1956). The servant Leo is part of a spiritual journey of a small group of travellers. In the course of the story Leo, who has been carrying the essential provisions and tools, suddenly disappears. Unrest and strife disturbs the remaining travellers, leaving them to realize that it was their servant Leo who acted as the group's focal point, leading them by serving.

Servant leadership hence stresses the importance for leaders to care for their followers thereby cultivating trust, initiative and moral responsibility. As the servant leader serves first, making the need of others his highest priority, he becomes the epitome of good and just conduct (Ciulla, 2006:29ff; Patzer, 2009:116ff; Yukl, 2006:420).

Greenleaf's servant leadership, although picked up again in recent publications (Liden *et al.*, 2008), has never gained the attention of concepts like transformational leadership. Still it remains a very good and explicitly normative illustration of what good leadership can mean.

Responsible leadership

Lastly, the concept of 'responsible leadership' represents another very young and promising strand found in the evolving literature on leadership and ethics. Responsible leadership places itself at the interface of leadership studies, ethics and business ethics. It has embraced the reflective paucity on the new challenges of present leaders and (their) corporations to act 'responsibly' in a globalized world under the threat of severe or even existential ramifications in the case of defective behaviour (Doh and Stumpf, 2005a; Maak and Pless, 2006a; Waldman and Siegel, 2008).

Among the different contributions it is that of Maak and Pless is most notable, as it is the most sensitive concerning the three illustrated problems of justification (Maak, 2007; Maak and Pless, 2006a; Maak and Pless, 2006b). Their work embeds responsible leadership in the stakeholder literature (Maak and Pless, 2006b; Maak and Pless, 2006c; Bass and Steidlmeier, 1999). Hence, leadership has to acknowledge an increasing cultural and moral diversity as well as the new role of the corporation in society. Maak and Pless define responsible leadership as 'a social-relational and ethical phenomenon, which occurs in social processes of interaction . . . [It] takes place in interaction with a multitude of followers as stakeholders inside and outside the corporations.' (Maak and Pless, 2006b:99). It becomes 'a values-based and through ethical principles driven relationship between leaders and stakeholders who are connected through a shared sense of meaning and purpose through which they raise another to higher levels of motivation and commitment for achieving sustainable values creation and social change.' (Pless, 2007:438). Maak and Pless go to great lengths to further specify their concept with a number of normative and operational roles, the leader's moral compass as well as a list of virtues to which leaders should adhere (see Maak and Pless, 2006b; Maak and Ulrich, 2007). Thereby Maak and Pless present important tools to analyse the challenges of present leaders.

More recent still is the politically extended concept of responsible leadership (Patzer, 2009; Patzer and Scherer, 2010; Voegtlin *et al.*, 2010). Inspired by the discussions on political CSR (Matten and Crane, 2005; Moon *et al.*, 2005; Palazzo and Scherer, 2008; Scherer and Palazzo, 2007) it reflects upon the leader's responsibility in the context of the theory of deliberative democracy and discourse ethics (Habermas, 1993, 1996; Bohman and Rehg, 1999; Cohen, 1999; Elster, 1998; Michelman, 1999; Rehg, 1994). This context provides a societal as well as an individual ethics that does not rely on cultural presuppositions, like religion or virtues, but draws its justification from the actual practice of the actors involved. Thereby the problems of coherent integration of the multiple tools in Maak's and Pless' conceptions are circumvented. The idea of a consensual agreement becomes the guiding idea in the daily leadership practice. The implementation of organizational structures that facilitate consensual coordination becomes the nucleus of corporate change towards responsible conduct. The politically extended responsible leadership can be understood as the proactive engagement in the process of societal self-determination resting on a procedural ethics and communicative reason. Leaders as powerful actors have to include affected actors, thereby facilitating the peaceful reconciliation of economic and social-political goals in a legitimate way.

Conclusion

The idea of good leadership is relevant in a multitude of academic and practical contexts from which it continuously receives important inputs and support. We propose to retain the notion of leadership ethics as an overarching label for these thoughts on good leadership in a globalizing society, thereby embedding aspects of morality, fairness, legitimacy and sustainability firmly into leadership studies (Ciulla, 2005b; Patzer, 2009). Leadership ethics as a field in the making carries the promise of a continuous exchange of thoughts, emancipated from the discussions on business ethics and leadership studies, regardless of the definitional, justificational and conceptual pluralism and challenges we sketched above. Still its future is determined by its ability to address the challenges present leaders face in their daily business and the conceptual hurdles we as researchers are confronted with:

First, leaders act under the conditions of globalization. Hence the postnational constellation with all its facets is becoming the prevalent context to reflect upon and to judge appropriate leadership conduct. This does not mean that leadership effectiveness has lost its relevance. Rather it implies the need to reconceptualize the meaning of effectiveness in a stakeholder-society. The successful mitigation of economical and societal pressures on leaders will determine the characteristics of good leadership in the twenty-first century. In a complex and dynamic global business world, adaption and change become vital for the survival of the organization. The globalization challenges have implications for leadership in change processes, and leaders as (social) change agents can help build a sustainable future.

Second, we believe that the success of this venture would be supported by a cooperative approach beyond paradigmatic boundaries. Beyond leaders challenged by globalization, ethics, work conditions and pollution there lies a multi-facetted research field. Organizational theory and business ethics have faced similar situations. In both fields we find separate strands of publications and the recurring complaints on the lack of integration. As leadership ethics still is on the brink of becoming a field it is up to us to influence its founding conditions. Obviously we do not argue in favour of *one* comprehensive approach, as such an endeavour would neglect the complexity of leadership ethics. Still we maintain that a vital discourse on paradigmatic assumptions, terminology, methodology and conceptual limits may prove fruitful in our mutual quest to understand the nature of good leadership.

Note

1 The cultural globalization was circumscribed by scholars with the catchword 'McDonaldization', which should stand for the process of converging cultural symbols and life forms that will, in the end, result in a global culture (see critically Beck, 2000; Habermas, 2001b; Sennet, 1998).

References

Albert, H. (1985). *Treatise on Critical Reason*. Princeton: Princeton University Press.
Antonakis, J., Cianciolo, A. T. and Sternberg, R. J. (2004a). Leadership: Past,

present, and future. In: J. Antonakis, A. T. Cianciolo and R. J. Sternberg (eds), *The Nature of Leadership*. London: Sage, 1–15.

Antonakis, J., Cianciolo, A. T. and Sternberg, R. J. (2004b). *The Nature of Leadership*. Thousand Oaks, London, New Delhi: Sage.

Avolio, B. J. (1999). *Full Leadership Development: Building the Vital Forces in Organizations*. Thousand Oaks: Sage.

Avolio, B. J. and Gardner, W. L. (2005). Authentic leadership development: Getting to the root of positive forms of leadership. *Leadership Quarterly*, 16, 315–338.

Bandura, A. (1986). *Social Foundations of Thought and Action*. Engelwood Cliffs: Prentice-Hall.

Bartlett, C. and Ghoshal, S. (2003). What is a global manager? *Harvard Business Review*, 81, 101–108.

Bass, B. M. (1985). *Leadership and Performance Beyond Expectations*. New York: Free Press.

Bass, B. M. (1990). *Bass & Stogdill's Handbook of Leadership: Theory, Research & Managerial Applications* (third edition). New York: The Free Press.

Bass, B. M. and Avolio, B. J. (1990). The implications of transactional and transformational leadership for individual, team and organizational development. *Research in Organizational Change and Development*, 4, 231–272.

Bass, B. M. and Avolio, B. J. (2004). *Multifactor Leadership Questionnaire: Manual Leader Rorm, Rater, and Scoring Key for MLQ* (form 5x – short). Redwood City: Mind Garden.

Bass, B. M. and Steidlmeier, P. (1999). Ethics, character, and authentic transformational leadership behaviour. *Leadership Quarterly*, 10, 181–217.

Beck, U. (1992). *Risk Society: Towards a New Modernity*. London: Sage.

Beck, U. (2000). *What is Globalization?* Cambridge: Polity Press.

Bennis, W. (2007). The challenges of leadership in the modern world. *American Psychologist*, 62, 2–5.

Bennis, W. and Nanus, B. (1997). *Leaders: Strategies for Taking Charge*. (second edition) New York: Harper Business Essentials.

Bies, R. J., Bartunek, J. M., Fort, T. L. and Zald, M. N. (2007). Corporations as social change agents: Individual, interpersonal, institutional, and environmental dynamics. *Academy of Management Review*, 32, 788–793.

Bohman, J. and Rehg, W. (1999). *Deliberative Democracy: Essays on Reason and Politics.* Cambridge, MA, London: MIT Press.

Brown, M. E. (2007). Misconceptions of ethical leadership: How to avoid potential pitfalls. *Organizational Dynamics*, 36, 140–155.

Brown, M. E. and Trevino, L. K. (2006). Ethical leadership: A review and future directions. *The Leadership Quarterly*, 17, 595–616.

Brown, M. E., Trevino, L. K. and Harrison, D. A. (2005). Ethical leadership: A social learning perspective for construct development and testing. *Organizational Behaviour and Human Decision Processes*, 97, 117–134.

Bryman, A. (1996). Leadership in organizations. In: S. Clegg, C. Hardy and W. R. Nord (eds), *Handbook of Organization Studies*. London: Sage, 276–292.

Burns, J. M. (1978). *Leadership*. New York: Harper Torchbooks.

Burns, J. M. (2003). *Transforming Leadership*. New York: Atlantic Monthly Press.

Burrell, G. and Morgan, G. (1979). *Sociological Paradigms and Organisational Analysis*. Aldershot: Ashgate.

By, R. T. (2005). Organizational change management: A critical review. *Journal of Change Management*, 5, 369–380.

Calas, M. B. and Smircich, L. (1988). Reading leadership as a form of cultural analysis. In: J. G. Hunt, B. R. Baliga, H. P. Dachler and C. A. Schreisheim (eds), *Emerging Leadership Vistas*. Lexington, Toronto: Lexington Books, 201–226.

Ciulla, J. B. (1995). Leadership ethics: Mapping the territory. *Business Ethics Quarterly*, 5, 5–28.

Ciulla, J. B. (2004a). Ethics and leadership effectiveness. In: J. Antonakis, A. T. Cianciolo and R. J. Sternberg (eds), *The Nature of Leadership* (302–328). London: Sage.

Ciulla, J. B. (2004b). *Ethics: The Heart of Leadership* (second edition). Westbury: Quorum Books.

Ciulla, J. B. (2005a). Integrating leadership with ethics: Is good leadership contrary to human nature? In: J. P. Doh and S. A. Stumpf (eds), *Handbook on Responsible Leadership and Governance in Global Business*. Cheltenham: Edward Elgar, 159–179.

Ciulla, J. B. (2005b). The state of leadership ethics and the work that lies before us. *Business Ethics: A European Review*, 14, 323–335.

Ciulla, J. B. (2006). Ethics: The heart of leadership. In: T. Maak and N. M. Pless (eds), *Responsible Leadership*. Oxford: Routledge, 17–32.

Cohen, J. (1999). Deliberation and procedure and substance in deliberative democracy. In J. Bohman and W. Rehg (eds), *Deliberative Democracy, Essays on Reason and Politics*. Cambridge, MA, London: MIT Press, 407–437.

Cradden, C. (2005). *Repoliticizing Management. A Theory of Corporate Legitimacy*. Aldershot, Burlington: Ashgate.

Crane, A. and Matten, D. (2007). *Business Ethics: Managing Corporate Citizenship and Sustainability in the Age of Globalization (second edition)*. Oxford: Oxford University Press.

Crane, A., McWilliams, A., Matten, D., Moon, J. and Siegel, D. S. (2008). *The Oxford Handbook of Corporate Social Responsibility*. Oxford, New York: Oxford University Press.

Danon-Leva, E. (2005). Global managers in the age of globalisation. *Global Business and Economics Review*, 7, 16–24.

Den Hond, F. and De Bakker, F. G. A. (2007). Ideologically motivated activism: How activist groups influence corporate social change activities. *Academy of Management Review*, 32, 901–924.

Doh, J. P. and Stumpf, S. A. (2005a). *Handbook on Responsible Leadership and Governance in Global Business*. Cheltenham, Northhampton: Edward Elgar.

Doh, J. P. and Stumpf, S. A. (2005b). Towards a framework of responsible leadership and governance. In J. P. Doh and S. A. Stumpf (eds), *Handbook on Responsible Leadership and Governance in Global Business*. Cheltenham, Northhampton: Edward Elgar, 3–18.

Donaldson, L. (1996). *For Positivist Organization Theory: Proving the Hard Core*. London: Sage.

Donaldson, T. and Preston, L. E. (1995). The stakeholder theory of the corporation: Concepts, evidence, and implications. *Academy of Management Review*, 20, 65–91.

Drath, W. H., McCauley, C. D., Palus, C. J., Van Velsor, E., O'Connor, P. M. G. and McGuire, J. B. (2008). Direction, alignment, commitment: Toward a more integrative ontology of leadership. *The Leadership Quarterly*, 19, 635–653.

Elster, J. (1998). *Deliberative Democracy*. Cambridge: Cambridge University Press.

Freeman, R. E. (1984). *Strategic Management: A Stakeholder Approach*. Boston: Pitman.

Friedman, M. (1970). The social responsibility of business is to increase its profit. *New York Times Magazine*, 13 Sept, 122–126.

Gilbert, D. U. and Rasche, A. (2008). Opportunities and problems of standardized ethics initiatives: A stakeholder theory perspective. *Journal of Business Ethics*, 82, 755–773.

Graetz, F. (2000). Strategic change leadership. *Management Decision*, 38, 550–562.

Graham, J. W. (1991). Servant leadership in organizations: Inspirational and moral. *Leadership Quarterly*, 2, 105–119.

Greenleaf, R. K. (1977). *Servant Leadership: A journey into the Nature of Legitimate Power and Greatness*. New York: Paulist Press.

Habermas, J. (1986). *Knowledge and Human Interests*. Cambridge: Polity Press.

Habermas, J. (1991). *The Structural Transformation of the Public Sphere: An Inquiry into a Category of Bourgeois Society*. Cambridge: Cambridge University Press.

Habermas, J. (1993). Remarks on discourse ethics. In: J. Habermas (ed), *Justification and Application*. Cambridge, MA: MIT Press, 19–111.

Habermas, J. (1996). *Between Facts and Norms: Contributions to a Discourse Theory of Law and Democracy*. Cambridge: Polity Press.

Habermas, J. (2001a). *The Inclusion of the Other: Studies in Political Theory*. (third edition) Cambridge, Massachusetts: MIT Press.

Habermas, J. (2001b). *The Postnational Constellation: Political Essays*. Cambridge: Polity Press.

Hempel, C. G. (1998). Studies in the logic of explanation. In: E. D. Klemke, R. Hollinger, D. W. Rudge and A. D. Kline (eds), *Introductory Readings in the Philosophy of Science* (third edition). Amherst, NY: Prometheus, 206–224.

Hesse, H. (1956). *The Journey to the East*. Picador.

Horkheimer, M. and Adorno, T. W. (1988). *Dialectic of Enlightenment*. Stanford: Stanford University Press.

Hunt, J. G., Baliga, B. R., Dachler, H. P. and Schriesheim, C. A. (1988).
Emerging leadership vistas: An introduction. In: J. G. Hunt, B. R. Baliga, H.
P. Dachler and C. A. Schreisheim (eds), *Emerging Leadership Vistas* (1–3).
Lexington, Toronto: Lexington Books.

Jensen, M. C. (2002). Value maximization, stakeholder theory, and the corporate
objective function. *Business Ethics Quarterly*, 12, 235–256.

Johnson, C. E. (2009). *Meeting the Ethical Challenges of Leadership: Casting Light
or Shadow*. (third edition) Los Angeles, London, New Delhi, Singapore: Sage.

Kellerman, B. (2004). *Bad Leadership*. Cambridge, MA: Harvard Business School.

Kobrin, S. J. (2001). Sovereignity@bay: Globalization, multinational enterprise,
and the international political system. In: A. M. Rugman and T. L. Brewer
(eds), *The Oxford Handbook of International Business* (181–205). Oxford:
Oxford University Press.

Kobrin, S. J. (2008). Globalization, transnational corporations and the future of global
governance. In A. G. Scherer and G. Palazzo (eds), *Handbook of Research on
Global Corporate Citizenship*. Cheltenham: Edward Elgar, 249–272.

Kuhn, T. S. (1962). *The Structure of Scientific Revolutions*. Chicago: University
of Chicago Press.

Laplume, A. O., Sonpar, K. and Litz, R. A. (2008). Stakeholder theory:
Reviewing a theory that moves us. *Journal of Management*, 34, 1152–1189.

Lewin, K. (1951). *Field Theory in Social Science*. New York: Harper & Row.

Liden, R. C., Wayne, S. J., Zhao, H. and Henderson, D. (2008). Servant
leadership: Development of a multidimensional measure and multi-level
assessment. *The Leadership Quarterly*, 19, 161–177.

Lipman-Blumen, J. (2005). *The Allure of Toxic Leaders. Why We Follow
Destructive Bosses and Corrupt Politicians – and How We Can Survive Them*.
Oxford: Oxford University Press.

Maak, T. (2007). Responsible leadership, stakeholder engagement, and the
emergence of social capital. *Journal of Business Ethics*, 74, 329–343.

Maak, T. and Pless, N. M. (2006a). *Responsible Leadership*. Oxford: Routledge.

Maak, T. and Pless, N. M. (2006b). Responsible leadership in a stakeholder
society – A relational perspective. *Journal of Business Ethics*, 66, 99–115.

Maak, T. and Pless, N. M. (2006c). Responsible leadership: A relational
approach. In T. Maak and N. M. Pless (eds), *Responsible Leadership* (33–53).
Oxford: Routledge.

Maak, T. and Ulrich, P. (2007). *Integrity Management. Ethical Orientation for
Business Practice* (released in German, titled: 'Integre Unternehmensführung.
Ethisches Orientierungswissen für die Wirtschaftspraxis'). Stuttgart:
Schäffer-Poeschel.

Matten, D. and Crane, A. (2005). Corporate citizenship: Toward an extended
theoretical conceptualization. *Academy of Management Review*, 30, 166–179.

Mendenhall, M. E., Osland, J. S., Bird, A., Oddou, G. R. and Maznevski, M. L.
(2008). *Global Leadership. Research, Practive and Development*. London,
New York: Routledge.

Michelman, F. I. (1999). How can the people ever make the laws? A critique of deliberative democracy. In: J. Bohman and W. Rehg (eds), *Deliberative Democracy, Essays on Reason and Politics* (145–171). Cambridge/London: MIT Press.

Mitchell, R. K., Agle, B. R. and Wood, D. J. (1997). Toward a theory of stakeholder identification and salience: Defining the principle of who and what really counts. *Academy of Management Review*, 22, 853–886.

Moon, J., Crane, A. and Matten, D. (2005). Can corporations be citizens? Corporate citizenship as a metaphor for business participation in society. *Business Ethics Quarterly*, 15, 429–453.

Moran, J. W. and Brightman, B. K. (2001). Leading organizational change. *Career Development International*, 6, 111–118.

Nicholls, A. and Cho, A. H. (2006). Social entrepreneurship: The structuration of a field. In: A. Nicholls (ed), *Social Entrepreneurship: New Models of Sustainable Social Change* (99–118). Oxford: Oxford University Press.

Palazzo, G. and Scherer, A. G. (2006). Corporate legitimacy as deliberation: A communicative framework. *Journal of Business Ethics*, 66, 71–88.

Palazzo, G. and Scherer, A. G. (2008). The future of global corporate citizenship: Toward a new theory of the firm as a political actor. In: A. G. Scherer and G. Palazzo (eds), *Handbook of Research on Corporate Citizenship*. Cheltenham: Edward Elgar, 577–590.

Patzer, M. (2008). Towards a political conception of leadership responsibility. Conference presentation at the 24th EGOS colloquium 2008, Amsterdam.

Patzer, M. (2009). Leadership and its responsibility under the conditions of globalisation (released in German, titled: 'Führung und ihre Verantwortung unter den Bedingungen der Globalisierung. Ein Beitrag zu einer Neufassung vor dem Hintergrund einer republikanischen Theorie der Multinationalen Unternehmung'). Berlin, Hannover: Patzer Verlag.

Patzer, M. and Scherer, A. G. (2010). Global responsible leadership: Towards a political conception. Conference presentation at the 26th EGOS colloquium 2010, Lisbon.

Pfeffer, J. (1993). Barriers to the advance of organizational science: Paradigm development as a dependent variable. *Academy of Management Review*, 18, 599–620.

Pies, I., Hielscher, S. and Beckmann, M. (2009). Moral commitments and the societal role of business: An ordonomic approach to corporate citizenship. *Business Ethics Quarterly*, 19, 375–401.

Pless, N. M. (2007). Understanding responsible leadership: Role identity and motivational drivers. *Journal of Business Ethics*, 74, 437–456.

Post, J. E., Preston, L. E. and Sachs, S. (2002a). Managing the extended enterprise: The new stakeholder view. *California Management Review*, 45, 6–28.

Post, J. E., Preston, L. E. and Sachs, S. (2002b). *Redefining the Corporation: Stakeholder Management and Organizational Wealth*. Stanford: Stanford Business Books.

Preuss, L., Haunschild, A. and Matten, D. (2009). The rise of CSR: Implications for HRM and Employee Representation. *International Journal of Human Resource Management*, 20, 975–995.

Rehg, W. (1994). *Insight & Solidarity. The discourse Ethics of Jürgen Habermas*. London: University of California Press.

Rokeach, M. (1973). *The Nature of Human Values*. New York: Macmillan.

Rost, J. C. (1991). *Leadership for the Twenty-First Century*. New York: Praeger.

Rost, J. C. (1995). Leadership: A discussion about ethics. *Business Ethics Quarterly*, 5, 129–142.

Scherer, A. G. (2003). *Multinational Organizations and Globalization* (released in German, titled: 'Multinationale Unternehmen und Globalisierung: Zur Neuorientierung der Theorie der Multinationalen Unternehmung'). Heidelberg: Physica-Verlag.

Scherer, A. G. and Smid, M. (2000). The downward spiral and the US model business principles: Why MNEs should take responsibility for the improvement of world-wide social and environmental conditions. *Management International Review (MIR)*, 40, 351–371.

Scherer, A. G. and Baumann, D. (2007). Corporate citizenship: Herausforderung für die Unternehmenskommunikation. In: M. Piwinger and A. Zerfaß (eds), *Handbuch Unternehmenskommunikation*. Wiesbaden: Gabler, 858–873.

Scherer, A. G. and Palazzo, G. (2007). Toward a political conception of corporate responsibility – Business and society seen from a Habermasian perspective. *Academy of Management Review*, 32, 1096–1120.

Scherer, A. G. and Palazzo, G. (2008). Globalization and corporate social responsibility. In: A. Crane, A. McWilliams, D. Matten, J. Moon and D. Siegel (eds), *The Oxford Handbook of Corporate Social Responsibility* (413–431). Oxford: Oxford University Press.

Scherer, A. G., Palazzo, G. and Baumann, D. (2006). Global rules and private actors – Toward a new role of the transnational corporation in global governance. *Business Ethics Quarterly*, 16, 505–532.

Scherer, A. G., Palazzo, G. and Matten, D. (2009a). Globalization as a challenge for business responsibilities. *Business Ethics Quarterly*, 19, 327–347.

Scherer, A. G., Palazzo, G. and Weaver, G. R. (2009b). The role of leadership, responsibility, and ethics in a globalized world: Behavioral issues of implementing CSR. Sub-theme proposal 26th EGOS Colloquium, 1–3 July, 2010.

Scherer, A. G. and Patzer, M. (2008). Paradigms. In S. Clegg and J. R. Bailey (eds), *International Encyclopedia of Organzation Studies* (vol. 4) (1218–1222). London: Sage.

Schneider, M. (2002). A stakeholder model of oganizational leadership. *Organization Science*, 13, 209–220.

Sennet, R. (1998). *The Corrosion of Character*. New York: Norton.

Sharma, P. and Bhal, K. T. (2004). *Managerial Ethics. Dilemmas and Decision Making*. Thousand Oaks/London: Sage.

Smith, D. C. (1995). Ethics and leadership: The 1990's. Introduction to the special issue of the Business Ethics Quarterly. *Business Ethics Quarterly*, 5, 1–3.

Stansbury, J. and Barry, B. (2007). Ethics programs and the paradox of control. *Business Ethics Quarterly*, 17, 239–261.

Suchman, M. C. (1995). Managing legitimacy: Strategic and institutional approaches. *Academy of Management Review*, 20, 571–610.

Sundaram, A. K. and Inkpen, A. C. (2004). The corporate objective revisited. *Organization Science*, 15, 350–363.

Thompson, G. F. (2008). The interrelationship between global and corporate governance: Towards a democratization of the business firm? In: A. G. Scherer and G. Palazzo (eds), *Handbook of Research on Corporate Citizenship* (476–500). Cheltenham: Edward Elgar.

Trevino, L. K. and Weaver, G. R. (1994). Business ETHICS/BUSINESS ethics: One field or two? *Business Ethics Quarterly*, 4, 113–128.

Trevino, L. K., Hartman, L. P. and Brown, K. W. (2000). Moral person and moral manager: How executives develop a reputation for ethical leadership. *California Management Review*, 42, 128–142.

Trevino, L. K., Brown, M. E. and Hartman, L. P. (2003). A qualitative investigation of perceived executive ethical leadership: Perceptions from inside and outside the executive suite. *Human Relations*, 56, 5–37.

Voegtlin, C., Patzer, M. and Scherer, A. G. (2012). Responsible leadership in global business: A new approach to leadership and its multi-level outcomes. *Journal of Business Ethics*, 105(1), 1–16.

Waddock, S. (2008). Corporate responsibility/corporate citizenship: The development of a construct. In: A. G. Scherer and G. Palazzo (eds), *Handbook of Research on Corporate Citizenship*. Cheltenham: Edward Elgar, 50–73.

Waldman, D. A. and Siegel, D. (2008). Defining the socially responsible leader. Theoretical and practitioner letters. *Leadership Quarterly*, 19, 117–131.

Walumbwa, F. O., Avolio, B. J., Gardner, W. L., Wernsing, T. S. and Peterson, S. J. (2008). Authentic leadership: Development and validation of a theory-based measure. *Journal of Management*, 34, 89–126.

Weaver, G. R. and Trevino, L. K. (1994). Normative and empirical business ethics: Separation, marriage of convenience, or marriage of necessity. *Business Ethics Quarterly*, 4, 129–143.

Weaver, G. R. and Trevino, L. K. (1998). Methodologies of business ethics research. In: C. L. Cooper and C. Argyris (eds), *The Concise Blackwell Encyclopedia of Management*. Oxford: Blackwell, 412–415.

Young, I. M. (2004). Responsibility and global labor justice. *Journal of Political Philosophy*, 12, 365–388.

Yukl, G. (2006). *Leadership in Organizations*. (sixth edition). New Jersey: Pearson Prentice Hall.

2 Perceptions and development of ethical change leadership

Rebecca Newton

Introduction

With the growing interest and importance of ethical leadership, in parallel with rapid and continuous organizational change, questions around *how leaders lead change ethically* is of paramount importance. The three sections outlined in this chapter examine key questions regarding ethical change leadership ('ECL') in organizational life.

In section one (*Perceptions of ethical change leadership*), we examine how ethical leadership is practically observed and therefore categorized as such, during organizational change. In section two (*Development of ethical change leadership*), we consider whether ethical change leadership can be developed, and if so, how. On this, we seek to translate hypotheses regarding ethical role modelling and the ethical context in the organization (Brown and Trevino, 2006) to organizational change: (i) being able to identify a proximate, ethical leader role model during organizational change experienced in one's career is positively related to ethical change leadership; and, (ii) an ethical context that supports ethical conduct will be positively related to ethical leadership of organizational change. In section three (*Practical implications*), we offer research-led suggestions for how leaders can promote ethical leadership within their changing organizations.

The findings presented in this chapter are based on qualitative research with experienced leaders who have recently or are currently involved in leading change. Findings will be of interest to both academics and practitioners who seek to ensure organizational change is led in a way that is not only beneficial for the organization, stakeholders and members, but also in a way that is ethical.

Acknowledgments

Our sincere thanks and appreciation goes to the senior leaders who contributed to this research: your willingness to share your ideas and experiences made this work possible. Thanks in particular to Brian Fishel, Catherine Baxendale, Andrew Meyrick and Jeff Lestz; and to all our anonymous contributors.

Section one: Perceptions of ethical change leadership

Over the last quarter of a century, there has been growing empirical investigation to support the interest in and need for a greater understanding of ethical leadership in organizations. One aspect of this field of study, however, remains largely unexplored: ethical leadership in the context of organizational change. In this section, we examine how ethical leadership is practically observed and therefore categorized as such, during organizational change. As noted by Brown (2007), few theorists and practitioners have focused on the *descriptive approach* – the perceptual aspects looking at how people actually perceive issues such as ethical leadership. We apply this descriptive approach to the context of organizational change.

Definitions of ethical leadership

Brown, Trevino and Harrison define ethical leadership as 'the demonstration of normatively appropriate conduct through personal actions and interpersonal relationships, and the promotion of such conduct to followers through two-way communication, reinforcement and decision-making' (2005:120). Such a normative approach concerning business ethics is typically how ethical leadership is defined, that is, how leaders 'ought' to behave in the workplace (Brown, 2007). The challenge with adopting such an approach in the context of organizational change is that, by its very nature, change implies that behavioural and organizational norms will be disrupted and moved. Lewin's 1951 framework for unfreezing, moving and refreezing implies such a shift is required for successful organizational change. To change an organization can mean changing the pattern of recurring behaviour (Katz and Kahn, 1966). Furthermore, a move away from the organization's 'norms' and what is considered 'normatively appropriate' behaviour may be precisely what is necessary in order to move the practices and organization to a more ethical position.

A more appropriate approach therefore may be to consider how ethical leadership is observed in practice and classified as such by organizational members or stakeholders involved in the change. This research will attempt to establish whether known characteristics of ethical leaders apply to the particular context of ECL. Trevino *et al.* (2000, 2003) found evidence that ethical leadership was related to a number of observable personal characteristics ('the moral person'), including being honest, trustworthy, fair, principled, caring about people, caring about the broader society, and to proactively influencing followers' ethical and unethical behaviour ('the moral manager'). Moral managers make ethics salient by communicating clear standards regarding ethics, purposefully role modelling ethical behaviour, and using rewards and discipline to hold people accountable for their ethical or unethical behaviour. Ethical leaders influence followers through both their personal actions and through interpersonal relationships (Brown *et al.*, 2005). Whilst we know ethical leaders influence followers, at the same time it is generally regarded that they should not be too concerned with how they are perceived by others, thereby allowing them to do the right thing even when it is unpopular (Brown, 2007). Thus we have ethical leadership observed in two ways: firstly, the personal or professional characteristics displayed by a leader and observed by followers; secondly, the proactive behaviour of a leader in influencing the actions of those around them and ensuring an ethical environment. According to Wright and Goodstein (2007), an organizational climate is perceived to be ethical when it is characterized by virtue. An ethical leader therefore would proactively encourage and foster such an environment, acting as a 'virtuous agent' in promoting an ethical climate (Fynn, 2008). This notion of a virtuous agent or catalyst can be applied to the context of change leadership.

Leading change

A major task for all organizations is effectively managing change (Carnall, 1990). Whilst minimal empirical research has been conducted into ethical leadership in the context of change, there is a substantial amount of work into ethical decision-making in organizations. This has implications for change leadership as decision-making forms a necessary (though not sufficient) part of the change leadership role. As an example, Ottaway's (1983) taxonomy of change agents identifies three groups:

- **Change generators**, who take decisions regarding what needs to change;

- **Change implementers**, who are responsible for seeing the change come to pass; and
- **Change adopters**, who take up the changes.

A change agent may hold any or all of these roles. The research into ethical decision making can be applied to better understand the Change Generator dimension of ECL.

In a comprehensive review of the studies into ethical decision-making (1996–2003), O'Fallon and Butterfield (2005) outline a number of factors which have been reported as relating to ethical decision-making. Included in these were what can be referred to as 'individual factors' found to be related to greater levels of ethical decision-making, such as more education, employment and work experience, and greater cognitive moral development and ethical judgment. However, they also concluded that some 'organizational factors' relate to greater levels of ethical decision-making; these include having a code of ethics, and having ethical climates and cultures within the organization. Many of these studies into decision-making in the field of descriptive ethics are built upon Rest's (1986) framework which outlines four basic components of moral decision-making: identifying the moral nature of an issue; making a moral judgment; establishing moral intent; and engaging in moral action. Such components may play a role in the decision-making component of ECL. These components, together with O'Fallon and Butterfield's 2005 factors linked to ethical leadership, were considered in the research conducted with experienced change leaders.

Senior leader perceptions and development of ECL

Qualitative research was conducted with informants, all of whom are senior members of their organization and have experience of observing and leading organizational change. Interviews were used to ascertain the leaders' perceptions and development of ECL.[1] Interviewees had experience within a wide range different industries including:

- Banking and finance
- Fast moving consumer goods
- Legal
- Retail
- Professional services
- Hospitality
- Public sector

Four in-depth case studies of how ethical change leaders are perceived are offered below.

Case study examples of ethical change leaders

INTERVIEW WITH DIRECT REPORT OF THE MANAGEMENT TEAM, ON THE GENERAL MANAGER, PROCTER & GAMBLE

15 years ago our division was going through a bad time; numbers were poor. A new General Manager was appointed. I considered him an ethical leader who led us through a lot of change as he listened to what people felt and what they perceived was going wrong. He introduced new values, behaviours and norms, which he expected people to aspire to, and he moved us into a new modern building which had a tangible impact on morale and mood. He introduced new culture, 'ways of working' and cross-functional working. He had respect for others, a more understanding approach to other functions, was more collective, flexible, and positive, and opened up the business. This resulted in improved business results. He – and subsequently our team – became a beacon for the business. Other parts of the business would come to see what we were doing and learn from us. He was very honourable, decent, trustworthy, inspired respect and followership.

As an example of how he led change ethically, there was a famous meeting in company folklore, where he gathered everyone to the new site and said, 'Business results are bad! We're going to move them to a place where we're proud.' He was overt, stark and completely honest with us with what was quite a harsh reality, but at the same time inspired us to change and build a new reality.

INTERVIEW WITH CATHERINE BAXENDALE, HR DIRECTOR COMMERCIAL AND MARKETING, TESCO UK

In the mid-late 1990s, Tesco embarked on a significant change to create the organization the new CEO wanted to lead. One of the key changes was around improving efficiencies – lean processes were put in place, simpler meetings, time management, meeting management, core skills, and some large governance changes such as how the Board operated and how trading operated each week. Everyone asked the question, 'How do we improve what we do for customers each year?' and a subsequent customer improvement plan was put into place. How do you engage an organization this big in such a change? Ethical leadership was key.

The new Board listened to people, asked for feedback, ran focus groups to ascertain people's ideas, and engaged the business in the process. One key was the introduction of our *Purpose and Values*. There was a manifestation of ethical leadership in this change programme. The Purpose and Values, introduced in 1997, were refreshed a couple of years ago, rolled out to all 14 countries we operate in, and this year we launched the 'Oscars Values Awards'.

The CEO wanted us to be ethical leaders. He had a vision of what he wanted us to be and ended up with some ground rules regarding what is and isn't acceptable in our organization.

Our values now are like a touchstone for the business – they provide us with a moral compass of what people should and shouldn't do in different places around the world and in different organizational contexts.

INTERVIEW WITH BRIAN FISHEL, SVP EXECUTIVE AND LEADERSHIP EXECUTIVE DEVELOPMENT, BANK OF AMERICA

Ethical change leadership is of growing importance in the world today because so many situations and decisions are ambiguous. Some key attributes of ethical change leaders are objectivity, transparency, trust, inclusion, creating space for productive dialogue and 'push-back'.

Ethical leadership comes into play every time someone has to make significant changes in their organization. A leader must consider many factors when making such decisions. First the leader must look objectively at performance and really focus on achieving the objective, but also the leader needs to make sure they're working off the right information.

Ethical change leadership means having the courage and conviction to speak up for what is ethically right and not get deterred by opposition. When people's opinions are different, it's important to ensure the right decision is made even if it means it's politically incorrect or unpopular. Integrity in decision-making process is fundamental to initiating successful change as a leader.

Ethical leadership in the context of change means taking a broad view of the issue; looking at things from the total enterprise. Whether it's driving to change an organization, driving a new product, etc., the reality is that as a leader it's vital to take that into account wider organizational needs in any change. The right decision within your unit or business might be the wrong decision for your company overall, and it can lead to unethical decisions when a leader maximises their own (team/unit) interests at the expense of the wider organization.

INTERVIEW WITH ANDREW MEYRICK, FORMER DIRECTOR OF FINANCE AND
PERFORMANCE OF TRANSPORT FOR LONDON INFORMATION MANAGEMENT ON THE
CIO AND LEADERSHIP TEAM

Whilst Director of Finance and Performance of TfL IM (1300 staff, £400m annual budget) I was privileged to be number two to the CIO. We had a major change programme to complete, bringing in outsourced work and also moving temps and contractors to permanent staff, whilst rolling out a ten-year plan of complete infrastructure change for TfL.

Challenged with some underperformance issues and a very tight timetable, we introduced 'Advocacy'. The Advocacy Network was created by a form of network marketing with each cell having a leader and five members. Their tasks were varied but after a two intensive days' training, they were sent out to be an ethical, fair and positive force in the change programme.

They were very successful as they became the measure of right and wrong, of fairness and reasonableness, whilst expounding, honouring everyone and respecting their viewpoints. We were trained in confrontation management, expected to train the teams and ensure that behaviours and values were a priority. This extended to the leadership team of which I was a member. We had a code of practice and behaviour and were each required to give a leadership pledge to the whole of IM. We developed a brand and identity to make people feel part of a large team going forward. The organizational change programme went by almost without incident to the extent that the unions were fully supportive as well.

What impacts perceptions of ECL?

Case study and interview research findings suggest the following components impact perceptions of ECL:

- **Honesty and transparency**. Being honest about the current reality, transparent regarding what needs to change and open about the vision for the future unit/organizational state;
- **Feedback**. Proactively ascertaining others' ideas and feelings, listening to them, gathering accurate data from which to make decisions, involving people across the unit/organization and where appropriate incorporating their perceptions of what needs to change;
- **Culture**. Change which either incorporates the existing culture or, if necessary, reworks organizational culture – values, behaviours, norms, and ways of working indicating what is and is not acceptable within that context;

- **'Right' decisions**. The right decisions are taken and corresponding change actions are made regardless of how popular or unpopular they may be. Right decisions on one hand mean responding to the needs of the individual person or individual situation, whilst always taking an enterprise view (regard for the bigger picture/organizational objective);

> To me ethical leadership during change is doing the right thing even in the eye of the storm. Staying the course even when everyone else is abandoning ship or doing the easy thing or taking the path of least resistance. Principled living is not necessarily the easy way to the working out of a situation.
>
> Jeff Lestz, Co-founder and CEO, Genistar Ltd
> (financial services)

- **Impact**. Ethical change leaders influenced people around them to engage in ethical behaviours. Their change interventions had a positive impact on the unit/organization and led to improved business results.

Overall, there was great consistency in the senior leaders' perceptions of ECL, and a resounding belief that it is of upmost importance to ensure successful and positive organizational change. Many of the ethical change leader qualities correspond to previous findings related to what is perceived as an ethical leader. Research suggests that characteristics of ethical leadership (such as the 'moral person' and 'moral manager', Trevino *et al.*, 2000, 2003) apply to the context of organizational change.

Section two: Development of ethical change leadership

Given the importance of ECL, the ensuing question is how to increase its presence in today's organization. This section presents the question, 'can ECL be developed, and if so, how?' In particular, we translate hypotheses regarding ethical role modelling and the ethical context in the organization (Brown and Trevino, 2006) to organizational change, hypothesising that:

1. being able to identify a proximate, ethical leader role model during organizational change experienced in one's career is positively related to ethical change leadership; and,
2. an ethical context that supports ethical conduct will be positively related to ethical leadership of organizational change.

Can ECL be developed?

> I definitely believe ethical change leadership can be developed
>   Catherine Baxendale, HR Director, Commercial and
>   Marketing, Tesco UK

Research results reveal a widespread belief amongst senior leaders that ethical leadership of change can be developed, albeit with some constraints. Largely, leaders considered that the development of ethical leadership itself was possible, and when ethical leaders were faced with the responsibility of leading change they would subsequently do so ethically. Not only was the development of ECL considered possible, it was largely considered a responsibility of senior leadership to foster throughout their organizations. There was some concern, however, that whilst the behaviours of ECL could be encouraged, including by the development of an ethical framework within the organization, it may not be possible to 'make someone ethical'.

> I believe you can teach people to think about problems in a way where ethics is at the centre. You can educate people regarding what is considered to be appropriate, you can provide them tools and resources to aid in their thinking and decisions, and you can help make them aware of their assumptions and box the boundaries of ethics. You can have mentors and coaches to serve as sounding boards to help make people conscious about their actions, and you can help people learn from their experience. But I don't know if I believe that you can make someone ethical. Ethical or non-ethical seems binary rather than a scale you can move people along.
>   Brian Fishel, SVP Executive and Leadership
>   Development, Bank of America Corporation

It is important to note therefore, that although the following factors are key to developing ECL, they do not necessarily imply the development of an ethical person who leads change. These factors are:

- being aware of, modelling and promoting a code of conduct for the change, outlining what is and what is not acceptable in that organizational context;
- seeking to gain others' input into changes;
- understanding the consequences of decisions taken and the impact of one's actions on others involved in the change;
- making the moral and 'right' change decisions within the context of that organization, and within the boundaries of government regulations and the law; and
- facilitating others to engage in the above during organizational change.

We sought to translate hypotheses regarding ethical role modelling and the ethical context in the organization (Brown and Trevino, 2006) to organizational change: (1) being able to identify a proximate, ethical leader role model during organizational change experienced in one's career is positively related to ECL; and, (2) an ethical context that supports ethical conduct will be positively related to ethical leadership of organizational change.

A proximate, ethical role model

There is considerable research evidence to suggest that ethical leader role models impact the development of one's own ability to lead ethically (Brown and Trevino, 2006; Mayer *et al.*, 2009). Having an ethical leader role model during organizational change throughout one's career was found to be positively related to senior leaders' own ability to lead change ethically.

> How does a leader become ethical or unethical? I believe they have been influenced by their mentors and people they look up to. It is not convenient to adopt the 'always do what is right' attitude in the society we live in. I believe the only way to develop ethical change leadership is to practice it and this will in turn influence others to do the same. My own personal experience of mentors has influenced me to be ethical.
>
> Jeff Lestz, Co-founder and CEO, Genistar Ltd

Research indicated that of particular importance was having an ethical leader role model who was *proximate* and *accessible* during change. That is, the senior leader participants had been able to tangibly observe how the leader carried out changes in an ethical manner. Some researchers have argued that top management influence is strongest on employee behaviour (Weaver *et al.*, 2005), and that they are responsible for establishing the organization's ethical values (Grojean *et al.*, 2004). Others, however, hold that supervisors are more likely to serve as ethical role models, given their proximity and intimacy of communication (Davis and Rothstein, 2006; Posner and Schmidt, 1984). Findings here supported the latter argument, and the 'proximate' claim of Brown and Trevino's (2006) hypothesis. Regardless of their hierarchical status within the organization, what influenced the interviewees' development of ECL was their proximity to ethical change leader role models. Their own ability to lead change ethically was influenced by their experience at some point over their career of being able to closely observe the ECL of their proximate managers, including the way they approached the change, involved stakeholders, made difficult (and often unpopular) decisions, and implemented the change process. Of particular influence was when that leader had sought their opinion, personally involved them in the change, encouraged debate, and challenged their perspectives of the change process. These change management findings echo Weaver, Trevino and Agle's (2005) claim that ethical role modelling is a 'side by side phenomenon' (p.12). A number of leaders claimed that even if the experience had been early on in their career, that ethical change leader role model *'left a lasting impression on how I manage change today'*. It is important to note the finding that where participants had experienced a leader who from their perspective was unethical in the way they led change, they too left an impression and had an impact on the way that participant led change.

Findings provided support for hypothesis (1): being able to identify a proximate, ethical leader role model during organizational change experienced in one's career is positively related to ECL.

An ethical context that supports ethical conduct

ETHICAL CLIMATE

Empirical evidence suggests organizational climate influences ethical leadership: an organization's ethical climate *signals and reinforces* to members what is appropriate or acceptable behaviour in that context (O'Fallon and Butterfield, 2005; Trevino *et al.*, 1998). Having an ethical organizational climate was considered by research participants to be an essential foundation for developing people who would lead change ethically. Research findings also suggest, that some climates may pose greater challenges than others when developing people who will lead change ethically (the example given was often the financial sector). So whilst development of ECL was considered possible, and having an ethical climate of upmost importance, there was recognition of the climatic differences and substantial sectoral challenges leaders may face when developing other ethical change leaders. This reflects Trevino and Brown's argument that 'the environment has become quite complex and is rapidly changing, providing all sorts of ethical challenges and opportunities to express greed' (2004:77).

In order to address such challenges, the extent to which change leaders understand the ethical boundaries within which they are called to operate was considered of particular importance. That is, ethical change leaders were developed within their particular organizational context and with a sound understanding of not only the laws and regulations governing their industry and changes, but also the organizational values and expectations of how change is carried out. This was often supported and reinforced by having a clear code of ethics.

CODE OF ETHICS

Most studies support the concept that a code of ethics is positively related to ethical decision-making (O'Fallon and Butterfield, 2005). Given the role of decision-making in change leadership, a code of ethics to guide leaders may foster ECL. This was supported in the research findings. In the TfL IM case study example above, a code of practice and behaviour stood as a code of ethics for how leaders pledged to roll out the change programme.[2] The Director interviewed attributed the change programme's success largely to the existence and adherence to this code. Such a code of conduct is a means of supporting ethical conduct.

Findings provided support for hypothesis (2): an ethical context that supports ethical conduct will be positively related to ethical leadership of organizational change.

Further keys to developing ECL

We have applied Brown and Trevino's (2006) hypotheses regarding role models and context and seen them supported in the case of ECL. Additional means of developing ECL were also identified in the research.

Case studies

Case studies were suggested by participants as a means of helping others develop their ability to lead change ethically. Discussions should be facilitated and different views expanded using internal organizational and external case studies. This was regarded a safe and important means of encouraging leaders to develop their ECL as they:

- explore different approaches and consequences to leading change;
- recognize different stakeholders involved in change;

- become mindful of the conflicting positions from which others might view the world so leaders are able to adopt a worldview rather than their own single view; and
- are encouraged to 'open their minds' through debate and discussion rather than being told simply what to do and how to lead change ethically.

Professional bodies

Membership of, and association with, professional bodies which encourage and support ethical trade was regarded as a means of fostering ECL. Particularly important was ensuring leaders had access to discuss options and decisions for change with such bodies and experts, and enabling leaders to gain inspiration from others.

Selection of change leaders

Key to organizational change is the concept of the 'change agent' – 'people, either inside or outside the organization, who are providing technical, specialist, or consulting assistance in the management of a change effort' (Beckhard, 1969:10). Change agents are responsible for assessing reality against organizational vision, identifying the need for change, taking decisions regarding what needs to change and leading the implementation of those changes. Decisions regarding who leads the change will ultimately influence the change success. Research participants took the view that it is ethical leaders who will lead change ethically. That is, rather than suggesting someone is or is not an ethical *change* leader, the key criteria is whether someone is or is not an ethical leader. An ethical leader who is consistent in this behaviour will be an ethical *change* leader when faced with change responsibilities. This has implications for the selection of the change agent. In order to develop ECL in an organization, those chosen to be responsible for decision-making and implementation of changes should be those who consistently demonstrate ethical behaviour. Developing ECL across an organization is therefore somewhat dependent upon selecting change agents who are ethical. This reinforces the importance of the 'virtuous agent' or 'catalyst' in organizational change (Fynn, 2008).

> The change team the CIO selected had certain qualities in common. He required honour, honesty and respect above all from this team and he

ensured that their behaviours were honed and well established. All petty
issues were ironed out rapidly and a successful change team was formed.

Andrew Meyrick, Former Director of Finance and
Performance of TfL IM

Leadership development programmes

Participants felt that leadership development programmes were an important
component in developing people within the organization who would lead
change ethically. Whilst no reports were made of teaching 'ethics' as a
subject within such programmes, it was regarded as a common thread that
underpinned the development programmes offered within interviewee
organizations. Leadership development programmes should have two
elements to accomplish this: (1) be built upon the organization's core values,
and (2) comprise at least in part of modules on organizational change.
Experiential and role-play scenarios were suggested as means of allowing
leaders to experiment with different change leadership scenarios they may
face, and as a window to open dialogue and debate regarding what decisions
and actions would and would not be ethical within their particular context.

Partnerships and organizational relationships

Senior leaders felt it was possible to develop ethical change leaders not only
within their organizations, but also through partnerships and relationships
with leaders in other organizations. Tesco is continuously presented with such
an opportunity through international outsourcing – based in Hong Kong with
hubs across Turkey, Cambodia, Pakistan, Sri Lanka, Bangladesh and China.
When looking to improve sourcing, key partnership considerations for Tesco
include the quality of products and legal and technical due diligence to ensure
the ethical factors meet required standards. Furthermore, strong organizations
also have the opportunity to drive change which will foster ethical leadership.
This represents a different form of ECL, where the change itself is the shift
towards ethical leadership by other organizations.

When sourcing goods from developing countries it is important to make
decisions based on lots of local implications rather than just focusing on
price and quality. The impact of sourcing on the local community and
economy is critical, and therefore demonstrating and fostering ethical
leadership plays an important part in this.

Catherine Baxendale, HR Director Commercial
and Marketing, Tesco UK

Rewards and sanctions

It was expected that rewards and sanctions may play a role in the development of ECL, given the evidence of their role in ethical behaviour (O'Fallon and Butterfield, 2005). Senior leaders in the research however did *not* highlight this as of particular importance when developing ethical change leaders, suggesting this may be an area for future research.

Section three: Practical implications

Practitioners can be incentivized to select for and develop ethical leadership within their organizations (Brown and Trevino, 2006). Supporting this claim, senior leaders involved in the research felt a responsibility to develop ethical change leaders within their organizations. The methods outlined for 'developing ethical change leadership' in section two above provide a number of practical ways in which ECL can be enhanced:

- providing proximate, accessible ethical change leader role models;
- ensuring an ethical climate supported by a clear code of ethics for the change;
- using case studies to increase awareness and encourage debate;
- providing access to professional bodies concerned with the development of ethical behaviour in organizational life;
- selecting ethical leaders for the change agent teams;
- engaging leaders in leadership development programmes underpinned by organizational values and consisting of modules on change management; and
- forming partnerships and organizational relationships which encourage ECL beyond the immediate walls of their particular organization.

Below, further research-led suggestions and considerations are offered to assist leaders in promoting ethical leadership within their changing organizations.

Increasing time and resources . . . or exposure and competence

Research findings suggest that ECL equates to not taking the short term, easy option. Therefore when planning organizational change, increased resources and more time may be necessary in order to ensure change is led ethically. The reality, however, is that timeframes are often tight and resources limited during organizational change. In order to compensate for this need, practitioners may expose leaders to change case studies and leadership development programmes to increase their experience and understanding of potentially ethically challenging scenarios, thereby speeding up their response and increasing their competence when faced with the actual change.

Impact on followers, norms and the 'ethical climate'

It is important for practitioners to note that during organizational change, the decisions and actions of change leaders are being closely observed. Uncertainty often surrounds organizational change, including organizational members' potentially threatened self-interest and fear of poor outcomes (Kotter and Schlesinger, 1979). This results in an increase in the degree to which leaders' decisions and actions are watched and assessed. As such, change leaders should be made aware that their actions may influence the establishment of new norms and acceptable conduct more than when the organization is in more stable phases.

Communication

Open, honest and transparent communication was one of the key ways in which ECL was perceived, according to research participants. Practitioners must encourage leaders to be mindful of common organizational change pitfalls which can prevent the development of ECL. Such pitfalls include secrecy around the change (whereas transparency is what is required for ECL), and subsequent lack of trust and sense of collaboration; and a *change* in the degree to which organizational members and stakeholders are informed and involved. Any decrease in information and involvement surrounding the change may be perceived by others as unethical behaviour, as it breaks from their expectation of organizational/team/unit norms and what is considered 'acceptable' based on past experience.

Ethical leadership and resistance to change

An area for consideration by practitioners, and future research by academics, is the impact of ECL on employee resistance. Employees in contemporary organizations are aware that in order to be successful, change in any form is necessary (Rousseau, 1998). Change, therefore, does not necessarily generate resistance. Equally important to what changes are carried out is the way in which these changes are led, as resistance is often to the management or leadership of change rather than the change content itself (van Dijk and van Dick, 2009). '. . . what some may perceive as disrespectful or unfounded opposition (to change) might also be motivated by individuals' ethical principles or by their desire to protect the organization's best interests' (Piderit, 2000:785). Therefore what may be observed as unethical change decision-making or implementation may increase employee resistance; ECL on the other hand may serve to reduce resistance during organizational change.

Conclusion

ECL is perceived as the demonstration of ethical decision-making processes and ethical implementation of organizational change. Whilst one may not be able to 'make a person ethical', it is possible to foster and develop ECL capabilities within an organization. Many factors influence the extent to which an organization develops leaders who behave ethically when faced with the many challenges and uncertainties of change, a number of which have been presented here.

Despite the fact that a large amount of research remains to be done in terms of understanding and promoting ECL, results from this research indicate that the extensive recent work on ethical leadership is largely applicable to the context of organizational change and can help to inform academics and practitioners in this field. Whilst there were substantial differences in the industries and change experiences of leaders enlisted in this research, it is encouraging to note three similarities. First, the senior leaders believe ECL does exist and have numerous examples of where they have experienced it (although not always to the degree they would like, or perceive as necessary). Second, they believe ECL can be developed and that this development is a responsibility of senior management within organizations. Finally, the senior leaders who shared their experiences hold the common belief that ethical change leadership is an increasingly important topic for study and a vital component of any organization's success in today's increasingly complex environment.

Notes

1 Key interview questions can be found in Appendix 1.

2 The Code of Ethics for the TfL 'Your IM' change leadership team can be found in Appendix 2.

References

Beckhard, R. (1969) *Organization Development: Strategies and Models*. Reading, MA: Addison-Wesley.

Brown, M. E. (2007) Misconceptions of ethical leadership: How to avoid potential pitfalls. *Organizational Dynamics*, 36(2), 140–155.

Brown, M. E. and Trevino, L. K. (2006) Ethical Leadership: A review and future directions. *The Leadership Quarterly*, 17, 595–616.

Brown, M. E., Trevino, L. K. and Harrison, D. (2005) Ethical Leadership: A social learning perspective for construct development and testing. *Organizational Behavior and Human Decision Processes*, 97, 117–134.

Carnall, C. (1990) *Managing change in organizations*. Englewood Cliffs, New Jersey: Prentice Hall.

Davis, A. and Rothstein, H. (2006) The effects of the perceived behavioural integrity of managers on employee attitudes: A meta-analysis. *Journal of Business Ethics*, 67, 407–419.

Fynn, G. (2008) The virtuous manager: A vision for leadership in business. *Journal of Business Ethics*, 78, 359–372.

Grojean, M., Resick, C., Dickson, M., and Smith, D. B. (2004) Leaders, values, and organizational climate: Examining leadership strategies for establishing an organizational climate regarding ethics. *Journal of Business Ethics*, 55, 223–241.

Katz, D. and Kahn, R. L. (1966) *The Social Psychology of Organizations* (second edition). New York: Holt, Rhinehart and Winston.

Kotter, J. P. and Schlesinger, L. A. (1979) Choosing strategies for change. *Harvard Business Review*, 57, 106–114.

Lewin, K. (1951) In: D. Cartwright (ed) *Field Theory in Social Science*. London: Tavistock.

Mayer, D. M., Kuenzi, M., Greenbaum, R., Bardes, M. and Salvador, R. (2009) How low does ethical leadership flow? Test of a trickle-down model. *Organizational Behavior and Human Decision Processes*, 108, 1–13.

O'Fallon, M. J. and Butterfield, K. D. (2005) A review of the empirical ethical decision-making literature: 1996–2003. *Journal of Business Ethics*, 59, 375–413.

Ottaway, R. N. (1983) The change agent: A taxonomy in relation to the change process. *Human Relations*, 36, 361–392.

Piderit, S. K. (2000) Rethinking resistance and recognizing ambivalence: A multidimensional view of attitudes toward an organizational change. *Academy of Management Review*, 25, 783–794.

Posner, B. and Schmidt, W. (1984) Values and the American manager: An update. *California Management Review*, 26, 202–216.

Rest, J. R. (1986) *Moral Development: Advances in Research and Theory*. New York: Praeger.

Rousseau, D. M. (1998) Why workers still identify with organizations. *Journal of Organizational Behavior*, 19, 217–233.

Trevino, L. K. and Brown, M. E. (2004) Managing to be ethical: Debunking five business ethics myths. *Academy of Management Executive*, 18, 69–81.

Trevino, L. K., Brown, M. and Hartman, L. P. (2003) A qualitative investigation of perceived executive ethical leadership: Perceptions from inside and outside the executive suite. *Human Relations*, 55, 5–37.

Trevino, L. K., Butterfield, K. D. and McCabe, D. L. (1998) The ethical context in organizations: Influences on employee attitudes and behaviours. *Business Ethics Quarterly*, 8, 447–476.

Trevino, L. K., Hartman, L. P. and Brown, M. (2000) Moral person and moral manager: How executives develop a reputation for ethical leadership. *California Management Review*, 42, 128–142.

Van Dijk, R. and van Dick, R. (2009) Navigating organizational change: change leaders, employee resistance and work-based identities. *Journal of Change Management*, 9(2) 143–163.

Weaver, G. R., Trevino, L. K. and Agle, B. (2005) Somebody I look up to: Ethical role models in organizations. *Organizational Dynamics*, 34, 313–330.

Wright, T. A. and Goodstein, J. (2007) Character is not "dead" in management research: A review of individual character and organization-level virtue. *Journal of Management*, 33(6), 928–958.

Appendix 1

Key questions for senior leader interviews

Topic 1: Ethical leadership during organizational change

- Please describe some examples of when you have practically observed 'ethical leadership' in the context of organizational change.
- What in particular made you perceive this person/people or their actions to be examples of 'ethical leadership' during change?

Topic 2: Development of ethical change leadership

- Do you believe it is possible to *develop* 'ethical *change* leadership'? If so, how? (Please be specific with regards to ethical change leadership rather than just leadership development in general.)
- In the examples provided in question one above, what factors do you believe contributed to the development of ethical change leadership?

Appendix 2

Box 1: TfL 'Your IM' change project leadership team code of ethics

Your IM

Leadership pledge

As the leaders of Your IM, and above all as TfL business leaders, we pledge to:

- Provide a clear vision for Your IM and a viable strategy to make it reality
- Challenge the status quo and develop solutions that move Your IM and IT in TfL forward
- Foster collaboration within Your IM and with our customers so that we operate as one team
- Encourage open and honest communication across Your IM, seeking your input and responding constructively to your feedback
- Work with you to create a consumer centric culture than ensures Your IM is a great place to work
- Provide you with the opportunities, empowerment and support to fulfil your potential within Your IM
- Recognize your contribution and build confidence across Your IM to always strive for more
- Set the standard and act as role models for Your IM
- Be a positive force for change within TfL
- Be good stewards and take care of Your IM

3 Justice and the ethical quality of leadership

Carl Rhodes

Introduction

The relationship between leadership and justice is something that has attracted increasing concern in the study of management (Colquitt and Greenberg, 2003; Van Knippenberg, De Cremer and Van Knippenberg, 2007; Janson *et al.*, 2008). This concern is expressed especially in terms of how the fairness with which leaders treat their followers is considered to be a core dimension of ethical leadership (Den Hartog and De Hoogh, 2009), which exerts an influence on the success and acceptance of organizational change (Daly and Geyer, 1994; Van Dijke and De Cremer, 2008). Indeed it is in conditions of organizational change that issues of ethics can become especially highlighted – the disruption of established ways of doing things resulting as it does in heightened sensitivities and the need to rethink the meaning of old norms and practices. In such conditions 'leaders are important sources of fairness and unfairness in organizations' (Van Knippenberg *et al.*, 2007: 131) to the extent that the metering out of justice is a central part of what leaders should be doing. Moreover it has been argued that justice can improve the quality of leadership as well as promote the acceptance of organizational change (Colquitt *et al.*, 2005).

While justice might just now be considered as a leadership virtue that can oil the wheels of change, the virtuousness of justice has a long and ancient tradition in Western thought. As far back as 350 BC, Aristotle (2000) lauded justice as a 'complete virtue' that rose above all of the others. Justice is thus privileged because it is a virtue that attends not only to the self, but to the self's relation to others. Justice is always about justice for others in the community. Central to Aristotle's conception of justice was fairness as it relates to the distribution of those resources, for example goods and money, that are to be shared amongst a community.

Clearly Aristotle's definition of justice immediately resonates with what we understand today as leadership. A leader's fairness has been identified as a core 'heuristic' with which followers make judgements about whether they can 'can rely on a given leader to lead them to ends that are good for the collective, rather than just good for the leader' (Janson *et al.*, 2008). A just leader is positioned as one who manages fairly and in the interests of others, while an unjust leader would be s/he who uses others for his or her own selfish ends. This chapter provides a critical interrogation and re-evaluation of this relationship between leadership and justice, especially in terms of the leadership of organizational change.

The chapter begins with a review and critique of existing approaches to how this relationship is theorized. Two main points of contention are raised. First that research into justice and leadership tends to assume that justice involves leaders treating others fairly, but that those others are solely motivated by self-interest. Second that while just leaders are proposed as being focused on the interests of others (i.e. employees), those interests are ultimately assumed to align with corporate or organizational interests. These two issues, it is argued, reflect an unquestioned managerialism that, while speaking the language of ethics and justice, actually considers justice largely from an instrumental perspective. Justice, by this account, is good, because it is good for business and as a result remains self- rather than other-centred. The second part of the chapter responds to these critiques by outlining the possibilities of an other-centred justice for leadership, taking inspiration from the ethical philosophy of Emmanuel Levinas (1969, 1985, 1998, 2006). It is argued that the multiple ethical demands faced by organizations put leaders in a position where ethical attention to those they lead is always divided, and hence compromised. Justice is here not so much a matter of 'effectiveness' but instead a persistent demand that is endemic to the very nature of leadership. As a result, the challenge for leadership is not to assert the value of its own just-ness, but to grapple with the aporia between the ethical necessity for justice and its own inevitable participation in injustice to others. Justice is not here regarded as a 'goal' that can be achieved through particular leadership or change management practices, but is an ongoing condition, the response to which defines the ethical quality of leadership.

Organizational justice and its leadership

Research into justice and fairness perceptions in organizations gathered steam during the 1960s and 1970s up to a point where it is now an established mainstay of management theory. As we shall see, however, in the hands of management scholars the meaning of justice takes on quite a different hue compared to the way that it has been considered elsewhere. For leadership in particular, the focus is less on the virtuousness of leaders, and more on their effectiveness in their professional roles. The imperative given to leaders is to ensure that the people they lead do not feel that they are being treated unfairly so that the leader can better achieve his or her organizational objectives.

The most common way that organizational justice is understood is in terms of its separation into three distinct 'dimensions'. Firstly, distributive justice as related to the ways in which resources are or are not perceived to be distributed fairly in organizations. Secondly, procedural justice in terms of the extent to which employees feel that the processes used for the distribution of resources are administered fairly. Thirdly, interactional justice, meaning how fairly people feel they are treated in interpersonal interactions in organizations. For each of these three dimensions justice has been researched in terms of the extent to which people perceive that they are treated fairly in and by their organizations. In these terms justice is less a matter of social equity or personal virtue, and more a matter of whether or not people believe that are treated in a way that makes them worse off than others. By implication organizational justice regards employees as self-serving and self-interested subjects whose motives are to ward off the possibility that other people are securing a greater advantage than they are.

In terms of organizational change, justice relates to whether people perceive that the process, outcome and interactions related to change are fair for them. Cropanzano and Stein confirm that '[o]rganizational justice research generally understands fairness [justice] as a subjective perception by a person or persons . . . [and that] . . . a workplace event is "fair" or "unfair" because an individual or individuals believes it to be so' (Cropanzano and Stein, 2009). This fairness can relate to almost any aspect of organizational life; however, particular attention has been paid to matters related to remuneration and benefits, recruitment, promotion, the management of work loads, as well as change management. Irrespective of the specific issue, however, it is always the individual's perception of whether or not they are treated justly that is privileged – justice is here much less about the possibility of virtuous behaviour or just institutions and more about whether other people (especially leaders) are perceived to be just or not. This approach harbours the assumption that employees are less interested in the ethics and fairness of their own behaviour and how they treat other people, and more interested in how others treat them. This relegation of justice as a matter of employee self-interest is deeply ironic. On the one hand it heralds the virtue of justice for employees, while on the other hand assumes that these recipients of justice are only in it for themselves.

In terms of followers, this dominant perspective on organizational justice is less about ethical social arrangements to do with how people relate to each other in a community, and, as suggested in Table 3.1, more about personal perceptions over whether I am happy about what other people are doing to me. Moreover, the organization and its leaders – those assumed to be responsible for justice – are further sanctified in their power because it is they only who are given credit for being able to behave on the basis of an ethically informed justice. As far as employees are concerned, their only interest in justice is assumed to be for themselves – the theoretical underpinning of organizational justice falsely rendering them solipsistic and disinterested in any social or political dimensions of their organizations other than those that lead to their own personal feelings of fairness and satisfaction.

The relationship between leadership and justice is cast in the following terms:

> The main question in leadership research has always been what makes leaders influential and effective. . . . Inspired by research in organizational justice . . . in recent years leadership research has increasingly engaged with the notion that to answer this question we need to understand the role of leader fairness.
> *(Van Knippenberg and De Cremer, 2008: 173)*.

This indicates a further irony in terms of how management thinkers have conceived of the relationship between leadership and justice. On the one

Table 3.1 *Dimensions of organizational justice*

Dimension	Explicit leader's roles	Implied follower's roles
Distributive justice	Fair distribution of resources such as pay and benefits – especially on the basis of merit	Ensure others do not receive a more advantageous share of resources than self
Procedural justice	Equal and fair application of rules and procedures to all employees	Ensure that others do not receive favouritism in application of rules and procedures
Interactional justice	Consistent communication and information sharing and treating all employees with respect	Ensure that self is not disrespected and that others do not receive more or privileged information

hand, just leadership is stated as being about a concern for the collective good rather than for the leader's own ends; on the other hand, what is claimed to be the value of studying leadership justice is that it has a 'substantial impact on the evaluation and effectiveness of leaders' (Janson *et al.*, 2008: 252) and their ability to stimulate self-esteem amongst followers (De Cremer *et al.*, 2005). But, in the performative nature of contemporary organizations what might be closer to the heart of a leader's own interests than his or her personal/organizational effectiveness? Other researchers have claimed that perceptions of leadership and justice amongst employees provide for enhanced cooperation amongst teams (De Cremer and Van Knippenberg, 2003) as well as an improved sense of social self-esteem amongst followers (De Cremer, 2003). Leadership justice has been shown too to increase followers' levels of commitment, which in turn means that they 'perform better, are less likely to leave the company, and engage more easily in organizational citizenship behavior' (De Cremer *et al.*, 2006: 555). Moreover, this is thought to be desirable because 'in groups and organizations it is often crucial that members devote extra time, energy, and effort to interdependent tasks and actions that benefit the group or organization' (De Cremer and Van Knippenberg, 2003: 858). The formula is laid bare – justice is of value because it makes people work harder in pursuing non-justice-related organizational imperatives. And as a corollary leaders should pursue justice not as a goal in its own right but as a means through which to achieve 'effectiveness' (Van Knippenberg and De Cremer, 2008). In other words, justice is subordinated to managerial power and organizational success.

There is a sleight of hand here that surfaces the subconscious (or at least non-explicit) managerialism of much leadership theory. The trick is to first claim that leaders should be other-centred or even self-sacrificial (De Cremer *et al.*, 2004), and next to uncritically assume that the interests of the others, collectively understood, align unproblematically with the corporate interests that the leader is supposed to represent anyway. If a leader is fair, we are told, s/he might be better accepted by the followers (Janson *et al.*, 2008) as well as being able to make them cooperate more effectively (De Cremer and Van Knippenberg, 2003) – all of this ultimately serves the achievement of the (non-justice-related) goals that the leader is employed to achieve. In sum the position is that '[l]eader fairness can be reliably linked to behavioural outcomes' such as performance and commitment (Van Knippenberg *et al.*, 2007: 129). It has further been suggested that the perception of whether a leader is interpersonally just is directly related to whether that leader is seen as transformational, which in turn positively influences 'employees' organizational citizenship behavior, performance, and organizational commitment' (De Cremer *et al.*, 2007: 1798). Conversely, when the outcomes an employee receives from the organization are perceived to be unjust, leaders who 'display behaviors that are perceived as valuable and useful towards the interest of the organization and its employees' (De Cremer *et al.*, 2004: 473) can mitigate the negative effects of that injustice.

Given that the overwhelmingly dominant focus of organizational justice research is on 'perceived' fairness, there is always the risk that justice can be used as a device of manipulating followers into consent in the name of the collective good. The advice given by leadership researchers does indeed smack heavily of manipulation rather than of a view that justice is virtuous on its own. For example according to Janson *et al.* (2008: 267) 'new leaders may find it very useful to engage their followers early on by enacting some noticeable act of fairness'. The imperative declared is that leaders should engage in dramatic acts to demonstrate justice, not that they should be just on the basis of any moral or ethical imperative. The same rings true at an organizational level, as represented in the view that 'ethical leadership in organizations is increasingly portrayed as crucial for sustained success in today's business world and recent scandals demonstrate that a lapse in ethics at the top can be costly for organizations' (Den Hartog and De Hoogh, 2009: 200) – ethics is here valued instrumentally because it leads to business success and cost savings. Organizational justice is not a justice that is privileged in the name of ethics, the name of community or the name of the good of others – instead justice is valued because, *inter alia*, it discourages disruptive behaviour, promotes the acceptance of organizational change, reinforces the sense of trustworthiness in people in positions of authority, reduces people's fear of being exploited, provides an incentive for worker cooperation, and also satisfies individuals' needs for control, esteem and belonging (Colquitt *et al.*, 2005:5–6).

Fortin (2008) gets to the heart of this set of intentions bluntly:

> Organization justice is concerned with people's fairness perceptions in their employment relationships. . . . Justice perceptions have been shown to have effects on people's motivation, well being, performance, attitudes, behaviours and other outcomes relevant for organizations and organizational members (p. 93)

Research into leadership and justice purports that the positive relationship between justice and effectiveness is a pleasant coincidence – one might wonder what would have happened if a concern for justice reduced effectiveness? Would this be a reason to abandon it? The logic of the leadership literature on the matter, by and large, suggests 'yes'. Justice, by this account, is only good if it's good for business. Again, despite the complexity of methods and analysis brought to bear on the positivistic pursuit of the study of justice and leadership, its political adherence to a pro-business and pro-capitalist state of affairs goes entirely unquestioned. As the ancient legal maxim suggests: *manifesta probatione non indigent* – in English, 'manifest things require no proof'. And, as far as leadership is concerned it seems that desirability and possibility of the alignment of interests between workers (aka followers) and organizations (as represented by leaders) is just manifest. Moreover, the assumption of this consensual state of affairs belies the managerialist subconscious mentioned earlier – the idea that corporations can enforce their will on others for their own good and that 'justice' is just another weapon in the arsenal used in the policing of that enforcement.

When it comes to considerations of justice in relation to organization change the same tendencies are present – albeit in an exaggerated form. In this context justice is also not regarded as something to be pursued for its own good, but is, instead, part of the managerial weaponry used to reduce employee resistance to change. As espoused by Daly and Geyer (1994), employees are more likely to accept organizational change if they *perceive* the process by which that change is implemented is fair. The point is that the perception of justice and fairness amongst employees is something that can be manipulated by leaders in order to implement large-scale change. As Tyler and De Cremer (2005:529) explain, 'leaders motivate their followers to accept change by exercising their authority via fair procedures'. Justice then is a way by which leaders can ensure support for their decisions and voluntary compliance with change initiatives (Van Dijke and De Cremer, 2008). When the goal of justice is to reduce resistance, justice is reduced to being a means to that end rather than an end in itself.

An ethical basis of just leadership

In the previous section it was argued that the so-called 'state of the art' (Van Knippenberg *et al.*, 2007) thinking in terms of the relationship between justice and leadership is imbued with some serious contradictions. While justice is presented in relation to treating people fairly and equally ahead of seeking unfair advantage for one's self, it simultaneously assumes that employees in organizations pursue justice out of self-interest, and that leaders in organizations pursue justice in the instrumental interests of the organization. In this way, while justice is premised on being other-centred, the dominant conception of organizational justice inadvertently rests on the primacy of self-interest. Employees are assumed to be interested in justice so as to ensure that they are not disenfranchised or taken advantage of. Leaders are interested in justice so as to ensure their own effectiveness. At the risk of being glib, we might say that 'organizational justice' does not do justice to the idea of justice!

The shortcomings of managerialist approaches to justice are, however, not a reason to give up on justice as it relates to leadership and change management. What these shortcomings call for is a way of thinking about organizational justice from a more genuinely other-centred approach – one that does not rest on the implicit assumption of the primacy of self-interest. To consider how this might be done, we now turn to the ethical philosophy of Emmanuel Levinas as a guide to how leadership might overcome its self preoccupation (*cf.* Knights and O'Leary, 2006). For Levinas any idea of justice must always be premised on ethics, such that to strive to do justice is inspired by an ethical concern for other people. As such, we must first consider Levinas' ethics before approaching how he understands justice. Levinas does not use the term ethics to refer to some system of procedures, practices or dispositions that can ensure a sense of 'goodness' or righteousness on the part of one who adheres to them. Neither does he develop a set of prescriptions intended to guide or inform how people might live or respond to situations in which they find themselves. Instead, Levinas' project is to delve into the very meaning of ethics – his is a 'proto-ethics' (Llewelyn, 1995:4) that attempts an 'ethics of ethics' (Derrida, 1978:138). By his own account Levinas' work 'does not consist in constructing ethics' as much as trying 'to find its meaning' (Levinas, 1985:90). Crucially, this meaning, for Levinas, begins with 'the other' – the actual other person who is thought of not as another of me but as radically different, particular and unknowable.

Levinas' ethics is conceived in the face-to-face relation between people. In this relation the other person, as a 'face', is always regarded as radically different to the self. Levinas holds extreme respect for the sanctity of the other person, a sanctity so revered that it never assumes that the other person can ever really be known. In this way, to lay claim to truly knowing another person would mean the ability to locate and categorize them within a system of knowledge – in so doing the other person is immediately rendered non-unique because s/he can be compartmentalized into categories and compared with other others. Levinas preserves the idea that the other person is so radically different that such knowledge is never fully possible, and, moreover, to pretend that it is means affronting the ethical uniqueness of that other person. So, while I may be face-to-face with the other, at the same time that other is infinitely different and certainly not capturable in any categories that I might choose to apply to him or her. For Levinas, it is the awe inspired by this infinity that gives rise to ethics – the absolute respect for the other person in face-to-face proximity.

The ethical relation that Levinas elaborates is quite different to how we might see 'normal' relations between people. Ethics is certainly not about exploiting others or about using them for our own advantage. It is not even about reciprocity and fair exchange – making sure that each person puts in and gets repaid the same amount from relationships. Ethics instead is an out of balance relationship – one that puts the other person first in the name of generosity, respect and humility. Ethics is a kind of giving without taking or expecting anything in return. This ethics, the meaning of ethics, is like a love that gives freely without thought of the pursuit of self-advantage or repayment. The ethical self is never self-sufficient and is always secondary to the other. With Levinas' ethics it is never 'me first'; Levinas describes the self as being hostage to the other. With ethics the self is not secure in its righteousness but is called into question 'by the presence of the Other' (Levinas, 1969: 43). From this questioning, the other person is not a reflection of one's self or a resource to be used for one's advantage, but calls into question the very idea that one might live one's life just for the purpose of satisfying selfish needs and desires. The ethical self is a vulnerable self – a self vulnerable to other people. With this '[G]oodness consists in taking up a position in being such that the other counts more than myself' (Levinas, 1969: 47).

Levinas' ethics is a very tall order – an ethics that seems almost impossible in the vastness of its demand for self-lessness. And practically it would seem that Levinas' ethics is hard to find in work settings, especially those where 'employees are viewed as numbers and not as people, let alone "faces" in the Levinasian sense' (Ten Bos and Willmott, 2001: 781). Leadership is also ethically questionable in that it so often focuses on the judging and monitoring of employees – for example through practices of performance management and employee development. Indeed, while the ostensible focus may be on the growth and development of the person, this done through a process which 'starts with a category and ends with a judgment relative to that category . . . [and] . . . through this move the "Otherness" of the Other, the exceptional, is neatly bracketed and "covered over"' (Introna, 2003: 212). In management and leadership it is the comparison between people, rather than each's specificity, that is paramount. We can take, for example, diversity management which, while seeking to promote the value of difference, has also been said to be 'an attempt to capture the elementary experience of self and other in the sphere of managerial control' – this control being exercised by compartmentalizing people into pre-defined categories of difference (e.g. on the basis of sex or race) and in so doing diminishing that difference into a form of sameness (Costea and Introna, 2008:187).

One might ask whether it might at all be possible to suggest that leaders should approach their work in a manner that is entirely attendant to the needs of other people. Perhaps the closest resonance to such concerns is Greenleaf's (1977) idea of 'servant leadership' (Chapman, 2006), based as it is on the idea that 'caring for persons, the more and less able caring for each other, is what makes a good society' (p.17). Indeed, servant leadership has been identified as an approach that brings with it a moral dimension absent in charismatic and transformation models – with leaders ranging from Jesus Christ and Martin Luther King Jr. to Adolf Hitler and Joseph Stalin all matching the general criteria established to identify charismatic leadership (Graham, 1991). The moral dimension that is located in servant leadership is said to be operationalized when leaders become other focused. The servant leader listens to people and empathizes with them, is devoted to serving the needs of others, is committed to people's personal growth, and serves to build communities at work (Spears, 1998).

Servant leadership appears very idealistic in that it assumes that leaders not only will, but *can*, lead in an way that displays caring for each and every other person, and can do so without at all conflicting with the organizational imperatives with which the leader is charged. In a sense servant leadership takes an interpersonal approach to leader–follower relations that does not adequately account for the complex and politically charged relationship that leaders are embroiled in in practice. Indeed for either Levinasian ethics or servant leadership to account for such realities in their ethical standpoint, these realities must be considered. Levinas himself, however does not stop at the ethical position of being 'for the other'; instead, his work attends directly to the complexities of what might actually be involved when such an ethics is brought to bear on the social and political realties of the world – in our case, the world of organizations. As we explore in the next section, these are the realities that mark the scene of organizational justice.

Impossible justice

As outlined above, for Levinas the meaning of ethics originates in the awe inspired in the face-to-face relation between two people where the other who one faces is infinitely different to oneself. Practically speaking, however, the social world we live in is not characterized by such dyadic relationships. While this dyadism might work in understanding where ethics originates, it is hardly 'practical' in the sense of relating directly to the complexity of relations to other people that we might actually encounter in social settings such as organizations. Levinas is very much aware of this, and it is this awareness that prompts his discussion of justice.

To begin with, organizations contain many people – they are not just about dyadic relationships. Leaders in particular encounter and are responsible for a variety of people and different interests, such that even if a leader were to abide by an ethics concerned with care for the other, such an ethics of generosity to any particular other person would always conflict with the potential to be generous to all of the other others. Cast in terms of servant leadership one would question whether a servant can indeed have many masters. If the servant is s/he who is devoted selflessly to the master, forsaking all others, then the servant leader is in trouble because such complete devotion must always be divided amongst many – devotion to the one other can only be full if one forsakes everyone else. One cannot offer the full potential of one's generosity to all, and in a social, community or organizational setting generosity is always divided.

Levinas explains the meaning of sociality for ethics in relation to what he refers to as the 'third party'. With this term he is interested in what happens to the ethics of the face-to-face when there are more than two people involved. It is at this point that Levinas moves from a philosophical exploration of the meaning of ethics to a position that is much more relevant to the understanding ethics in relation to leadership and organizations. For Levinas, as soon as a third person joins the scene of the relation of the face-to-face things get much more complicated – and this complication is where justice becomes relevant. As Levinas puts it:

> It is the third party that interrupts the face to face of a welcome of the
> other man, interrupts the proximity or approach of the neighbour, it is the
> third man with which justice begins.
>
> *(Levinas, 1998:150)*

The reason that this is the beginning of justice is because the presence of
a third party diverts attention from the face-to-face relation with the one
other, to the face of an 'other other' as well as bringing into question the
relationship between those two others. One's attentions and resources
must now be divided and therefore full devotion and responsibility to
the one other is no longer possible – ethics, while still being meaningful
and possibly remaining as a motivating force is now subject to inevitable
compromise. When one is responsible for more than one other person, as
leaders are, there is some need to share and to divide – one's generosity
must be directed at many people at the same time. Moreover, it is with
this requirement for sharing and division that justice is called for; justice,
as in the justification for how things get divided and whether that division
is fair. One might still be motivated by ethics, but that ethics can now
only be enacted imperfectly through justice. This is not an easy position
to be in as far as Levinas' ethics is concerned because division requires
comparison between people – the very comparison that defies what
Levinas means by ethics. Put starkly, the implication is that 'ethical
leadership is unattainable' (Knights and O'Leary, 2006:126). Moreover,
as explored below, it is this tension between ethics and justice that
characterizes just leadership. In this sense, just leadership is no longer
about trying to ensure followers perceive one's actions as just in order
to improve one's own effectiveness – instead it is about navigating the
ethical quandaries and dilemmas that leading other people, and being
responsible for them, inevitably raise.

The dilemma of justice is about how to make decisions when faced with
multiple and conflicting demands from other people. For leaders this
might mean, for example, conflicting demands from different followers,
or conflicting demands between what is good for employees and what is
good for the corporation (the latter being a political and practical reality
that is radically absent in discussions of organizational justice, given its
ever-present yet silent pro-capitalist bias). Dealing with such conflicts
means, for leaders, the requirement to compare all of the demands, and
decide which ones to try to serve, which to neglect, or how to compromise
between them. Of course such decisions might be made pragmatically
or instrumentally in relation to what is best for the leader him or herself,
but if justice is to be considered then the decision must be based on some

notion of what is the fairest decision, even though that decision will not satisfy everyone. This is the challenge of just leadership.

As we saw earlier, current research into organizational justice tends to assume that justice for employees can be attained without any necessary conflict with organizational goals. While such a convenient perspective might make for an easy justice, it fails to account for the entire history of organizational and industrial conflict. Of course if, in a change management context, a leader has to, for example, retrench employees in the name of improving efficiency there will be a conflict between the demands of different interests. It is the potential dilemma that such a conflict presents that is the site where justice is demanded. Moreover, while it may be within the interests of the employees to maintain employment, and within the interests of capital to maximize returns, these two sets of interests are not necessarily commensurable. Justice can demand a judgement that entails someone's interests going unmet.

Justice, for Levinas, entails 'a comparison of what is in principle incomparable' (Levinas, 2006) – a comparison between at least two others who are radically different and essentially incomparable. On account of this, organizational justice is always already in an ethical conundrum – ethics demands justice to be applied in organizations, but justice, because it requires compromise between people, can never live up to the absoluteness of the ethical demands that invoked it. This is, following Levinas, the vexing condition that characterizes just leadership. The question for leadership then is how might these impossible dilemmas be resolved or responded to? Of course one way to address this is through the institution laws, norms or policies designed to guide judgement and decision making. Consistency of policy is one way that leaders can try to ensure justice – at least distributive and procedural justice. In a change management situation, for example, this might mean having a transparent mechanism for selecting who gets retrenched in a downsizing process. The inevitable yet impossible condition that Levinas' ethics invokes, however, is that by offering equal treatment for all the absolutely singular ethical relationship of the face-to-face is irrevocably yet unavoidably broken.

What does this mean then for leadership and justice? To begin with we can say that a concern for justice highlights the unavoidable politics that the leadership function is always located in. Justice is concerned with how these political issues are managed. As we discussed earlier, a disruption caused by a third party means that one must respond to more than one other – make a choice between them and decide which one to put first. This portends an ongoing oscillation between ethics and politics (Simmons, 1999) where leaders are caught up in contexts where they might try at once to be responsible to one other (say an employee) only to find that they face demands from other others (say another employee, a boss or a customer) and that these demands are not commensurable. Dealing with these competing and incommensurable calls for responsibility is the location where justice impinges on leadership. Moreover, in this 'dealing' there is no guarantee that everyone will perceive that matters are fair.

It is not so much that leaders can declare themselves as being just on the basis of some or other criteria, nor even on whether followers 'perceive' that they have been treated justly. Rather justice is something that places demands on leadership – demands to take responsibility and to decide. Justice demands that leaders negotiate the inevitable but necessary tensions between ethics and justice as well as recognize that it is the presence of those tensions that are the signs of ethical self-questioning in organizations and of just leadership (Byers and Rhodes, 2007). This is not a justice that seeks to manage other people's perceptions of whether or not they believe they are treated fairly – to do so would mean that justice is achieved when people merely stop complaining about being treated unfairly. Instead, just leadership is an ongoing engagement with the anxieties, dilemmas, contradictions and double-binds that occur in the conflict between the ethical demands of all of the others. This justice must be done in the name of an ethical caring for and generosity towards every single unique other person, while at the same time requiring compromise between them. The challenge for the just leader is not only to treat everybody equally and without favouritism, but to do so in the name of caring for those people while knowing that they cannot all be cared for fully.

The quality of just leadership does not lie just in the extent to which individuals perceive that they personally are treated justly, but also in the way that leaders, individually and collectively, exercise their power. Any leadership practice that has a material effect on other people is open to deliberation in terms of ethics and justice. Following Levinas, with these deliberations leaders must concern themselves with all of the others their actions affect, while at the same time being prepared to answer to each other person. This is what Introna (2007) calls 'singular justice' in that it must be delivered face-to-face – any principles, laws or generalizations about justice are thus applied not to everyone, but individually to each person, at least in the sense that each person receives them separately.

As we have been discussing, following Levinas, true justice must grounded in ethics – in the face-to-face relation with the other person to whom we are responsible, who is radically different from us, and whose very presence demands generosity, hospitality and charity. But, while ethics is the only possible justification for justice, it is also the case that justice always violates ethics because it involves a comparison of the ethically incomparable. The implication for leadership is that justice is not about ensuring that people report that they are treated fairly, but rather about engaging in, and taking responsibility for, the ethical dilemmas that trying to be just entails. This justice is not a state of being that can reached, measured and self-righteously proclaimed, but rather it is a motivating force that calls into question and trouble the practice of leadership in all of its dimensions.

Conclusion

Organization change is a process that is characterized by multiple and complex ethical challenges for organizations and their leaders. In such contexts, this chapter has argued that dominant approaches to organizational justice that focus on how leaders can influence the perceptions of justice amongst their followers are both naive and self-serving. Naive in that they do not account for the complex ethical dilemmas faced by leaders in times of change. Self-serving in that they assume that the purpose of just leadership is to promote leadership and organizational effectiveness – justice is just a means to a corporately sanctioned end. Despite this, justice remains a pressing issue for those organizations who wish to manage and lead change ethically.

In seeking to develop an alternative way of conceiving of organizational justice, the chapter has drawn on the ethical philosophy of Emmanuel Levinas. In so doing the concern has turned away from the embedded assumptions that leaders seek justice for their own effectiveness and followers seek justice for themselves – indeed, these are assumptions that render justice as merely another form of self-interest. What the concern has turned towards is the opening up of a space for a more affirmative and other-focused notion of organizational justice – one based on generosity and hospitality while at the same time being mired in the political realities of organizational life. This just leader is less interested in his or her own instrumental effectiveness, instead grappling with his or her conflicting responsibilities. This 'grappling' is central to the quality of the ethical leadership of change, such that the meaning of what it might mean to be effective is put into question by the demand to do justice to all other people to which one owes responsibility. There is no end to the quest for justice – indeed it is this quest that is a condition of the leadership of change, as well as one of its most indefatigable challenges.

References

Aristotle (2000) *Nicomachean Ethics*, (trans. R. Crisp), Cambridge: Cambridge University Press.

Byers, D. and Rhodes, C. (2007) Ethics, alterity and organizational justice, *Business Ethics: A European Review*, 16(3), 239–250.

Chapman, N. (2006) A poetics of servant leadership, *The International Journal of Servant Leadership*, 2(1), 377–398.

Colquitt, J. A. and Greenberg, J. (2003) Organizational Justice: A fair assessment of the state of the literature, in: J. A. Greenberg (ed.), *Organizational Behavior: The State of the Science* (second edition), Mahwah, NJ: Lawrence Erlbaum, 165–210.

Colquitt, J. A., Greenberg, J. and Zapata-Phelan, C. P. (2005) What is organizational justice: A historical overview, in: J. Greenberg and J. A. Colquitt (eds) *The Handbook of Organizational Justice*, Mahwah, NJ: Laurence Erbaum, 3–57.

Costea, B. and Introna, L. (2008) On the mystery of the other and diversity management, in: L. Introna, F. Ilharco and E. Fay (eds) *Phenomenology, Organisation and Technology*, Lisbon: Universidade Catolica Editora, 187–207.

Cropanzano, R. and Stein, J. H. (2009) Organizational justice and behavioral ethics: Promises and prospects, *Business Ethics Quarterly*, 19(2), 193–233.

Daly, J. P. and Geyer, P. D. (1994) The role of fairness in implementing large-scale change: Employee evaluations of process and outcome in seven facility relocations, *Journal of Organizational Behavior*, 15(7), 623–638.

De Cremer, D. (2003) Why inconsistent leadership is regarded as procedurally unfair: The importance of social self-esteem concerns, *European Journal of Social Psychology*, 33, 535–550.

De Cremer, D. and Van Knippenberg, D. (2003) How do leaders promote cooperation? The effects of charisma and procedural fairness, *Journal of Applied Psychology*, 87(5), 858–866.

De Cremer, D., Van Dijke, M. and Bos, A. E. R. (2007) When leaders are seen as transformational: The effects of organizational justice, *Journal of Applied Social Psychology*, 37(8), 1797–1816.

De Cremer, D., Van Dijke, M. and Bos, A. E. R. (2004) Distributive justice moderating the effects of self-sacrificial leadership, *Leadership and Organization Development Journal*, 25(5), 466–475.

De Cremer, D., Van Dijke, M. and Bos, A. E. R. (2006) Leader's procedural justice affecting identification and trust, *Leadership and Organization Development Journal*, 27(7), 554–565.

De Cremer, D., Van Knippenberg, B., Van Knippenberg, D., Mullenders, D. and Stinglhamber, F. (2005) Rewarding leadership and fair procedures as determinants of self-esteem, *Journal of Applied Psychology*, 90(1), 3–12.

Den Hartog D. N. and De Hoogh, A. H. B. (2009) Empowering behaviour and leader fairness and integrity: Studying perceptions of ethical leader behaviour from a levels-of-analysis perspective, *European Journal of Work and Organizational Psychology*, 18(2), 199–230.

Derrida, J. (1978/2001) *Writing and Difference*, London: Routledge.

Fortin, M. (2008) Perspective on organizational justice: Concept clarification, social context integration, time and links with morality, *International Journal of Management Reviews*, 10(2), 93–126.

Graham, J. W. (1991) Servant-leadership in organizations: Inspirational and moral, *The Leadership Quarterly*, 2(2), 105–119.

Greenleaf, R. K. (1977/2002) *Servant Leadership*, New York: Paulist Press.

Greenleaf, R. K. (1998) *The Power of Servant Leadership*, San Francisco: Berrett-Koehler.

Introna, L. D. (2007) Singular justice and software privacy, *Business Ethics: A European Review*, 16(3), 264–267.

Introna, L. D. (2003) Workplace surveillance 'is' unethical and unfair, *Surveillance and Society*, 1(2), 210–216.

Janson, A., Levy, L. Sitkin, S. B. and Lind, E. A. (2008) Fairness and other leadership heuristics: A four-nation study, *European Journal of Work and Organizational Psychology*, 17(2), 251–272.

Knights, D. and O'Leary, M. (2006) Leadership, ethics and responsibility to the other, *Journal of Business Ethics*, 67(2), 125–137.

Levinas, E. (1969) *Totality and Infinity*, Pittsburgh: Duquesne University Press.

Levinas, E. (1985) *Ethics and Infinity*, Pittsburgh: Duquesne University Press.

Levinas, E. (1998) *Otherwise Than Being or Beyond Essence*, Pittsburgh: Duquesne University Press.

Levinas, E. (2006) *Entre Nous*, London: Continuum.

Llewelyn. J. (1995) *Emmanuel Levinas: The Genealogy of Ethics*, London: Routledge.

Muhr, S. L. (2008) Reflections on responsibility and justice: Coaching human rights in South Africa, *Management Decision*, 46(8), 1175–1186.

Simmons, W. (1999) The third: Levinas' theoretical move from an-archical ethics to the realm of justice and politics, *Philosophy and Social Criticism*, 25(6), 83–104.

Spears, L. (1998) *Insights on Leadership: Service, Stewardship, Spirit, and Servant-Leadership*, New York: Wiley.

Ten Bos, R. and Willmott, H. (2001) Towards a post-dualistic business ethics: Interweaving reason and emotion in working life, *Journal of Management Studies*, 38(6), 769–793.

Tyler, T. R. and De Cremer, D. (2005) Process-based leadership: Fair procedures and reactions to organizational change, *The Leadership Quarterly*, 16, 529–545.

Van Dijke, M. and De Cremer, D. (2008) How leader prototypicality affects followers' status: The role of procedural fairness, *European Journal of Work and Organizational Psychology*, 17(2), 226–250.

Van Knippenberg, D. and De Cremer, D. (2008) Leadership and fairness: Taking stock and looking ahead, *European Journal of Work and Organizational Psychology*, 17(2), 173–179.

Van Knippenberg, D., De Cremer, D. and Van Knippenberg, B. (2007) Leadership and fairness: The state of the art, *European Journal of Work and Organizational Psychology*, 16(2), 113–140.

Part II
Ethical change leadership: issues and challenges

4 Virtuality and materiality in the ethics of storytelling answerability

Implications for leadership and change

David M. Boje and Rohny Saylors

Introduction

Ethical leadership, given scandals from Enron to the current epidemic of 'toxic assets' bailouts, would appear to be in decline. Instead of increased ethical practices, many corporations engage in apparently more apologist versus positive ethical rhetoric. The storytelling of organizations has become nonsensical (and by virtue, obfuscating) because it contradicts empirical conditions. An international sports brand is given an ethics award, while facts of its sweatshop contractor material conditions are well researched! Clearly the material conditions of sweatshop capitalism were not considered valid criteria in that ethics award. Perhaps the plight of ethical leadership and change lies in the limitations of social constructionism philosophy. This chapter explores an alternative philosophy, 'social materiality' as a different approach to ethics, change and leadership. Social materiality contributes an ethics of storytelling, answerability for constructing one's life as an ethical living storytelling, in intra-activity with material conditions. Social materiality is about how virtuality and materiality are intra-penetrating one another, whereas social constructionism dualizes them. Answerability is a Bakhtinian ethical concept, to be that person, standing in the once-occurrent, non-recurrent moment of Being-ness, who intervenes in the Now, who does the right thing, out of an awareness of one's complicity in the material-virtual situation that is riddled with storytelling, inseparable from storytelling. A contribution this chapter makes is sorting out the intra-play of materiality and storytelling which social construction would render just virtuality. Social materiality storytelling has its consequences for answerability ethics in leadership and change. Some autoethnographic examples are presented to explore these relationships.

Storytelling and materiality are intra-weaving in the new quantum physics

Each paradigm in physics has its ripple effects in defining new horizons of leadership and change. After Newtonian physics, organizations were conceived of as mechanistic systems, with interchangeable human parts, that made process reengineering possible vis-à-vis Taylorism. Taylor missed the Einstein relativity theory shift in physics, but this was not missed by Henri Bergson, Mikhail Bakhtin, and Gilles Deleuze. Their work has rippled through leadership and change studies (Boje, 2008a, 2008b, 2011a, 2011b). In the new quantum physics work by Karen Barad (2003, 2007), there is an important intra-play of living things and living discourse.

The implications of this newest shift in physics paradigms are only beginning to be explored rigorously in academia. Our theory is that it prompts a re-theorizing of storytelling and materiality. In our proposed integration, there is this intra-weave of strands of storytelling and materiality that is greatly affecting the ethics of leadership and change in quite a variety of institutions which are now at a crossroads. This is not the materiality of either the mechanistic physics of the relativity physics, but constitutes an approach to materiality, as living things (living at the subatomic level, and intra-active with human consciousness). Such integration was anticipated in the work of Bergson (1992/1932), as well as by Bakhtin (1981).

There is now an important transformation of leadership and change in both the virtual and material world, in a new way of doing this merger that has its own ethical consequences. But, at the crossroads, which way do we merge? Do we envision leadership and change that is more of the same domination project, or do we advocate for liberation from that domination and envision a different relationship to Nature (the perceived world of social constructionism)? Materiality and virtuality have been merged with storytelling in a way that has lead to the destruction of Nature, entombment of humans, and oppressive organizational hierarchies. This process has been accelerating over the past several decades, as can be seen in the increasing preference for leadership and change based in the metaphysics of domination. The metaphysics of domination is how hegemonic actors overcome the metaphysics of practical pragmatism. The metaphysics of practical pragmatism connects the material and virtue with storytelling in a way that respects persons and Nature and is answerable.

Our purpose in this chapter is to trace this merging and weaving at this crossroads, and sort out some of the implications for change leadership and ethical theories and practices so that we can choose to head in another direction – away from the past (apologist ethics) and future (positivist ethics), rooting us in the now, helping us truly enact an ethics of action and answerability. Our contribution is showing the intra-penetration of storytelling with the material world, and storytelling's already existent virtual connectivity (the 'virtual-real' in Lacanian sense). We will use autoethnographic material to explore this in our own life worlds. We participate in acts of leadership and change in the university, in the arts scene, and in the union. In each venue, virtuality and materiality have been merging. The problem is that mainstream theories of leadership, ethics, and change management have not kept pace with that merger. We begin by looking at the false duality of positive and negative thinking.

How positive thinking ignores its negation and how positivism blinds itself to material conditions

More 'positive thinking' combined with 'positivism-empiricism' continues to mask the power and privilege sustained in a project of economic organizations that is the destruction of Nature and the Social to create a technological world steeped in gratification, in what Herbert Marcuse (1964:167) calls 'metaphysics of domination' of Nature and humans. The other road is what Marcuse (1964:166) calls a 'qualitative physics' that comprehends, and promotes, a different change project where the technological apparatus of organizations of production 'partakes in the metaphysics of liberation' of Nature and humans. Marcuse follows John Dewey (1929:95–100) who saw an alternative to 'active manipulation and control' in a path to 'contemplative enjoyment' of 'aesthetic enjoyment of properties of nature.' For Marcuse, qualitative physics is the dialectic processes of these two poles, each of which is an expression of a different metaphysics: domination versus liberation. Aristotelian qualitative physics allows for attendance to many things that are 'real' but that require critical thinking to understand. Marcuse argues that focusing on positive thinking and empirical positivism is one-dimensional. Practical pragmatism stands in stark contrast to this simplistic perspective because it looks at the real as that which humans use, including the negative. This allows for the negation inherent in qualitative physics, something that positive thinking and empirical positivism removes. The supposed virtue of this removal is extoled by positivism as it is through the removal of negation that that positivism is set up as the successor to qualitative physics. That negation, which positive thinking produces, remains a blind spot because of the prohibition of doing any sort of critical thinking or deconstruction of how positive thinking and positivistic thinking have merged to cover over projects of the domination of Nature.

Change practices, in a dialectical view, have been developed in a pre-established tradition of the use of technological rationality to enact the domination of Nature. Positive positivism has been unable (or unwilling) to examine its own 'great vehicle of *reification*' (Marcuse, 1964:169). 'This sort of empiricism substitutes for the hated world of metaphysical ghosts, myths, legends, and illusions a world of conceptual or sensual scraps, of words and utterances which are then organized into a philosophy' (Marcuse, 1964:187).

And the current name of that philosophy is social constructionism, which purges storytelling of the metaphysical ghosts, myths, legends, and illusions to create a world of sensemaking scraps, where the linguistic turn and narrative turn combine and organize a duality with material conditions, and overlook that vehicle of reification which Berger and Luckmann (1967) once appreciated in social construction of everyday reality, theorized as a dialectical enactment of subjectification reified into objectification, then taking the whole great vehicle of reification for granted. The new versions of social constructionism, as Bruno Latour (2005) makes abundantly clear, treat materiality as illusion and deception in a theory of the social, and a theory of construction that needs reassemblage, reimagining, and resituation. The present technological organization of human domination and wider Nature exploitation is validated, legitimated, and camouflaged by the new social constructionists, who no longer walk in the footsteps of Berger and Luckmann. We fear that this departure will serve to hinder the growth of ethically enacted behavior in organizations, and only serve to further perpetuate the use of apologist instead of enacted ethics.

Marcuse's (1964:180–190) *One-Dimensional Man*, Eckhart Tolle's (2005:200–220) *A New Earth*, and Gregory Cajete's (2000:79) *Native Science*, all look at quantum physics in relation to the materiality of storytelling. Where this seems to be pointing towards, from a paradigmatic approach: Tolle is smitten by the positivistic philosophy, but on occasion comes quite close to Marcuse. Marcuse (1964) is smitten by critical theory and critical thinking, and looks at positivism as empiricism's way of continuing the old physics. Cajete (2000) wants a Native Science rooted in ecology and community, not in late modern capitalism. Where do all three meet? For Tolle negative thinking includes blame, criticism, resistance, defensiveness, shouting back – all these are dysfunctional (Tolle, 2005:14–215). Instead, Tolle wants us to see the power of the universe, be humble, and refrain from expression. This lets us see all the vast space around the thing, and enter no-thingness, silence, and stillness. Now the place where Tolle does converge with Marcuse is the dance between thingness and no-thingness. For us narrative is all about thingness (in old physics) and the storytelling we want to do is about no-thingness, where Being is background to the thing-existence. Being is background to what happens that narrative fixates, and Being is background to living story content emerging and unfolding.

Marcuse does not want to keep the negative apart from the positive in discourse or in behaviour. For Marcuse (1964) positivity bars access to the realm of negativity, by prejudging negative. This positivistic psychology is calling for radical acceptance of empirical facts given by organizations, bars critical appraisal of factors behind them, and is therefore for Marcuse (1964:182), 'one-dimensional and manipulated.' Positivist cleansing is a restricted experience of sensemaking, such that the thing-world becomes the object of positive thinking and made equivalent to empirical thinking, but misses the universe of experience. The acts of repression, regression, restriction, and reduction are 'the transformation of critical thinking into positive thinking [that] takes place mainly in the therapeutic treatment of universal concepts' (Marcuse, 1964:183). For Marcuse this is an ethical problem, because it leaves the status quo where it is. Further in connection to Cajete, 'the neo-positivist critique still directs its main effort against metaphysical notions' (Marcuse, 1964:184).

Next we begin our look at living materiality. For Greg Cajete (2000) the modern project of enlightenment bans animalism and vitalism. He argues that the term "animism" is derogatory and dismissive, implying a regressive, or savage, thought processes. Practical pragmatism is in agreement with Cajete, who prefers the concept of cosmology. Cosmology is a posthumanist understanding of our connections to the earth, to animals and to the universe. Further, Cajete does not think that critical theory has reconnected to earth, and just focuses on the social, and its social constructions. So one-dimension is different for Cajete from how it is for Marcuse. Cajete, for example, thinks that Paulo Freire (1970) does not go far enough in Pedagogy of the Oppressed because all the dialogical action is at the level of the social, without any ecological currency. And what Marcuse (1964) calls 'false consciousness' (p. 184) is for Cajete (2000) a very different false consciousness: the pragmatic status quo of the social that in its repression under that guise of positive thinking conceals repressive material conditions. For Marcuse the struggle between the positivistic and the negativistic is the basis of the dialectic. To have one side of the dialectic is to reduce the dynamic to one-dimension. And this positivism moves into academic world of concreteness, empiricism that substitutes for the 'hated world of metaphysical ghosts, myths, legends, and illusions' and instead we get this narrative world of conceptual, sensual scraps, words and utterances organized into the positivistic philosophy of positive science, positive OB, and positive leadership.

For Marcuse the technological organization (following Heidegger's critique of technology) accepts the verdicts of technique and invalidates Aristotle's essence, Hegel's Geist, and Marx's *Vedignlichung* as negative to civilization and the march of progressive rationalization. This becomes for critical theory the oppressive reality of the labouring class. (Marcuse, 1964:187–189). Marcuse makes an important point. Further, in *Das Kapital*, Marx – exploring an organic systemicity, concludes that mankind instinctively, naturally creates duality within all aspects of social organizing such that the actor is both affected by and affecting an environment; but this concept is rooted in the notion of linearity and decisional transposition. We are trying to get away from this sort of decision making. However, current repressive ideology is now embodied in the material processes of production and consumption. We think that *storytelling organizations* (Boje, 1991, 1995, 2008a) are engaged in what Marcuse calls 'productive publicity, propaganda, and politics' (p. 190).

Leadership and change management is somewhat entangled in a web of domination of nature and humans, which does not allow for any transcendence from the metaphysics of domination to the metaphysics of liberation. The reason for this is that the prohibitions in positive thinking philosophy do not allow reflexivity on the reification process or on the other negations that are a consequence of the prohibitions. One of the prohibitions in positive thinking is a refusal to think critically about the instrumental ethics of technological projects of an organization enacting the project of the domination of Nature while blocking the metaphysics of liberation with all kinds of detours. The complicity of leadership and change management in the domination of Nature project is masked by the ideology of positive thinking and its irreverent alliance with positivism.

Leadership and change theory keeps muddlingly tinkering with the conceptual maps, which continue to be a veil over the transgressions of leadership and change practices. The metaphysical 'ghosts' as Marcuse (1964:170) calls them, are the unexamined premises and complicities of positive-positivism in the project of domination.

Next we look at 'creative mind' in the work of Henri Bergson. Bergson (1992/1932), working out the implications of relative space-time, sees spatiality as a multiplicity where consciousness and sensemaking unfold outwards and then 'turns back within itself' and 'the matter [and] life which fill [the world] are actually within us; the forces which work in all things we feel within ourselves' (1992/1932:124). Bergson (p. 128) says 'Kant's error' was trying to transport intuition outside the domain of sensemaking, making it pure reason and the *a priori* (predicate). And Weickian sensemaking, as Bergson (1992/1932:128) anticipates, 'cannot get out of time nor grasp anything else than change.' It stays retrospective, and cannot grasp movement, only change:

> But the time in which we are naturally placed, the change we habitually have before us, are a time and a change that our sense and our consciousness have reduced to dust in order to facilitate our action upon things.

Bergson's alternative to Kant – and, we think, to Weick – is of course the durée of the immediate present, where a series of pasts are co-present with the present and it is that infinite present that revivifies narrative, and 'gives us joy' (1992/1932:129). In this space exists freedom from the BME, linear ethical decision making that is so pervasive in current organizational paradigms. In this space, managers can choose to have a multitude of possible futures instead of being fixed into trying to transpose similar pasts on complex, unknowable futures. There are implications of this analysis of Bergson in the work of Bakhtin, which leads us into our approach to virtuality.

The virtual world never was distinct and different from the material world

The material world Mikhail Bakhtin (1981) describes in his chronotopes essay is all about how virtuality empties out timespace of its aliveness. In the Rabelisian purge Bakhtin sees a way towards metaphysics of liberation, a way to balance all the adventure chronotopes (romance, everyday, biographic, and chivalric) combining in the historical inversion chronotope with the folkloric ones that have a non-domination relation with Nature (Rebalesian purge, Rogue-Clown-Fool, grotesque humor, and idyllic). The difference with Marcuse, is that Bakhtin preferred a dialogical to a dialectic approach. In the dialectic, the adventure and folkloric chronotopes would be dualized into opposed choices. In the dialogical there is an interactivity and inter-penetration which affords potential for generativity of unforeseen possibilities.

Here and now, at the crossroads, virtuality is thoroughly interspersed with materiality. Our contemporary virtual world is made up of an assemblage of material things: servers, computers, cables, Wi-Fi impulses, electric circuit boards, memory chips, cellphones, and so forth. In every leadership role we are now using virtuality, having virtual meetings on Skype, using a laptop to store and retrieve stuff once stored in file cabinets that are now stored in virtual folders. A lot of material actants intra-penetrate virtuality. 'Actant' is Bruno Latour's (2005) term for a non-human, non-animal agent, one smitten with materiality.

Since most leadership and change theories are historically rooted in the social sciences, which have made materiality and the socially constructed a duality, resituating the duality, de-dualizing materiality – virtuality is important. Latour's (2005) criticism of social constructionism is that the social is not social enough and needs non-human actants, and that this construction makes anything material become a fiction, a non-existent. Yet, the social is corporeal and the constructions have material agencies and actants. Interaction in one time, one place, with one agency, one actant, and singular pressure is the ultimate fiction. Latour, along with Barad (2007) distrusts the term interaction. Barad (2003, 2007) uses the term 'intra-action' to denote the importance of what is going in between materiality and discourse.

For example, (Barad, 2003:814, footnotes 18 and 19) says:

> Bohr argues on the basis of this single crucial insight, together with the empirical finding of an inherent discontinuity in measurement 'intra-actions,' that one must reject the presumed inherent separability of observer and observed, knower and known.

> The so-called uncertainty principle in quantum physics is not a matter of 'uncertainty' at all but rather of indeterminacy.

Social construction, on the other hand, defines discourse as virtual, as non-materiality, and thus the dualism. This for Latour and for Barad is a denial of materiality. If our thesis is correct, and virtuality is already thoroughly intra-penetrated with materiality, then the social constructionist paradigm is coaching leadership and change down an errant and fictive path. This is concerning to say the least – given the typical power distance between individuals and organizations in terms of how their ethical decision making activities intra-penetrate their environment.

There are important storytelling implications of antenarrative-virtuality-movement as actualizing virtual-real. For example, Ronald McDonald has become more real than any other real, flesh and blood based, leader (Boje and Rhodes, 2005a, 2005b; Boje *et al.*, 2011). Practical pragmatism says that intentions to use something toward some end make something real. From this perspective, then, in the 1960s when followers used Ronald McDonald more as a leader than any flesh and blood leader, Ronald McDonald became more real than real. Executive Jim Cantalupo experienced 14 consecutive months of same-store sales decline. It was a downward spiral, and to reverse it, he has the virtual-real Ronald McDonald restylized to be younger, thinner, more athletic, and loving those new salads, and coordinates this with getting rid of the supersize fries and burgers, after Morgan Spurlock released the film, *Supersize Me*. In 2004 when Jim Cantalupo dies, Ronald is the one giving the eulogy and a virtual image of a tear rolling down Ronald's cheek is a full-page advert in the business press. Betty Crocker was fabricated by General Mills executives in the 1921, when the last name of male executive William Crocker was put with the first name 'Betty' as a marketing strategy. The famous signature of Betty Crocker was from a secretary. In 1924 Betty Crocker got her voice on American Radio. Betty Crocker by 1936 was created from blended features and official likenesses of real women. As a virtual leader Crocker was changed over eight decades including being younger in 1955, professional by 1980, and in 1996 more multicultural (more ethnic) (Boje *et al.*, 2011:524–5). Being more real than real, in American, Betty Crocker by 1940s was second most famous woman after Eleanor Roosevelt. Akin to Ronald McDonald then, Betty Crocker is a third order simulacrum, who is virtualized as the 'good woman' (ibid). In contrast, Aunt Jemima of the Quaker Oats Company was the idealized image of a black woman: maid, cook, and slave; a counterpart to 'Uncle Tom' (ibid, p. 525). She also undergoes changes during the century, from a plump, smiling African-American woman, to being played by a series of actresses, and to a cartoon character. Like Ronald she had several make-overs. Unlike Ronald, Crocker and Jemima are not the transformational leader that

Ronald became. Ronald has a seat on the board of directors, an office in the executive suite, and officiates at McDonald's corporate gatherings. Ronald therefore is a full transformational leader, not just a stereotype changing with the tastes of consumers.

What is the difference of social materiality and social constructionism?

This is not a relativistic social construction, its more an ethnomethodology (following Garfinkel) of one's answerability of the web of living stories from the standpoint (Smith) of an ethical answerability, to intervene, to change, to lead differently to those standing on the line, in the cycle would imagine. If an aesthetic creation of living story answerability were treated seriously as ethical conduct, then leadership would take more account of complicity, and develop more dialogical ways of participation in governance. The lines of hierarchy and the cyclic programming of behaviour keeps alternative forms of participation out of awareness.

What is answerability ethics?

This answerability ethics requires a method of awareness of one's presentness, in eventness (Boje, 2008b). Bakhtin's (1993:22) review of ethical systems is subdivided into content-ethics and formal ethics. Content ethics tries to find special moral or universal norms that have definite content, and can be universally applied.

Bakhtin's first objection to content ethics is that there are no universal ethical norms. Norms are grounded in particular religious or social science disciplines. I can agree as a business person that a certain economic or organizational proposition regulates my performed work acts. I may or may not agree that such a proposition has my agreement. Content ethics does not admit that I have a consciousness, not of sensemaking-content, but from the standpoint of actual performance. Oftentimes a content-ethics is about some kind of discussions of how a particular norm, once adopted, will be beneficial to business and its customers. There is also academic discussion whether business needs this or that norm to be profitable and/or socially responsible.

Bakhtin's second objection to content ethics is its assumption of universality. If a norm is to be adopted because it is regarded a valid judgment by some religious or social science discipline, the trap of thinking of ethics as universals comes into play. At this point content-ethics attempts to become no different than formal ethics.

Bakhtin's main critique of formal ethics is that a Kantian ethics starts with the insight that 'ought is a category of consciousness' (for Kant it is a theoretical *a priori* to sensemaking consciousness of the transcendental), but making it only an act of categorical-consciousness means that the deed loses its 'compellentness' and 'historicity' (1993:25). There are certainly many instances when a Kantian approach that performed act must conform to universal and to legal law, is a very good idea. Yet, there is more going on than the universal or legal surrender of one's actual performed business acts. The key problem Bakhtin has with Kant is that universal ethics casts out the actual act and makes performance pure conformity to the law, and shuts off the historicalness of the performed act. The result is that people become passively-obligatory actors in their performed acts. Once this disconnect exists, ethical decision making no longer becomes a function of answerability.

How does answerability ethics relate to storytelling ethics?

Answerability is entirely different to the narrative of abstracted events, done in retrospection backshadowing, or some narrative prospective sensemaking, or foreshadowing of the future. In living story webs of eventness, in presentness, there is what Morson (1994) calls a sideshadowing. One is in an embodied experience of eventness, discerning the shapes of time that are neither linear (as in beginning, middle, end BME narratives) nor cyclic (as in stage by stage repeating, recurring business models, so popular strategy). Some other shaping of time is in the living story sideshadowing. This chapter develops an ethics of storytelling answerability for leadership and change. The difference with traditional narrative, is that living story answerability is for procedural awareness of one's complicity, rather than a search for abstract form. In the moment of Being, answerability of acts of business encompasses several moments. The several moments encompassed by the answerable act include the historical storytelling and the sensemaking of the acts and deeds of people living their life in business. The ideal and the immediate present, once-occurrent living story enters into the composition of answerable motivation for performed acts. Emergent storytelling of answerable acts is once-occurent, in the eventness of Being. It is not about epistemology (knowledge) it is about ontology (Being-ness) of storytelling's relationship to answerable acts.

Living story in the now-ness and here-ness

From Bakhtin, Derrida, de Certeau, Morson, to Dorothy Smith, there is what we call once-occurrent living story answerability, an attention to the actualities of presentness, without retreat to backshadowing (for instance, regret) or foreshadowing (for instance, worry). The shapes of time we want to explore in living story answerability are Deleuzian spirals and rhizomes. If one can create life as a living story, as an eventness of spiral or more rhizomatic assemblage, one is stepping outside the lines and cycles of utilitarian ethics, and outside the rhetoric of ethics. One is entering the weave of living stories, in an embodied eventness and presentness, in sideshadowing. I think that being in the Now is something that requires careful cultivation. In this cultivation, we want to learn a competency, to 'feel the energy field' (Tolle, 1997:81). When we can pay more attention to the higher Vibratory Energy Frequency (VEF) and learn to watch the lower VEF and let it pass through us, there is a transformation that occurs, in what Bakhtin (1993) calls the once-occurrent event-ness of Being. Interestingly enough, the higher VEF is found in stillness meditation, in the emotion-volition (as Bakhtin calls it) of ethical answerability. For Tolle, the emotion-volition of lower VEF includes egoic ones: envy, rage, revenge, and so on of the victim-hero narrative-past.

This leads us to: by making Doing, Being and Stillness into a single process, leadership without duality becomes emergent.

We are now asking, following Tolle (2005:46), 'Is there joy, ease, and lightness in what I am doing?' We are trying to learn to use my heart-compassion sword to cut through three types of storytelling, so I can be totally centered in the Now Spiral.

Consider Figure 4.1 as a process.

First, one cuts through the retrospective-narrative-past that is petrified. Second, one cuts through the linear and cyclic antenarratives. Finally, one cuts through the living story web of relationships so we can with love, recover our fragmented selves. It is only then that I can *see* (Trungpa, 1973) with *emotion-volition* (Bakhtin, 1993; also in part in Tolle, 2005). We also find these concepts in *The Tibetan Book of the Dead*, the teachings of Mantak Chia, etc.

In the Savall *et al.* (2008) book, which many of you now have, the focus is on *intervention research* that is quite different from Appreciative Inquiry

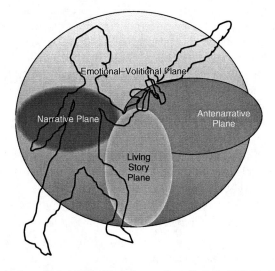

Figure 4.1   *Architectonic null storytelling hologram – from D. Boje (2011b: 117).*

(and other action research approaches). To me Savall is a modern-day Aristotle, focused on the virtues of habits of thought and action. For Savall the vices are the problem/dysfunctions. What I am adding by my work with Zen (as well as the Bible text that Tolle (1997, 2005) cites) is that when you take away a dysfunction (vice) you take away 'who' that person is in their narrative role, function, and identity. They get really defensive. They have invested many years in their role of victim or hero in relation to that dysfunction. They also fear the future without the linear/cyclic antenarrative that replicates the dysfunctions. When you step through the door, marked 'Now Spiral' then as Tolle (1997:45) puts it, 'should a situation arise that you need to deal with Now, your attention will be clear and incisive if it arises out of present moment awareness'.

For instance one of the authors offers an ethnographic account for contextual purposes:

> I had this happen to me in a moment of emergency. I was riding my Harley Davidson Electroglide about 80 (OK 85) MPH on the 405 highway headed north out of LA into the valley. There were four lanes of traffic either direction. I started to notice a yellow bucket bouncing in a pickup truck bed in front of me. And a child in the pickup was looking out at the yellow bucket and at me. I came out of my automatic unawareness, and began to watch the bucket. It took a bounce and was now on the highway. I steered left and the bucket moved left. I steered right and it moved right. In an emergency I become totally aware and present in the Now. It was clear that no past way of riding would help. And no worry about the future

would change the path of the Yellow Bucket, Here and Now. I entered a timeless state. I could see the people in a van watching me, and some more in the other lane in various cars watching me. I was boxed in by vehicles, behind, to my left and ahead. I acted intuitively in the situation. With my right hand I turned the throttle all the way up. I loosened the grip of my left hand, and like some kind of knight on horse, I speared the bucket, as it was about to wedge in-between my front wheel and frame. I did not have a spear. My left arm was the spear, and I picked the bucket up by its spinning handle, timing the tumbles of the bucket, till it spiralled into an opening, all in such slow motion, nothing seemed to be moving, not the Harley, not the other vehicles. I raised the Yellow Bucket up over my head, like some kind of trophy. I could hear the cheers from the people around me, and see their expressions of joy and ease. I carried the bucket home with me and kept it for many years.

This was one moment where I was totally centred in the Now. I was not in clock-time. I was not in psychological-time. It is how I felt at our table, with Jack and several mentees and a few other folks there. Being in the Now is not about multi-tasking on a cell phone or doing text messaging. When I see that I know they are not with me. When I see me typing on my keyboard while people are at table, I know I am not there, not in the moment of Being, not fully present.

The Harley Yellow Bucket account is what Boje (2011a) calls an 'onto-story', an ontological storytelling, is more accurate. Ontological storytelling is not a social construction one often finds in action research and appreciative inquiry. It is not a past narrative. It is not a linear-cyclic antenarrative. To me, it is stepping through that door marked 'Now Spiral.' It is stepping onto the spiral. Being totally present in the Now, there are these choices one can make between doors. There are no problems, not even the Yellow Bucket, on the Now Spiral, just the spiral turning one situation now, then another now, which I can leave alone or accept. Each situation can be left alone or dealt with. Dysfunctions or problems cannot survive in the actuality of the Now Spiral. If I lose myself in the web of living story relationships, in all the dependencies, expected reciprocities, etc. that are also Now, then I have no energy awareness of the Now, because the living stories are busy becoming stuck narratives or worry antenarratives (linear or cyclic).

It takes practice to be in the Now. Recently, I was involved in Beingness exercise and loved the four-seven-eight breath exercise that Barb (I think that is her name) did in the Sunday workshop. Breath to count of four in, hold it to count of seven, and breath out to count of eight (repeat four times). This is her way to move from head to heart-space. Opening up a heart-space, not a head space is what one does upon entering the Now Spiral. Clear some sacred space, free of unease-narrative-past, and worry-antenarrative-future (linear-cyclic). That is stale energy that just folds the past onto the future. The Now Spiral energy is in what the Bible calls 'being still' where those birds 'do not worry' about their future.

Another author offers the following ethnographic account:

> I first experienced Being through intense physical exertion
> – participation in a martial arts tournament. These tournaments are typically held over the course of a day, and if you keep winning you can end up sparring sometimes up to six or seven opponents throughout the day. A match consists of three, three-minute rounds of which in order to win, I must score by landing a kick or punch to my opponents head (and of course they are trying to reciprocate). Over time, exhaustion sets in, but you are still engaged in an activity in which if focus is lost – often the event is lost (by virtue of a painful blow somewhere to the body).
>
> The first time I participated in one of these events, I was pummeled. I was thinking, worried about all of the onlookers, remembering my training, trying to anticipate opponent movement, etc. – in other words I wasn't in the now: I was in the past or future, and I paid for it. An interesting thing happened during the last match of the day of this tournament however. I was faced with an opponent that was much larger, and much more experienced. When the match began, something amazing happened – I wasn't even cognizant of it at the time, but knowing that I was in danger of being beaten quickly and easily, I stilled my mind (involuntarily). For six brief minutes, I wasn't thinking about anything but pure self-protection through my most basic techniques. I wasn't thinking, I was acting, I was Being. I still lost.

However, for those of you who have trouble with the subsequent section, and finding the Now Spiral – I suggest the following very basic exercise. Go outside to somewhere safe and start running. Keep running until winded. Then run more, and more. Run as fast and hard and long as you can until you collapse – and in that few moments of intense exertion see if your mind is focused on anything but your burning legs and lungs – you've just achieved Being. Moving on . . .

There is no energy for the Now Spiral.

The steps are simple to find the Now Spiral.

1. Stop, look and listen until you see the doors marked linear, cyclical, and spiral in this very moment of the Now.

2. Close the linear and cyclic doors, but watch them through the glass window in the doors.
3. Open the Spiral Door and step through into a room where there is only timelessness (no clock-time, and no psychological-time).
4. Fitzgerald and Hoxsey (2010), Boje (2010), and Gary Morson (1994) put it, one needs to look at the side-shadows, and see the shapes, texture, momentum, light, and color, and hear the sounds, and feel the life energy of the Spiral in the Now in Being-ness, in event-ness as well as the backshadows and foreshadows.

Figure 4.2 summarizes the backshadow narratives, the sideshadows of living story, and the foreshadows of antenarrative possibility waves.

For many years much work has been done to deconstruct those fossilized narratives of the past and then to deconstruct the linear/cycle antenarratives. We thought the living story web in the Present situation held the answer. But, now we are finding that the living story web is so fragmented and entangling that we must cut all the spider-web cords, and let all the energy return to them and to you. Step through the door just in the side shadow, located beneath psychological-time, and above clock-time. Touch the Now Spiral energetic frequency vibrations. One of the authors has been studying this quantum energy for the past few years.

Organization strategy exists in clock-time and psychological-time. It rarely is in the Now, except in emergencies, when it is often too late to act. Life is real materiality, not just social construction. It's both, and moving from social construction action research (or appreciative inquiry) is what is needed.

In *Intervention Research*, there is intra-play of storytelling and materiality

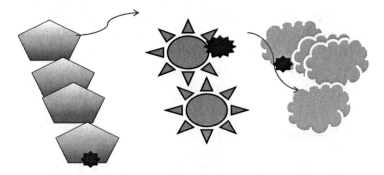

Figure 4.2 *Shadows and Storytelling – Adapted from Boje (2011b: 47) by permission. Backshadows (past), sideshadows (now), foreshadows (future)*

in the Now Spiral. 'Ultimately there is only one problem: the time bound mind itself' (Tolle, 1997:43).

Until an organization accepts its dysfunctions, and stops the denial-defensive posturing, they attach to fossilized-narrative-past or fragment into webs of living story-now-problems, or expect the antenarrative-linear/cyclic-hope or worry-antenarratives to fulfill happiness, and bring about rescue. Meanwhile little or no attention awareness is on the Now Spiral.

Too much attachment to narrative-past brings emotions of guilt, regret, resentment, grievance, sadness, bitterness, and forgiveness (list of emotions from Tolle, 2005:42). Too much progress-linear-cyclical-antenarrative-futuring and too much fragmentation of self into living story webs of Now obligation brings suffering and loss of personal and collective energy. These three storytelling dimensions sap energy from the Now that is the Spiral of joy, happiness in the Aristotlelian sense of habits of virtue, actions and thought; or Bakhtin's answerability ethics in the once-occurrent event-ness of Being in emotion-volition awareness). For us, this is different than mindfulness. The main problem corporations face is too much instrumental mindfulness, not enough Being-full-ness.

The quality of your connectedness and intra-activity with the Now Spiral shapes the future of the storytelling and the course of action choices in the Now. The Now Spiral is Now in connection to the future as an intrinsic part of the Now-situation, Here and Now. The linear and cyclic antenarratives perceive the future as part of the narrative-past, relayed, again and again. Belief that replaying the past-narrative will be a progress-antenarrative-future creates much of the present hellish dysfunctions of Storytelling Organizations (Boje, 1991, 1995, 2008a).

Strategy has become a 'mind-projected future' (Tolle's terms, 1997:41). It is a future-time that is an illusion. Corporate culture is retrospective-sensemaking-pastness-narrative, and those organizations are stuck in their past narratives. Then there are organizations so busy Doing in webs of living story relationships, they cannot Be-in-the-Event-ness of Being. Collective manifestations of Storytelling Organizations are in dis-ease when they are stuck in the narrative-past, the linear-cyclic-antenarrative-future, or in fragmented living-stories-now. Cut all the storytelling attachments. Including attachments to linear-cyclic-antenarrative-futures there is what Tolle calls an 'implicit assumption that the highest good lies in the future and therefore the end justifies the means' (2005:41). This is what I call instrumental ethics (Boje, 2008b), and is different from

Aristotelian, virtue, Kantian categorical-principle-ethics, and Bakhtinian-answerability ethics. It is the preference for instrumental ethics, and a lack of the other ethical paths that is creating such havoc, suffering, and duplicity in organizations.

We would like to theorize with you for a moment. There is a Gap between the storytelling and the timespacemattering. It is within the stillness of the Gap, that one can practice meditation in the Now, and possibly observe the intra-play of storytelling and timespacemattering. The intra-play is highly agential, highly efficacious. It is what Karen Barad (2007) calls agential realism. Put it to the test. Spend a few more of your moments in the higher VEF of what we are calling the Now Spiral Antenarrative (NSA) and in the Gap between all storytelling and what Barad (2007) calls timespacemattering. Before you begin consciously cut your cords with all your fragmented selves distributed in the present across your living story webs of relationships. A few moments in the Gap allows you to increasingly observe not only the NSA but the lower VEF of stuck-in-the-past narratives and their retrospection-projection into linear-cyclic antenarratives of lower VEF.

Storytelling organizations get caught up and attached to lower VEF rooted in narrative habits, fragmented living story webs, and linear/cyclic antenarratives. By stepping into the 'moment-by-moment practice of being' (Tolle, 2005:80): into Bakhtinian eventness of answerability, we can begin to see what Kurt Lewin (1951) meant by energetic force field of an organization, and the force fields of its participants.

When you notice, as a consultant, your attention drifting to the organization's narrative-past, its present-living-story-fragmented-selves, or the linear-cyclic-antenarratives, then as they say in *Matrix Energetics* (Richard Bartlett), 'notice what you notice' and draw your attention back to the Gap and NSA of once-occurrent event-ness of Being. Organizations drift into victim-hero-narrative reaction-reenactments, and into worry-linear-cyclic-antenarratives. This means they get attached and habituated to the VEF storytelling. In stillness observe the lower VEF coursing through the organization, its corporeal materiality.

Then visit the Gap between all storytelling and all timespacemattering, for even a momentary glimpse, then that observational awareness attention is transformational of VEF, at least so we are told by Bennett's (2010) *Vibrant Matter*, Barad's (2007) *Meeting the Universe Halfway*, Bartlett's (2007) *Matrix Energetics* and his (2009) *The Physics of Miracles*, and to some extent, Latour's (2005) *Reassembling the Social* and Bakhtin's (1993) *Toward a Philosophy of the Act*.

It is the Gap and NSA meditation in timelessness that allows one to break free of habitual narrative scripts and their linear/cyclic antenarrative projections, while reclaiming the fragmented selves from webs of living story webs that are energy-draining. Gap and NSA also lessen the illusion of linear time narratives and belief in the Newtonian physics materiality, and make it more possible to the aliveness of energetic quantum physics of the intra-play of timespacemattering and storytelling.

All kinds of lower VEF take root in storytelling organizations (Boje, 1991, 1995, 2008a, 2008b), making them highly toxic and highly dysfunctional places to work. Practice in being in the Gap, observing all the storytelling, all that VEF, with full observational attention, takes heaps of practice. It's a sort of Zen discipline, an Eastern meditation, an adventure in Native or Indigenous storytelling-materiality.

The Gap is a ripple wave, Bakhtinian in nature, from his Dialogic Imagination on light-beam (cited in Boje, 2008a). Observing the Gap is key to transmuting from narrative-past and its projective linear/cyclic antenarrative pathologies to the NSA. The key is spending quality timelessness in the Beingness of Now, long enough to detach from the past-future, and create some new choices of connectedness in the present-future of NSA. In quantum physics, observing, 'noticing what you notice in the Now' is key to energetic frequency transformation.

'Instead of mentally projecting yourself away from the Now, go more deeply into the Now by going more deeply into the body' meditation (Tolle, 1997:76), which is kind of like those realization body meditations we have all done. If we can add to this keeping our attention, for a moment, on the timespacemattering in the Now, we have a way to not lose our selves in the storytelling and its intra-activity with timespacemattering.

The collective egoic narrative (dys)functions, roles, and identities have lower VEF. Yet these lower VEFs take over in the projective linear/cyclic antenarrative futuring, especially in strategic planning, and in action research. Savall *et al.*'s (2008) *Intervention Research* that I write about is more about finding the virtue ethics, the answerability ethics, the changes in the habits of thoughts and action that have become dysfunction narratives.

In the Now Spiral, there can be those fractal spirals, the ones that spin off in egoic reactive emotion (jealousy, envy, forgiveness, etc. that are plagues to any professor's life). One of the authors expounds:

I am writing to you, since I know you like spirals, and fractals. I have started to imagine how the Now Spiral can have some fractals of joy, and others that split off into the Egoic emotion-volitions. I am trying to sort out some relation between Tolle and Bakhtin. Both use the terms emotion and volition, but for Tolle these are the worst of the Egoic, and he has a more appreciative enquiry take, except that Tolle embraces the emotion-volition. Bakhtin sees E-V as a way to get into the once-occurrent eventness of Being (1993, Philosophy of the Act book). Both Tolle and Bakhtin are more into the Now than any Western Europeans I know, or any Americans, other than Native Americans or those involved in Zen mediation practice. For Bakhtin, he is not just about positivity (AI), but is always looking at forces and counter-forces of heteroglossia (what in open systems theory is deviation-counteracting and deviation-amplifying forces). And once in the *Dialogical Imagination* book, Bakhtin talks about light-ray energy.

The leaders, in our organizations, in their current state, are rarely if ever paying attention to the Now, being truly present in the Here and Now. They are either stuck in retrospective-narrative-petrifications (Czarniawska, 2004) or in the progress-antenarrative-fulfillment types (linear and cyclical). As Tolle puts it in *The Power of Now*, the 'loss of Now is loss of Being' (1997:49). Your organizations seems both stuck in the past, and recycling it into linear progress and cyclic antenarratives. These leaders are not in the Now in the joy of Being. It comes from socialization into psychological linear/cyclic time.

Conclusion

An ethical approach to change leadership would go outside the line, and into the co-generation of emergent spirals, and assemblage clusters that are neither pre-determined, nor fatalistic progress futures. It would empower decision makers to approach ethical decision making not only from a new direction, but from a new dimension. In other words, ethical leadership needs to not only be a virtue (through petrified narrative) based enterprise, but also a contemporaneous virtue – a vehicle through which all decisions can be approached.

Achieving this outcome means achieving a greater level of Being in organizational decision making, and subsequently a paradigm shift from the dominant nature of BME linear transposing. From a managerial perspective this means a willingness to embrace a greater level of diversity, uncertainty and complexity from a Being perspective.

Empowering managers to do this means surrendering a minute amount of the rational control structure of an organization, and converting it into a space where Beingness can occur. Organizations operating in this capacity (Apple, Oracle, etc.) are enjoying success in a new and 'tough' economy.

The enactment of the ideas contained within this chapter will require openness to divergent ideas, willingness to change, and corporate training and development. However, it is our supposition that an organization in crisis or in need of wholesale ethical change will benefit from an enhanced Being-ness in terms of their living story intra-activity.

References

Bakhtin, M. M. (1981). *The Dialogic Imagination: Four Essays*. Austin, TX: University of Texas Press.

Bakhtin, M. M. (1990). *Art and Answerability*. Austin, TX: University of Texas Press.

Bakhtin, M. M. (1993). *Toward a Philosophy of the Act*. Austin, TX: University of Texas Press.

Barad, K. (2003). Posthumanist performativity: Toward an understanding of how matter comes to matter. *Journal of Women in Culture and Society*, 28 (3), 801–831. Online at www.kiraoreilly.com/blog/wp-content/uploads/2009/06/signsbarad.pdf.

Barad, K. (2007). *Meeting the Universe Halfway: Quantum Physics and the Entanglement of Matter and Meaning*. Durham, London: Duke University Press.

Bartlett, R. (2007). *Matrix Energetics: The Science and Art of Transformation*. New York: Simon and Schuster and Hillsboro, OR: Beyond Words.

Bartlett, R. (2009). *The Physics of Miracles: Tapping into the Field of Consciousness Potential*. New York: Simon & Schuster and Hillsboro, OR: Beyond Words.

Bennett, J. (2010). *Vibrant Matter: A Political Ecology of Things*. Durham, NC: Duke University Press.

Berger, P. and Luckmann. (1967). *The Social Construction of Reality: A Treatise in the Sociology of Knowledge*. Garden City, NY: Anchor Books.

Bergson, H. (1992/1932). *The Creative Mind*. New York: Citadel Press.

Boje, D. M. (1991). The storytelling organization: A study of story performance in an office-supply firm. *Administrative Science Quarterly*, 36(1), 106–126.

Boje, D.M. (1995). Stories of the storytelling organization: A postmodern analysis of Disney as 'Tamara-Land'. *Academy of Management Journal*, 38, 997–1035.

Boje, D. M. (2001). *Narrative Methods for Organizational & Communications Research*. London: Sage.

Boje, D. M. (2008a). *Storytelling Organizations*. London: Sage.

Boje, D. M. (2008b). *Critical Theory Ethics For Business and Public Administration*. Charlotte, NC: Information Age Press.

Boje, D. M. (2010). Sideshadowing appreciative inquiry: One storytellers' commentary (on article by Fitzgerald, Oliver and Joan Hoxsey). *Journal of Management Inquiry*, 19(3), 238–241.

Boje, D. M. (2011a). *Storytelling the Future of Organizations: An Antenarrative Handbook*. New York/London: Routledge.

Boje, D. M. (2011b). *The Quantum Physics of Storytelling*. Unpublished manuscript. Online at bit.ly/nSQyqb.

Boje, D. M., Pullen, A., Rhodes, C. and Rosile, G. A. (2011). The virtual leader. In: A. Bryman, D. Collinson, K. Grint, B. Jackson and M. Uhl-Bien (eds), *The Sage Handbook of Leadership*. Los Angeles, London, New Delhi: Sage, 518–530.

Boje, D. M. and Rhodes, C. (2005a). The leadership of Ronald McDonald: Double narration and stylistic lines of transformation. *The Leadership Quarterly*, 17(1), 94–103.

Boje, D. M. and Rhodes, C. (2005b). The virtual leaders construct: The mass mediaization and simulation of transformational leadership. *Leadership Journal*, 1(4), 407–428.

Boje, D. M. and Rosile, G. A. (2008). Specters of Wal-Mart: A critical discourse analysis of stories of Sam Walton's ghost. *Critical Discourse Studies*, 5(2), 153–179.

Cajete, G. (2000). *Native Science: Natural Laws of Interdependence*. Sante Fe, NM: Clear Light Publishers.

Czarniawska, B. (2004). *Narratives in Social Science Research*. London: Sage.

Dewey, J. (1929). *The Sources of a Science of Education*. NY: Liveright.

Fitzgerald, S. and Hoxsey, J. (2010). Appreciative inquiry as a shadow process. *Journal of Management Inquiry*, 19 (3), 220–233.

Freire, P. (1970). *Pedagogy of the Oppressed*. London: Penguin Books.

Latour, B. (2005). *Reassembling the Social: An Introduction to Actor-Network-Theory*. Oxford, New York: Oxford University Press.

Lewin, K. (1951). *Field Theory in Social Science: Selected Theoretical Papers*. Oxford: Harpers.

Marcuse, H. (1964). *One-Dimensional Man*. Boston: Beacon Press.

Marx, K. (2008). *Das Kapital: an Abridged Edition*. Oxford, New York: Oxford University Press.

Morson, Gary Saul (1994). *Narrative and Freedom: The Shadows of Time*. New Haven, London: Yale University Press.

Savall, H., Zardet, V. and Bonnet, M. (2008). *Releasing the Untapped Potential of Enterprises Through Socio-Economic Management*. Geneva, Switzerland: ILO (International Labour Office) Bureau of Employers' Activities.

Tolle, E. (1997). *The Power of Now*. Vancouver: Namaste.

Tolle, E. (2005). *A New Earth: Awakening to Your Life's Purpose*. Camberwell, Victoria: Penguin Group.

Trungpa, Chögyam (1973). *Cutting Through Spiritual Materialism*. Boston: Shambhala.

5 Mind the gap

Hypocrisy monitoring and integrity striving as a source of ethical leadership

Ronald L. Dufresne and Judith A. Clair

> Integrity is a ubiquitous ideal in leadership: citizens clamor for it from politicians, employees desire it from managers, religious faithful expect it from clergy, and stockholders demand it from corporations. Everyone seems to want integrity in their leaders . . .
>
> *(Palanski and Yammarino, 2007:171)*

> [R]ecognizing our hypocrisy is a source of power. When we become willing to monitor our hypocrisy, we discover that intense personal shame drives us to close our integrity gaps. Accepting the truth about our hypocrisy helps us to transform ourselves and others.
>
> *(Quinn, 2004:24)*

Introduction

In the quote above, Palanski and Yammarino remind us that integrity is at the center of leadership; it is much desired, and the implication is that a lapse of integrity would deeply harm one's leadership. Take for example the recent scandal in the spring of 2010 involving Paul Levy, CEO of Beth Israel Deaconess Hospital of Boston. Paul Levy, who is widely acknowledged as a highly-admired and effective healthcare leader, found himself faced with a scandal over an inappropriate relationship with a woman subordinate. The scandal overshadowed Levy's long recognized tenure of hands-on, transparent, and innovative leadership. One must reflect on the possibility that jaws may not have dropped so widely open if Levy was not already known to be a CEO-of-the-people, whose leadership is deeply rooted in courageousness, compassion, honesty, and integrity. While in the long term Levy may survive and even flourish as the gossip and rubber-necking subsides, the incident is a powerful reminder that integrity is easily lost when leaders' words and deeds become misaligned, in other words, when leaders act in ways that appear to be hypocritical.

But, perhaps it is less lapses of judgment of admired leaders that are a problem in this situation and more our understanding of integrity that is at fault for the ease with which admired leaders' identities becomes tarnished. Both popular understandings and scholarly research on the connection between integrity and leadership paints a picture whereby one meaningful misstep can shift leaders' identities from integrity-centered to hypocritical. But, as Quinn (2000) so aptly reminds us, aren't we all hypocrites? To be human is to experience moments in which our deeds become misaligned with our stated values, our highest ideals, and our truest and deepest beliefs. There are many reasons that this occurs, which we explore in depth later in the chapter, but the reality is that *no person* is capable of full integrity because there will always be moments of hypocrisy.

If we embrace this idea, it shifts the conditions that we hold for hypocritical leaders to become leaders with integrity. Specifically, whereas the dominant view is that *having* integrity is critical for leadership effectiveness and ethical leadership, Quinn's (2004) view, and the one we will further explore in this chapter, is that embracing hypocrisy and *moving in the direction of* integrity are indeed more important for leadership effectiveness and ethical leadership. This is an important, albeit subtle, shift from the prevailing view on integrity and leadership. Our assertion is that seeing one's hypocrisy and taking steps to repair it may be at the center of what it means to be an ethical leader. In our view, the process of seeking and working to close hypocrisy gaps is a critical aspect of effective and ethical leadership. In this chapter , we therefore propose a new concept to describe this process of closing hypocrisy gaps: *integrity striving*. We assert that integrity striving involves meaningful daily efforts to recognize and close hypocrisy gaps.

In sum, in this chapter we examine integrity – the match between espoused principles and values and embodied principles and values – and its shadow, hypocrisy in leadership. Our central premise is that every leader engages in hypocrisy. Effective and ethical leaders are those who are mindful of their hypocrisy and strive to close these hypocrisy gaps as a way of seeking integrity. We therefore discuss how the monitoring and remedying of hypocrisy gaps relates to effective and ethical leadership.

This chapter is organized into 6 sections. In section 1 we explore traditional definitions of hypocrisy and integrity. In section 2 we discuss existing views about the role of integrity in effective and ethical leadership. In section 3, we explore how leaders instead cross the line to become hypocrites. In the next two sections of the chapter (sections 4 and 5), we explore the ways in which leaders can build integrity in light of hypocrisy. In section 4, we explore the deep links between identity, integrity and hypocrisy and discuss how identity management is at the heart of building a path toward integrity striving. In section 5 we explore in depth what it means to engage in integrity striving. We conclude our chapter with closing thoughts in section 6.

Understanding hypocrisy and integrity

To explore the relationship hypocrisy and integrity have with leadership, we must first define what we mean by hypocrisy and integrity. This is, it turns out, not as straightforward as it might seem. With regard to integrity, scholars state that it is a value that is commonly touted as an expectation and a requirement of effective leadership (Palanski and Yammarino, 2007). However, there are multiple definitions of integrity, and it is unclear how each conceptualization uniquely relates to leadership outcomes (Becker, 1998; Gosling and Huang, 2010; Palanski and Yammarino, 2007). Just as there is conceptual confusion in the literature regarding integrity, there is also conceptual confusion regarding what is meant by hypocrisy and about how hypocrisy relates to leadership. In this section, we explore various definitions of hypocrisy and integrity, and provide our views on meanings that guide our theorizing in this chapter.

Hypocrisy

Cha and Edmondson (2006:59), reflecting on the paucity of scholarly work on hypocrisy, cite the Oxford English Dictionary (1989) of a hypocrite as one "who pretends to have feelings or beliefs of a higher order than his real ones." This implies hypocrisy to be the espousal of values, beliefs, or principles that may be socially acceptable, yet are not genuine. This definition, as Runciman (2008) and Barden, Rucker, and Petty (2005) mention, is rooted in the Greek root *hypokrisis*, which referred to a leader's playing a part. Other authors more simply define hypocrisy to be an incongruity between one's espoused beliefs and one's behavior (Furia, 2009; Stone *et al.*, 1997), or more colloquially, not practicing what one preaches. Within both definitions in the sense that the espoused beliefs represent socially desirable principles. This sense is reflected in the common reference to the La Rochefoucauld quote, "Hypocrisy is the homage vice pays to virtue" (Furia, 2009; Kane, 2005; Runciman, 2008). The espoused beliefs, then, are likely to be virtuous espousals.

Kris (2005) argues that hypocrisy is the opposite of integrity. Of course, given our preceding discussion concerning the need for authors to be explicit about what exactly they mean by integrity, this begs the question of how Kris (2005) defines the concept. We define hypocrisy as the mismatch between actions and words, where those words are socially desirable. Note that integrity and hypocrisy, in our view, are not perfect conceptual opposites. In our view, it is possible to lack integrity if one's behavior fails to embody socially-desirable and defensible principles, even if one does not publicly espouse those principles. For example, if one lies solely for personal gain, thus violating a social norm of truth-telling, he would be viewed as lacking integrity – even if he never publicly claimed to value truth-telling or to be a truth-teller. However, in this case, he would not be viewed as a hypocrite. A liar, yes, but not a hypocrite. To be a hypocrite, he would have to espouse the value of truth-telling and violate that espousal. In keeping with the view that hypocrisy entails, at least in part, a false claim to virtue, our definition would be safe from the observation, "but at least Hitler wasn't a hypocrite," since his espousals were clearly not in keeping with socially-defensible principles. (See Figure 5.1 below for a graphical representation of the relationship between integrity and hypocrisy.)

Before leaving this section, it is also important to distinguish between

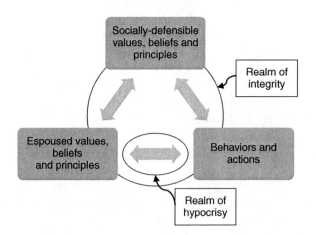

Figure 5.1 *The relationship between integrity and hypocrisy*

actual hypocrisy and *perceived* or *attributed* hypocrisy. Actual hypocrisy implies some objectively "real" mismatch between espoused values and behavior. If the espousal was performed in public and the behavior performed in private, it is possible that only the leader would or could be aware the actual hypocrisy. On the other hand, attributed hypocrisy would be a perception of hypocrisy in the mind of an observer, even if the incongruence didn't "really" exist. In this respect, attributed hypocrisy would be the inverse of Simon's (2002:19) behavioral integrity, which he defines as "the perceived pattern of alignment between a leader's words and deed."

Integrity

Palanski and Yammarino (2007) have identified five different meanings of integrity in the scholarly literature. These meanings include integrity as wholeness, integrity as authenticity, integrity as word-deed consistency, integrity as consistency in adversity, and integrity as ethicality (Palanski and Yammarino, 2007). Integrity as wholeness builds from the etymology of the word, from the same Latin root shared by integer, to highlight the completeness and consistency of all aspects of one's person across time and space. In Palanski and Yammarino's (2007:174) words, integrity as wholeness shows "an overall consistency of behavior, thoughts, and emotions across time and situations." Integrity as authenticity relates to the Shakespearean concept of "to thine own self be true." In this sense, integrity means being aware of one's private values and motives, and behaving accordingly. Integrity as word-deed alignment, however, hinges on making one's values and motives public and then behaving accordingly. Simons' (2002) conceptualization of behavioral integrity fits with this version of integrity. He defines behavioral integrity as "the perceived pattern of alignment between a leader's words and deeds" (Simons, 2002:19). Integrity as consistency in adversity is a conceptualization that highlights the importance for someone with integrity to be able to resist temptation and remain true to one's principles even when faced with adversity (Palanski and Yammarino, 2007). Lastly, integrity as ethicality has been used as somewhat of a catch-all conceptualization, including meanings such as morality, honesty, trustworthiness, respectfulness, openness, and compassion (Palanski and Yammarino, 2007).

Certainly, many of these conceptualizations are highly related and perhaps overlapping. Throughout all of these meanings runs a theme of consistency, among such components as explicit values, tacit values, societal values (e.g., honesty is good), and actions. The differences emerge as a function of which components are salient to the conceptualization. Authors have attempted to reconceptualize integrity in a way that transcends the differences among the definitions, seeking a fundamental perspective on what integrity *really means*. One of the motivations here is the idea that those conceptualizations of integrity as consistency between an individual's values – be they espoused as words or tacit – and his or her actions runs the risk of being ethically void. The thought experiment proposed by these authors is: did Hitler have integrity (Becker, 1998; Gosling and Huang, 2010)? Using a strict word-deed consistency view, the answer would seem to be "yes," since Hitler opened espoused the same principles his actions embodied. Since this Hitler-with-integrity view fails the face validity test of what common language usage of integrity implies, Becker (1998) and Gosling and Huang (2010) propose accounts of integrity that reconcile a theoretical conceptualization of integrity with the common usage of integrity.

Both Becker (1998) and Gosling and Huang (2010) argue for embedding the values or principles with which behavior should be consistent in some broader sociological fabric. Relying on a Randian Objectivist perspective, Becker (1998) argues that, to have integrity, one's individual values need to be "morally justifiable" (p. 157) as rationally pursuing "long-term survival" (p. 157), and then one must act in accordance with those individual values. Relying on an integrative social contracts theory (ISCT) perspective, Gosling and Huang (2010) address the multiple levels of principles and norms that underlie action with integrity. For these authors, one's word in the wholeness, word-deed alignment, authenticity, and consistency-in-adversity meanings of integrity translate into making and fulfilling nano-level social contracts. These nano-level social contracts consist of interpersonal commitments, such as when a manager makes a statement of principle or value (Gosling and Huang, 2010). The "Hitler problem" of integrity formulation in the ISCT perspective is addressed by an additional level of principle or value. Underlying the interpersonal nano-level social contract are hypernorms and macro- and micro-social contracts. These three components reflect the acceptability of the principle or value to humanity or to one's communities; principles need to be defensible to be valid (Gosling and Huang, 2010).

Together, this emerging view of integrity highlights consistency among one's actions, one's stated values, and the defensible social values. This view accounts for the five perspectives outlined by Palanski and Yammarino (2007). In our view, including the aspect of defensible social values or principles addresses a conceptual problem (i.e., the Hitler-with-integrity problem). At the same time, however, we feel this would be an empirically uncommon problem to encounter. It would seem to be uncommon for one to espouse values that are anathema to broader societal norms. Nonetheless, abiding by repeated calls (Becker, 1998; Gosling and Huang, 2010; Palanski and Yammarino, 2007) to define what we mean by integrity, we therefore define the concept to mean an alignment among one's actions, words, and socially-defensible principles.

Existing views on the role of integrity in leadership

As Palanski and Yammarino (2009) claim, there has been relatively little research exploring the explicit link between integrity and leadership. There has been, however, more leadership research in which integrity plays a more implicit role. This integrity-and-leadership perspective tells a consistent story, largely informed by the current formulations of transformational and authentic leadership. Transformational leadership concerns the type of leadership that strives to connect more deeply with followers, changing and challenging them to aspire to become leaders themselves (Bass and Riggio, 2006; Burns, 1978). The four components of transformational leadership are idealized influence, inspirational motivation, intellectual stimulation, and individualized consideration (Bass and Riggio, 2006). Within these four components are hints at the role of integrity in transformational leadership. Idealized influence, for example, concerns how transformational leaders serve as role models, where they are admired, respected, trusted, and emulated by their followers (Bass and Riggio, 2006). Given the centrality of trust in transformational leadership (Dirks and Ferrin, 2002), it is important to highlight the role of integrity in trust development. Mayer, Davis, and Schoorman (1995) argue that integrity is one of the three key factors explaining one's trustworthiness. These authors, however, fall prey to the problem (Becker, 1998; Gosling and Huang, 2010; Palanski and Yammarino, 2007) of not clarifying what they mean by integrity. In fact, they write, "in the evaluation of trustworthiness it is the perceived level of integrity that is important rather than the reasons why the perception is formed" (Mayer *et al.*, 1995:720). Simons (1999) clarifies these linkages, arguing that word-deed consistency (i.e., behavioral integrity) leads to trust, which in turn is an important antecedent to transformational leadership. Thus, the greater the integrity, the more effective the transformational leadership.

Related to the transformational leadership perspective is authentic leadership (Avolio and Gardner, 2005), which is a recently developed perspective on leadership. The authentic leadership perspective is so recent, in fact, that there is no clear consensus on definitions or frameworks. Gardner *et al.* (2005) define authentic leadership as consisting of leaders who are authentically self-aware, self-accepting, and whose behavior remains true to their thoughts and beliefs. Similar to transformational leadership's concern for trusting relationships and follower development, Gardner *et al.*'s (2005) view also includes authentic relationships with followers, marked by transparency, trust, guidance toward higher aims, and care for followers' development. Shamir and Eilam (2005) take a narrower view, framing authentic leadership as concerning leaders who are true to themselves, and whose leadership is rooted in personal values and convictions. Throughout these conceptualizations, authentic leadership hinges on a leader's awareness of his or her own values and how well his or her behaviors embody those values. It stands to reason, then, that this increased self-awareness would lead to greater integrity in the sense we mean it in this chapter. Avolio and Gardner (2005:330) state: "Accompanying the basic meaning of authentic leadership . . . is the notion that the leaders' espoused values/beliefs and their actions become aligned over time and across varying situational challenges." Integrity, it would seem, plays a vital role in authentic leadership, where the greater the integrity, the more authentic the leader is.

An additional perspective on integrity and leadership is offered by Trevino, Hartman, and Brown (2000) on ethical leadership. Ethical leadership, Trevino *et al.*'s (2000; Trevino and Brown, 2004) work, hinges on a leader being both a moral person and a moral manager. A moral person is one who is honest, fair, and trustworthy, whereas a moral manager uses his or her position to pursue that which is ethical. Clearly, the form of integrity Trevino *et al.* (2000) use here is integrity as ethicality (Palanski and Yammarino, 2007). Interestingly, Trevino *et al.* (2000) also explore a perspective on hypocritical leadership, which is what, in their view, occurs when a morally-weak person tries to behave like a morally-strong manager. In this case, "employees become cynical and distrust everything the leader says" (Trevino *et al.*, 2000:138). Personal integrity, then, is required for a leader to be viewed as an ethical leader.

Put together, the extant literature on the connection between integrity and leadership paints a picture whereby leaders with – and perceived to have – greater integrity are associated with increased trustworthiness, more authenticity, greater capacity to transform those around them, and more ethicality. While hypocrisy and leadership has received scant attention relative to the attention paid integrity and leadership, the implied view offered by the transformational and authentic leadership literature, and the explicit view offered by Trevino *et al.* (2000), indicates that not walking the talk would be detrimental to leadership effectiveness. In the next section we develop a perspective that problematizes this view and explores how hypocrisy could serve a vital role in ethical leadership.

How leaders become hypocrites

How do leaders – especially well-meaning leaders who are good and ethical persons – come to experience themselves and to be viewed by others as hypocritical? We earlier defined hypocrisy as a mismatch between espoused principles, beliefs, and values and behaviors. In this section, we explore the various kinds and sources of mismatches among principles, beliefs, values and behaviors that provoke a sense of hypocritical leadership.

First, it is possible for the espoused words to be knowingly untruthful, where the leader has no intention of walking the talk. Imagine a manager who knows a downsizing is looming, yet he tells his employees he would never lay any of them off. Espousing this principle can avoid short-term pain, yet it also sets the stage for hypocrisy when the downsizing occurs.

Second, a leader may espouse beliefs or principles that are aspirational in nature, principles the leader wishes to be able to embody through his or her deeds. Whereas the motivation behind the first reason was to deceive, for this second reason the motivation is to inspire either themselves or others (Brunsson, 1989; Davis, 1993; Runciman, 2008; Simons, 2002). Brunsson (1989: 233–234) goes as far as writing: "hypocrisy [is] necessary to the creation and preservation of high morals." Furia (2009) refers to this as "strategic hypocrisy" since the objective is to suffer hypocrisy in the short-term to strive for longer-term integrity.

Third, a leader may have espoused values in one point in time, only to have her value set shift over time. Later, when she embodies a different (unspoken) value with her behaviors, there would be an incongruence with the previously-espoused values. Similarly, Brunsson (1989) and Furia (2009) argue how the decoupling of words and deeds over time can lead to the charge of hypocrisy, and Barden *et al.* (2005) explore the effects of shifting values over time. These first three reasons can lead to both actual and attributed hypocrisy, since these forms of hypocrisy would be visible to both observers as well as a leader who chooses to observe his or her own congruence.

Fourth, hypocrisy can arise when a leader simultaneously espouses what could be competing values, where the behavior might only be able to match one of those values (Furia, 2009). For example, a manager might espouse the values or principles of both caring for their employees' development as well as focusing on the efficient profitability of her department. While she might genuinely feel committed to both of these values, if she decides against funding an employee's training because it would impact her bottom line, she opens the door to hypocrisy. This problem is further compounded due to the multiple stakeholders to whom a leader must respond (Brunsson, 1989; Furia, 2009; Kane, 2005; Simons, 2002), since satisfying one stakeholder's interests may lead to sacrificing another's and generating hypocrisy. A challenge to satisfying stakeholders' interests is that hypocrisy can also arise because different stakeholders can interpret values or principles differently. Cha and Edmondson (2006) discuss the phenomenon of value expansion, whereby a leader's espoused values might be reinterpreted in light of some larger societal values to mean something different than perhaps what the speaker initially intended. Thus, even if the leader mindfully embodies the espoused principle or value he or she intended with his or her behavior, observers may still perceive incongruence with the value as they understand it and attribute hypocrisy.

Beyond the reasons for hypocrisy that are seated in the values or principles part of the equation, there is an additional reason stemming from the behavioral component. Related to the aspirational hypocrisy and competing stakeholder reasons provided above, it is also evident that hypocrisy can arise because a leader's ability to take action may be constrained in some systemic way. A leader may espouse a value she has every intention of upholding with her behavior, only to learn that she there are compelling systemic reasons why that behavior isn't possible. An example that comes to mind is of President-Elect Barack Obama publicly committing not to permit any recent lobbyists to serve in his administration, only to realize there were some capable, otherwise-qualified candidates for positions who had been lobbyists. What sounded good in theory actually tied his hands in practice, and he proceeded, as President, to issue exceptions to his stated principle.

Lastly, and probably most endemically, there is an underlying reason for hypocrisy that concerns the overall espoused values-behavior relationship. This wellspring of hypocrisy is what Argyris calls Model I theories-in-use (Argyris, 1976; Argyris and Schön, 1974). Model I includes governing variables such as defining situations unilaterally, seeking to win and not lose, and stressing the "rational," or non-emotional aspects of life. These governing variables in turn lead to behavioral strategies aimed at maintaining unilateral control over self and others. Together, these components conspire to stifle learning and lead to self-sealing and un-self-critical thinking (Argyris, 1976; Argyris and Schön, 1974). People operating with Model I theories-in-use avoid testing their beliefs because they are unaware of the possibility of their beliefs being incorrect. They also tend to externalize negative feedback, since taking it personally would come too close to "losing." The net effect is a systemic mismatch between espoused theories – articulations about how the world should work – and theories-in-use, which are what actually drives behavior, and concomitant lack of awareness of this mismatch (Argyris, 1976; Argyris and Schön, 1974).

Identity, integrity, and hypocrisy

Given the many challenges that can lead to hypocrisy we explored in the section above, it would seem difficult for a leader to avoid hypocrisy altogether, either actual or attributed! Indeed, hypocrisy seems instead to be ubiquitous, or, as Kane (2005:4) writes, inevitable. According to Quinn (2000:75), "As painful as it might be for us to accept, the truth is that we are all hypocrites."

The prevailing view outlined in the previous section is that having integrity, not hypocrisy, is a requirement for effective leadership. Specifically, having integrity is necessary for the ethical leadership that results from transformational, authentic, and moral leadership. Leaders with integrity foster trust with their followers and inspire others around them to behave ethically in service of higher ideals. However, if Quinn (2000) is correct in noting we are all hypocrites, how, then, is ethical leadership possible?

Quinn (2000, 2004) has been at the forefront of formulating an answer to this question. His work on advanced change theory argues that deep transformation emerges when, among other things, change agents are internally-directed by constantly checking for fit between values and behavior and other-focused by putting common interest above self-interest (Quinn, 2000). Leaders who wish to transform themselves and systems around them, then, need to embrace their hypocrisy, monitor their hypocrisy constantly, and work to remedy their hypocrisy gaps.

This is an important, albeit subtle, shift from the prevailing view on integrity and leadership. Whereas the dominant view is that *having* integrity is critical for leadership effectiveness and ethical leadership, Quinn's (2000) view, and the one we will further explore, is that embracing hypocrisy and *moving in the direction of* integrity is indeed more important for leadership effectiveness and ethical leadership.

Confronting one's hypocrisy, Quinn (2000, 2004) writes, is a painful endeavor. Realizing one's behavior does not conform to one's espoused values might trigger feelings of failure, which can feel like "losing" (Argyris, 1976; Argyris and Schön, 1974). It is no surprise, then, that many leaders commonly avoid embracing their hypocrisy. Most people tend to naturally view themselves in kinder light, minimizing what they would characterize as negative self-perceptions (Fiske and Taylor, 1991; Swann and Read, 1981).

Palmer states in his classic book *The Courage to Teach*:

> But, by identity and integrity I do not mean only our noble features, or the good deeds we do, or the brave faces we wear to conceal our confusions and complexities. Identity and integrity have as much to do with our shadows and limits, our wounds and fears, as with our strengths and potentials . . .
>
> Identity and integrity are not the granite from which fictional heroes are hewn. They are subtle dimensions of the complex, demanding, and lifelong process of self-discovery. *Identity* lies in the intersection of the diverse forces that make up my life, and *integrity* lies in relating to those forces in ways that bring me wholeness and life rather than fragmentation and death.
>
> (Palmer, 1998:13)

Palmer's focus is on the art and practice of teaching, not leading organizations per se. However, his sage words are relevant to both settings. According to Palmer, at the center of links between identity and integrity is a practice of seeking the undivided self – honoring, creating, detecting, and repairing linkages between worthy values, beliefs, and behaviors.

Palmer's reflections suggest that seeing one's hypocrisy and taking steps to repair it may be at the center of daily identity management practices; in other words, the steps the leader takes in daily interactions with others to build private and public self-insight about hypocrisies that will inevitably occur and/or that will be perceived by others. To be able to do so, a person must first be capable of seeing and experiencing the wholeness of the self – in all of its paradoxes, conflicting values and behaviors, and failures and successes at living up to one's ideals and to others' needs. Without at least catching glimpses of one's wholeness, a leader is unable to see the hypocrisy in the first place, let alone repair it. Skills at hypocrisy repair do not just involve navel-gazing oriented reflection. As social constructionists assert (*cf.* Bartel and Dutton, 2001; Goffman, 1959), identity is built and maintained through social interactions. Leaders must also be able to gain insight into how others view them, experience them, and especially, how others have seen and experienced their integrity and hypocrisy.

This can be challenging for several reasons. First, as Palmer (1998) explains, individuals who are vulnerable daily to others at work can over time lose a sense of connectedness among the various aspects of one's self. In business, this is likely to occur because of the fatigue that can build up over time when showing various parts of one's private and public self feels threatening and is not valued. Living in an environment where a tough exterior and emotion-free functioning is the practiced norm can provoke fragmentation of the self – leaving the vulnerable pieces at home or outside of one's normal daily functioning. Over time, to reduce a sense of vulnerability, leaders may learn to disconnect and disengage parts of themselves from one another. Values and behaviors that one hopes to be tightly coupled become only loosely connected (or not connected at all). In search of security from critique or judgment, leaders may tend instead toward defensive and protective behaviors that seek to buffer the self from harm. Palmer (1998) refers to this as a "self-protective split" of personhood from practice. Just as the lifetime smoker may have difficulty breaking his or her addiction to cigarettes, when self-protective splits have become a lifelong practice, it may be difficult to sew the parts of one's identity back together.

Further, building insight into one's hypocrisy requires two kinds of behaviors. First, it requires leaders to demonstrate openness to receiving feedback from others about the nature of their integrity and others' experiences of their hypocrisy when it occurs. Second, it requires so-called "followers" to have the courage to provide insight and feedback to leaders about their strengths and faults. While leaders and so-called followers both may espouse openness to others' input and to providing input, in practice a plethora of research demonstrates individuals' aversion to feedback seeking and feedback giving (Jackman and Strober, 2003). Therefore, both of these behaviors take a great deal of courage, and may rarely occur in organizations.

This is especially likely to be the case in organizations characterized by a lack of identity safety (Davies, Spencer and Steele, 2005). Scholars have used the term "identity safety" to characterize an organizational environment in which a person feels vulnerable to being stereotyped and devalued based on one or more social identities. We extend the use of this term to describe organizational environments, situational contexts, or interactive moments in which a person feels that his or her core self is threatened by the possibility of being prejudged and evaluated negatively and/or unfairly. Based on this broad definition, many of our organizational environments certainly fall into the category of identity unsafe. This is the case because judgment – of one's performance, behaviors, commitment and engagement, and so on – is at the very heart of life in organizations. Such threats are likely to further be fueled in many modern organizations characterized by threats of downsizing, shrinking resources, and lost opportunities. In such environments, it is no surprise that individuals find that they defend rather than remain open and responsive to providing and receiving feedback from others about the state of their integrity and acts of hypocrisy.

A new way of framing hypocrisy and integrity with leadership: Integrity striving

In our view, as painful as it may be, the process of seeking and working to close hypocrisy gaps represents a critical aspect of ethical leadership. The first step in this process is to recognize that integrity and its shadow, hypocrisy, are continuous – rather than dichotomous – variables. Leaders have varying degrees of the quality with which they walk their talk and varying degrees of importance of the values underlying their espousals (Furia, 2009; Schwartz, 1994). Viewing hypocrisy as a continuous variable minimizes an either-or proposition that can be crippling, whereby one instance of hypocrisy brands one as a hypocrite for life. For example, a leader may espouse different types of values, including self-enhancing values such as the pursuit of personal success, or self-transcendent values such as concern for social justice (Schwartz, 1994). These values may be of differential centrality to the leader (Furia, 2009), and the leader may embody these values with their behavior with varying degrees of fidelity. The complexity of the leader's degree and type of hypocrisy thus defies a simple label of hypocrite or non-hypocrite.

If the goal of completely eliminating hypocrisy is an unrealistic one for leaders to undertake (Kane, 2005; Quinn, 2000), leaders can instead focus on reducing their hypocrisy. We propose a new concept to describe this process of closing hypocrisy gaps: *integrity striving*. Reflecting back to our definition of integrity as an alignment among one's actions, words, and socially-defensible principles, integrity striving first entails a mindful accounting of the degree of alignment among the three components, then undertaking change efforts to close the hypocrisy gaps.

Since our definition of integrity is rooted in a contractualist theory of ethics (Donaldson and Dunfee, 1994; Scanlon, 1998), our concept of integrity striving is necessarily a process of ethical leadership. Leaders would need to assess and close the gap between their personal values, beliefs, principles, and priorities and those that would be defensible to the community (i.e., the implicit social contract, Donaldson and Dunfee, 1994; Scanlon, 1998). Leaders would also need to close the hypocrisy gap between their stated values and principles and the values and principles that are embodied by their behavior, and in so doing also narrow the gap between their behaviors and socially-defensible principles. The process of integrity striving would result in leadership with less hypocrisy and more congruence with principles that benefit the community.

Given the three components of integrity, integrity striving entails first assessing the congruence among those components. A leader should consider how well her espousals fit with socially-defensible values, how well her actions fit with socially-defensible values, and how well her actions fit with her espousals. Part of this diagnosis would include recognition of the centrality or importance of her different values. Given our definition of integrity, it would seem that the more important espousals would be regarding benevolent values such as honesty or loyalty and universal values such as equality or social justice (Schwartz, 1994).

The process of integrity striving also requires leaders to work to close the hypocrisy gaps once recognized. As Quinn (2000) notes, a leader's first focus should be internally-directed, aimed at reducing actual hypocrisy; only then can the leader move to focus on closing attributed hypocrisy gaps. Having prioritized their values, leaders should first strive to close hypocrisy gaps concerning their espoused central values.

Our concept of integrity striving by closing hypocrisy gaps builds on Argyris and Schön's (1988) formulation of reciprocal integrity, which is itself embedded in a Model II theory-in-use. A Model I theory-in-use, as described above, is an implicit world view that is unilateral in nature, tacitly designed to maximize winning and minimize losing, resulting in untested assumptions and self-sealing thinking (Argyris, 1976; Argyris and Schön, 1974). Model II, in contrast, is governed by the pursuit of valid information, even and especially when it disconfirms previous assumptions, and the free and informed choice of all parties in a relationship. Leaders employing this theory-in-use seek mutuality with those around them, minimizing the need for defensiveness. A critical action strategy stemming from Model II is the combining of advocacy and inquiry, whereby one shares a belief or an inference and publicly tests these propositions through open inquiry (Argyris, 1976; Argyris and Schön, 1974).

Reciprocal integrity (Argyris and Schön, 1988) is a process wherein a leader can articulate and advocate principles and values, as well as how those principles and values might best be embodied and then test these advocacies with those around them. Building from a case provided in Cha and Edmondson (2006), imagine a leader who espouses the value of *community* in his organization. He may define the value as developing a sense of oneness or belonging at work, and may advocate various fun and morale-building activities that can enhance the sense of community at work. Cha and Edmondson (2006) explore how, in what appears to be a Model I theory-in-use, a leader did just this – advocating his unilateral view of what *community* means and what it looks like. The members of the organization, who were not included in the original value articulation, generated their own unilateral perspective on what community meant; this is a common Model I dynamic where bald advocacy begets more advocacy, which Argyris and Schön (1988) call "schismogenetic." Later, when the leader made a decision to expand the business, it was a decision that, in the eyes of his followers, violated their interpretation of community (which included related values such as equality, openness, and family). There is evidence here of attributed hypocrisy at a minimum, and there may also be actual hypocrisy as well.

Model II-informed reciprocal integrity (Argyris and Schön, 1988) would have taken a more mutual approach to co-constructing the value and testing the degree to which all members of the community were embodying the value of *community*. We are aware that this cannot be practically accomplished with all principles that a leader may value. However, those values that are central enough for a leader to espouse should merit public and mutual testing. In Cha and Edmondson's (2006) study, for example, the CEO espoused five core values, all of which were self-transcendent (Schwartz, 1994). While no doubt difficult, we feel it would be reasonable for a leader to engage with these core values with reciprocal integrity.

The closing of hypocrisy gaps is therefore a reciprocal endeavor. Quinn (2000) describes his advanced change theory as engaged in the emergent reality. Part of a leader's emergent reality entails seeking valid feedback, testing his or her inferences about what values mean and whether or not he or she is embodying those values. Seeking reciprocal integrity is also similar to Kernis' (2003) description of authenticity. In his conceptualization, authenticity entails being self-aware, engaging in unbiased processing of evaluative information, behaving in a manner true to oneself, and having open and truthful relationships (Kernis, 2003). Together, these components mirror a Model II theory-in-use since they entail a willingness to advocate through words and behavior a set of values and beliefs and to inquire of others the degree to which one is embodying these values and beliefs.

Engaging in Model II-informed reciprocal integrity and developing authenticity should allow a leader to recognize and work to close hypocrisy gaps. These are the processes of integrity striving, and they should reduce both actual and attributed hypocrisy. However, as Kim and colleagues (Kim et al., 2009; Kim et al., 2004) note, people tend to weigh negative data about integrity more heavily than positive data about integrity. That is, it may take consistent, repeated observations of a leader's integrity for someone to judge the leader as having high integrity (and low hypocrisy), yet a single instance of leadership hypocrisy would be enough for an observer to see the leader as having low integrity (and high hypocrisy). Even if observers adhere to our admonishment to view hypocrisy and integrity as continuous variables, they may still exhibit a type of bias toward the extremes where they essentially re-dichotomize them. While Kim et al. (2009) conceptualize integrity as ethicality, it would seem that similar logic would hold when taking our view of integrity as well. Put differently, hypocrisy is a stickier label than integrity, and once attributed, a leader would need to engage in further work, even beyond reducing actual hypocrisy, to reduce the hypocrisy attribution.

The literature on trust repair offers a useful template to consider as we explore what leaders can do to reduce attributed hypocrisy. Trust repair considers what a trustee and trustor might do to regain trust that was lost due to a violation (Lewicki and Bunker, 1996). In a recent article making sense of several years of trust repair research, Tomlinson and Mayer (2009) develop a model to explain the phenomenon. Fundamentally, the issues at play in determining the proper recourse are the type of trust violation (i.e., based on the trustee's ability, benevolence, or integrity) and the internal versus external locus, the controllability, and the stability of the cause of the breach.

While our present focus is on reducing a hypocrisy attribution rather than repairing trust, and Tomlinson and Mayer (2009) do not share our specific definition of integrity, it is most instructive to navigate through what they argue can be done in response to an integrity-based trust violation. Tomlinson and Mayer (2009) build their model on the work of Weiner (1986, 1995), exploring the development and management of attributions. Since Weiner (1986) argues that individual characteristics are largely seen by others as controllable by the individual, it stands to reason that the only two levers for the management of integrity-based trust attributions are the locus of causality and the stability of the cause. For a trustee to regain someone's trust, he or she must explain the trust violation as being caused by something external to the actor, and/or to argue that the cause is unstable and therefore unlikely to occur again in the future.

Tomlinson and Mayer (2009) proceed to propose the types of social accounts (Bies, 1987; Cody and McLaughlin, 1990; Scott and Lyman, 1968) that could best externalize and render unstable the attributions. The first social account is a denial, whereby the trustee claims not to be responsible for the violation, so he shouldn't be held to account (Tomlinson and Mayer, 2009), thereby hoping to externalize the attribution of a lack of integrity. An excuse, the next account, allows the trustee to admit a role in the violation, yet also introduces mitigating circumstances that he hopes to externalize the attribution and render it unstable to the extent the unique circumstances are unlikely to repeat in the future (Tomlinson and Mayer, 2009). The last germane account Tomlinson and Mayer (2009) explore is apologizing, which is an account that accepts an internal locus of causality, yet hopes to minimize the stability attribution since the trustee, if the apology is full and extensive, is committing not to commit the violation again. Relatedly, promising to change behavior in the future can also minimize the stability attribution, as can engaging in behavioral change by consistently embodying trustworthy behavior and making substantive amends (Bottom *et al.*, 2002; Schweitzer *et al.*, 2006).

For our purposes, it would seem as though denial is an untenable account for reducing a hypocrisy attribution. This is not to say that denials have not been tried, or that they would never work, however, if we take seriously the ideas that we are all hypocrites (Kane, 2005; Quinn, 2000) and that leaders should engage in reciprocal integrity striving (*cf.* Argyris and Schön, 1988), it would be hollow to advise leaders to follow a Model I theory-in-use and pretend like they have not engaged in hypocrisy. Of the social accounts pertaining to integrity Tomlinson and Mayer (2009) and Schweitzer *et al.* (2006) propose, therefore, excuses, apologies, promise-making remain viable. Furthermore, these accounts would be most effective if they, too, stem from an honest, reciprocal, and mutual engagement in integrity striving.

To reduce attributed hypocrisy, then, a leader may accept that the hypocrisy existed (or exists), and provide a full explanation of how and why it occurred, using a combination of reason-giving, apologizing, and promise-making. We prefer to reframe "excuse-making" as "reason-giving," since the latter is more in line with what we intend by integrity striving. Such reason-giving can help leaders explain the competing values they are attempting to balance, the ways in which their behaviors are systemically constrained, or how their values have changed since a previous espousal (Barden *et al.*, 2005). Apologizing and promise-making are both important ways leaders can communicate their commitment to integrity striving going forward. Using Tomlinson and Mayer's (2009) framework, the intent of these accounts in service of integrity striving is to portray how the leader's hypocrisy is unstable; the more the leader engages in integrity striving, the less stable is the leader's hypocrisy since it should be lessening. Providing social accounts can thus reduce attributed hypocrisy. It is important to note, however, that leaders should first attend to the direct approach of closing actual hypocrisy gaps (Stone *et al.*, 1997); only then should leaders worry about attributed hypocrisy gaps.

Conclusion

Given the realities of organizational life, how can leaders ever hope to move toward a state of hypocrisy repair? We leave the reader with the sage advice offered by Livsey and Palmer (1999:16): "If we want to grow . . . we must learn to talk to each other about our inner lives, our own identity and integrity." By this, they mean that we must learn to share our strengths and weaknesses, our hopes and our despair with others, and to confront them on our own. In doing so, Livsey and Palmer (1999) further assert, we must address our expectations about this process (e.g., how will we do it?), our fears about it, and how our institutions encourage us or discourage us from behaving in this way.

In sum, integrity and hypocrisy are closely related – figure and shadow. Identity is a close relative of the pair. The feeling that we are identity-vulnerable and the experience of being fearful represent two crucial parts of leaders' experiences in organizations. These feelings of vulnerability and fear can hold leaders back from seeing their hypocrisy and engaging in hypocrisy repair. However, if we reframe hypocrisy from a weakness and a fault of failed leaders to a reality of everyday human behavior (be it actual or attributed), then hypocrisy repair also becomes normalized as just part of one's daily practice of seeking to be more effective and more whole. Suspending judgment about hypocrisy allows leaders to appreciate the paradoxes inherent in being human – that to be human is to be hypocritical, and to engage in hypocrisy repair is just a part of becoming a more effective and whole person.

These ideas may seem hopelessly unrealistic sounding. For the so-called public leader, judgment is never suspended. Media and the public look for and may even relish the moments where leaders demonstrate hypocrisy in word and/or in deed. However, our view is that accepting that it is unrealistic to hope to suspend judgment, to seek out feedback about one's hypocrisy, and to repair it when it inevitably occurs represents a loss of hope for the future.

References

Argyris, C. (1976) Theories of action that inhibit individual learning. *American Psychologist*, 31, 638–654.

Argyris, C. and Schön, D. A. (1974) *Theory in practice*. San Francisco: Jossey-Bass.

Argyris, C. and Schön, D. A. (1988) Reciprocal integrity: Creating conditions that encourage personal and organizational integrity. In: S. Srivastva and associates (eds), *The Search for High Human Values in Organizational Life*. San Francisco: Jossey-Bass, 197–222.

Avolio, B. J. and Gardner, W. L. (2005) Authentic leadership development: Getting to the root of positive forms of leadership. *The Leadership Quarterly*, 16, 315–338.

Barden, J., Rucker, D. D., and Petty, R. E. (2005) "Saying one thing and doing another": Examining the impact of event order on hypocrisy judgments of others. *Personality and Social Psychology Bulletin*, 31, 1463–1474.

Bartel, C. A. and Dutton, J. E. (2001) Ambiguous organizational memberships: Constructing organizational identities in interactions with others. In: M.

A. Hogg and D. Terry (eds), *Social Identity Processes in Organizational Contexts*. Philadelphia: Psychology Press, 115–130.

Bass, B. M. and Riggio, R. E. (2006) *Transformational Leadership* (second edition). Mahwah, NJ: Lawrence Erlbaum Associates.

Becker, T. E. (1998) Integrity in organizations: Beyond honesty and conscientiousness. *Academy of Management Review*, 23, 154–161.

Bies, R. J. (1987) The predicament of injustice: The management of moral outrage. In: L. L. Cummings and B. M. Staw (eds), *Research in Organizational Behavior*. Greenwich, CT: JAI Press, 289–319.

Bottom, W. P., Gibson, K., Daniels, S. E., and Murnighan, J. K. (2002) When talk is not cheap: Substantive penance and expressions of intent in rebuilding cooperation. *Organization Science*, 13, 497–513.

Brunsson, N. (1989) *The Organization of Hypocrisy: Talk, Decisions and Actions in Organizations*. Chichester: Wiley.

Burns, J. M. (1978) *Leadership*. New York: Harper & Row.

Cha, S. E. and Edmondson, A. C. (2006) When values backfire: Leadership, attribution, and disenchantment in a values-driven organization. *The Leadership Quarterly*, 17, 57–78.

Cody, M. J. and McLaughlin, M. L. (1990) Interpersonal accounting. In: H. Giles and W. P. Robinson (eds), *Handbook of Language and Psychology*. New York: Wiley, 227–255.

Davies, P. G., Spencer, S. J., and Steele, C. M. (2005) Clearing the air: Identity safety moderates the effects of stereotype threat on women's leadership aspirations. *Journal of Personality and Social Psychology*, 88, 276–287.

Davis, N. (1993) Moral theorizing and moral practice: Reflections on some of the sources of hypocrisy. In: E. R. Winkler and J. R. Coombs (eds), *Applied Ethics: A reader*. Cambridge, MA: Blackwell, 164–180.

Dirks, K. T. and Ferrin, D. L. (2002). Trust in leadership: Meta-analytic findings and implications for research and practice. *Journal of Applied Psychology*, 87, 611–628.

Donaldson, T. and Dunfee, T. W. (1994) Toward a unified conception of business ethics: Integrative social contracts theory. *Academy of Management Review*, 19, 252–283.

Fiske, S. T. and Taylor, S. E. (1991) *Social Cognition* (second edition). New York: McGraw-Hill.

Furia, P. A. (2009) Democratic citizenship and the hypocrisy of leaders. *Polity*, 41, 113–133.

Gardner, W. L., Avolio, B. J., Luthans, F., May, D. R., and Walumbwa, F. (2005) "Can you see the real me?" A self-based model of authentic leader and follower development. *The Leadership Quarterly*, 16, 343–372.

Goffman, E. (1959) *The Presentation of Self in Everyday Life*. New York: Anchor Books.

Gosling, M. and Huang, H. J. (2010) The fit between integrity and integrative social contracts theory. *Journal of Business Ethics* (forthcoming).

Jackman, J. M. and Strober, M. H. (2003) Fear of feedback. *Harvard Business Review*, 81(4), 101–107.

Kane, J. (2005) Must democratic leaders necessarily be hypocrites? Paper presented at the Australasian Political Studies Association Conference. University of Otago, New Zealand. September.

Kernis, M. H. (2003) Toward a conceptualization of optimal self-esteem. *Psychological Inquiry*, 14, 1–26.

Kim, P. H., Dirks, K. T., and Cooper, C. D. (2009) The repair of trust: A dynamic bilateral perspective and multilevel conceptualization. *Academy of Management Review*, 34, 401–422.

Kim, P. H., Ferrin, D. L., Cooper, C. D., and Dirks, K. T. (2004) Removing the shadow of suspicion: The effects of apology versus denial for repairing competence – versus integrity-based trust violations. *Journal of Applied Psychology*, 89, 104–118.

Kris, A. O. (2005) The lure of hypocrisy. *Journal of the American Psychological Association*, 53, 7–22.

Lewicki, R. J. and Bunker, B. B. (1996) Developing and maintaining trust in work relationships. In: R. M. Kramer and T. R. Tyler (eds), *Trust in Organizations: Frontiers of Theory and Research*. Thousand Oaks, CA: Sage Publications, 114–139.

Livsey, R. C. and Palmer, P. J. (1999) *The Courage to Teach: A Guide for Reflection and Renewal*. San Francisco: Jossey-Bass.

Mayer, R. C., Davis, J. H., and Schoorman, F. D. (1995) An integrative model of organizational trust. *Academy of Management Review*, 20, 709–734.

Oxford English Dictionary (second edition). (1989) Prepared by J. A. Simpson and E. S. C. Weiner. New York: Oxford University Press.

Palanski M. E. and Yammarino, F. J. (2007) Integrity and leadership: Clearing the conceptual confusion. *European Management Journal*, 25, 171–184.

Palanski, M. E. and Yammarino, F. J. (2009) Integrity and leadership: A multi-level conceptual framework. *The Leadership Quarterly*, 20, 405–420.

Palmer, P. J. (1998) *The Courage to Teach: Exploring the Inner Landscape of a Teacher's Life*. San Francisco: Jossey-Bass.

Quinn, R. E. (2000) *Change the World: How Ordinary People Can Accomplish Extraordinary Results*. San Francisco: Jossey-Bass.

Quinn, R. E. (2004) *Building the Bridge as You Walk On It: A Guide for Leading Change*. San Francisco: Jossey-Bass.

Runciman, D. (2008) *Political hypocrisy: The Mask of Power, from Hobbes to Orwell and Beyond*. Princeton: Princeton University Press.

Scanlon, T. M. (1998) *What We Owe to Each Other*. Cambridge, MA: Harvard University Press.

Schwartz, S. H. (1994) Are there universal aspects in the structure and contents of human values? *Journal of Social Issues*, 50, 19–45.

Schweitzer, M. E., Hershey, J. C., and Bradlow, E. T. (2006) Promises and lies:

Restoring violated trust. *Organizational Behavior and Human Decision Processes*, 101, 1–19.

Scott, M. B. and Lyman, S. M. (1968) Accounts. *American Sociological Review*, 33, 46–62.

Shamir, B. and Eilam, G. (2005) "What's your story?" A life-stories approach to authentic leadership development. *The Leadership Quarterly*, 16, 395–417.

Simons, T. L. (1999) Behavioral integrity as a critical ingredient for transformational leadership. *Journal of Organizational Change Management*, 12, 89–104.

Simons, T. (2002) Behavioral integrity: The perceived alignment between managers' words and deeds as a research focus. *Organization Science*, 13, 18–35.

Stone, J., Wiegand, A. W., Cooper, J., and Aronson, E. (1997) When exemplification fails: Hypocrisy and the motive for self-integrity. *Journal of Personality and Social Psychology*, 72, 54–65.

Swann, W. B. and Read, S. J. (1981) Acquiring self-knowledge: The search for feedback that fits. *Journal of Personality and Social Psychology*, 41, 1119–1128.

Tomlinson, E. C. and Mayer, R. C. (2009) The role of causal attribution dimensions in trust repair. *Academy of Management Review*, 34, 85–104.

Trevino, L. K. and Brown, M. E. (2004) Managing to be ethical: Debunking five business ethics myths. *Academy of Management Executive*, 18, 69–81.

Trevino, L. K., Hartman, L. P., and Brown, M. (2000) Moral person and moral manager: How executives develop a reputation for ethical leadership. *California Management Review*, 42, 128–142.

Weiner, B. (1986) *An Attributional Model of Motivation and Emotion*. New York: Springer-Verlag.

Weiner, B. (1995) *Judgments of Responsibility: A Foundation for a Theory of Social Conduct*. New York: Guilford Press.

6 Moral agency in strategic change

Coping with ethical tensions through irony

Henrika Franck and Saku Mantere

> How do we make sure that they don't become fat and lazy?
>
> *Manager at an MNC*

Introduction

Good ethics is good business. You have probably heard that, but did you believe it? Scholars argue about whether ethical decisions lead to better results than unethical. But what is ethics in decision making, and how can it be enacted? This chapter examines how moral agency – the agency to make 'ethical' decisions – is enacted in a strategic change process. The first section examines how strategic discourse puts boundaries on what is possible to enact, the second section looks into sense-making and ethics and the third section outlines a case of strategic change and the tensions that were built up in between strategy and moral agency. The case shows that moral agency is inherent in human behaviour but is restricted or even made impossible in strategic discourse. One way of coping in this tension is through the use of irony.

Strategic thinking – sameness

Strategy is typically conceived to be a rational technique for an organization to meet challenges and succeed in changing business environments. The various strategic schools; the 'design' school (Andrews, 1960), the 'planning' school (Ansoff, 1965) the 'positioning' school (Porter, 1980) and the 'vision' school (Hamel and Prahalad, 1994) all embrace the idea that a supreme end that is conciliated by a person or a coalition, drives strategy. There is an underlying assumption that some individuals determine the strategic objective and a vision that must be accepted and enacted by others. Durand and Calori (2006) call this the 'end prevalence dimension of sameness' that is illustrated by opportunism and goal compliance (Ghoshal, 2005). Top management has a strategic intent and communicates what they see as the preferred future position of the firm, and this should guide the actions of the agents by means of selection and retention (Lovas and Ghoshal, 2000). The strategy occurs via organizational members whose actions conform to leaders' views to achieve the strategic intent (Hamel and Prahalad, 1989). Organizational members are left to be goal compliant to reach ambitious collective objectives. This view on strategy can be seen as relying on the notion of sameness, where the aim is to unite both the organization and its stakeholders under the same objective formulation. Sameness, in all levels of identity construction, corresponds to what remains intact – unchanged, that is, the intrinsic dimensions that define the individual, group or institution as recognizable through time. Sameness posits itself against otherness in clear terms – that is, based on the persistence of difference; sameness is related to otherness because what 'is' the case is always in relief from, rather than separate from, what 'is not'.

Strategy has been criticized to disable agency through the subjugation of management (Knights and Morgan, 1991), as a form of symbolic violence (Oakes *et al.*, 1998), as a constitutive force that doesn't pay attention to the interrelationships of the subjects and objects of knowledge (Ezzamel and Willmott, 2004) and an ideology that helps legitimize existing power structures and inequalities in resources (Shivastava, 1986). Knights and Morgan see corporate strategy as a set of discourses and practices which transform managers and employees alike into subjects who secure their sense of purpose and reality by formulating, evaluating and conducting strategy' (1991:252). They suggest that strategy is a discourse that shapes the very sense of what it is to be human. They treat strategy as a problematic, rather than natural feature of organization life. Their main argument is that strategy discourse causes power effects that disables some actors and empowers others. To gain power, the actor has to accept the logic of strategic discourse, which leads individuals to secure their sense of identity and reality through participation in discourses of strategy. This has implications on the agency of the individual in strategy. Power is gained by using and participating in the 'right' discourse, may it be rationalization of failure or a masculine conception of power. Oakes *et al.* (1998) also draw attention to the power-aspect on strategy and saw power as a form of symbolic violence.

These views can be read to suggest that strategic management would disable managerial moral agency. In this chapter, we adopt a less pessimistic view, adopting the question of moral agency *within* the domain of influence of strategic management as an empirical question. In our empirical analysis of a major strategic change process within an MNC, we focus on the ethical coping of managers engaged in strategy discourse. We find that moral agency during strategic change is riddled with tensions, but that individuals rely on a number of coping tactics to navigate this tension. We discuss irony as example tactics of coping in the tension.

Moral agency – otherness

We build on Paul Ricoeur's work on moral agency as our theoretical lens. Ricoueur founds moral agency as a tension between the concepts 'sameness' and 'otherness', which have important correlates with strategic management. Ethics is founded on our acceptance and relation toward our peers, superiors and subordinates. The question that arises is: 'Do we relate to others with respect to their otherness or do we seek to colonize them into sameness with ourselves?' As otherness is inherently alien to us and we have a tendency to reduce it to sameness, moral agency involves an endless challenge. Otherness is inextricably bound to the persistence of pattern as sameness.

In management research and strategy sameness, or the realization of sameness, or its pursuit, dominates. This is the kind of identity most managers are encouraged to express. Yet there is a tension here because otherness creeps in always. It is the other, rather than the same that is perhaps the single major ethical aim for an individual seeking to lead a good life. This can give rise to a dilemma to a manager, engaged in strategy work: how is it that one navigates the tension between the need to subordinate others (subordinates, customers, competitors, allies, and so on) behind a performance-oriented goal, and the need to accept others as ends in themselves? Paul Ricoeur (1992) saw identity being formed in the dialectic relation between otherness and sameness, and for him, 'other' is not just a simple antonym to 'same' like 'other than self' or 'contrary', but otherness is constitutive of identity as such. In other words, otherness is both a comparison when defining identity *and* an integrative part in forming it. Selfhood reconciles and ties the self to the other through commitment and promise. Ricoeur distinguishes between three levels of otherness; Otherness from the institution, otherness from the other person and otherness from oneself. In all such identity is a condition of reciprocity and so, for Ricoeur, ineluctably ethical: identity is sustained insofar as others' lives are considered of equal value and interest to one's own. The self is formed, then, through the aim of self-esteem in which who we are is firstly bound up in a sense of the good life, secondly is realized in the company of others and thirdly is sedimented through just institutions (Ricoeur, 1992:172).

If the 'good life' is the goal of ethics, it is lived with and for others. This is the basis for Ricoeur's reflection of ethics. He designates this concern for the other as solicitude. Ricouer thus takes from Aristotle the ethics of reciprocity, of sharing, of living together, but he wants to extend his analysis of the ethical goal of the good life from interpersonal relations to institutions, and he extends the virtue of solicitude for the other to the virtue of justice. By institution, Ricoeur means those structures of living together found in historical communities, structures that extend beyond simple interpersonal relations but are bound up with the latter through their function of the distribution of roles, responsibilities, privileges, goods, and rewards. Ricoeur asks if justice is found on the level of ethics and teleology or only on the deontological level of morals. Ricoeur's own answer is that justice has two sides: the side of the good which is an extension of interpersonal relations, and the legal side where it implies a judicial system of coherent laws.

This view of identity formation runs contrary to that established in the management literature, most notably the identity of strategists, for whom the aim as a strategist is to annul or contain otherness to a point of possession and control. The discipline of strategy can be seen as relying on the 'sameness' – principle, where the aim is to unite both the organization and its stakeholders under the same objective formulation. The attitude towards the 'other' in strategic management is as something to be conquered, absorbed, dealt with and codified. This sameness permeates most strategy practice and theory, as strategy research is about the idea of something uniform, predictable and stable. On Ricoeur's terms, this can give rise to a dilemma to a manager, engaged in strategy work: how is it that one navigates the tension between the need to subordinate others (subordinates, customers, competitors, allies, and so on) behind a performance-oriented goal, and the human capacity for sympathy and reciprocity by which otherness can be admitted to form and frame conceptions of identity? This apparent tension of aims is summarized in Table 6.1.

Drawing on Ricouer, moral agency is defined as:

> The action caused by the recourse to the ethical aim when norms lead to conflict and antinomies.

Table 6.1 *Strategic aims versus ethical aims*

	Strategic aim	*Ethical aim*
Individual	Goal compliance, uniformity, collective goals.	*To live the good life . . .*
		Concern for self, unity of life, self-esteem, honesty.
Group	Goal compliance, uniformity, collective goals.	*. . . with and for others . . .*
		Concern for others as individuals, solicitude, sympathy, reciprocity.
		Honesty.
Organization	Strategic intent and a preferred future position of the firm	*. . . in just institutions*
	that should guide the actions individuals.	Past moral norms and traditions, rituals of and routines, justice, duty, norm.

This is an agency that leads to purposive action, which is action taken to alleviate ourselves from a negative situation in which we find ourselves, in contrast to purposeful action that presupposes having a desired and clearly articulated end goal that we aspire towards (see Chia and Holt, 2006, 2009). To understand how moral agency is enacted, sensemaking serves as a guide to meaning construction of the organizational reality.

Ethics in organizations: A sensemaking perspective

It is debatable whether ethics is an individual or an organizational issue. Some argue that it is individual (Soares, 2003; Watson, 2003), and others claim that structures and ethics are linked (Du Gay, 2000). The latter idea not only presumes that ethics informs organizational practice, but also leads to research that assumes that individuals in an organization can be studied by an external observer who determines what is 'right' and what is 'wrong' (Clegg *et al.*, 2007). However, there is an emerging body of literature that assume that ethics is situated and contextual (Kjonstad and Wilmott, 1995; Paine, 1994; Ten Bos, 1997; Andrews, 1989). The starting point for this perspective is that a moral being knows that there are good and bad things, but it doesn't mean knowing for sure which things are good and which are bad (Bauman and Tester, 2001).

In this chapter we adopt a non-normative view on ethics in organizations, treating it as a sensemaking issue tackled by individuals. Previous research has implied some sensemaking processes in responses to ethical issues. For example, in an empirical study Sonenshein (2009) concluded that in a strategic change implementation, the employees took the meaning of strategic issues and reinterpreted them as either leading to harmful consequences or the violation of a right. Also research on the 'moral recognition phase' focuses on how individuals encode information about issues using moral schemata that recognize that a decision or action will affect others (Jones, 1991; Rest, 1986). Instead of an objectivist view on ethics that focuses on questions like 'have I processed this issue as having ethical implications?', a sensemaking view focuses on questions such as 'what story am I telling?' and how these stories may differ across individuals and time, instead of the more objectivist approach (Sonenshein, 2009). Sensemaking serves to reduce knowledge gaps (Ashforth *et al.*, 2008), but in order to analyze how identities are constructed and unfolded, the notions of sensebreaking and sensegiving can be used (Pratt, 2001; Weick, 1995; Ashforth *et al.*, 2008). Sensebreaking accentuates knowledge gaps, as it raises questions like 'Who am I?; What is my life purpose?; What makes me different from other people?; Am I really the same person from one year to the next?' These are the questions asked when identity is enacted. Sensegiving occurs when the individual attempts to construct meaning of others towards a preferred redefinition of organizational reality (Gioia and Chittipeddi, 1991:442). All these questions motivate an ethical exploration.

Sources of data and analysis

To develop a process of moral agency in strategic change, we use a case study at a multinational corporation undergoing strategic change. ICE (all names are pseudonyms) is an MNC with operations in 18 countries. It consists of a corporate headquarters and seven business units. ICE was listed on the stock exchange in the late 1990s after a merger between two companies, and has grown substantially since then. After the IPO, the company was losing on the stock market and the organization was in crisis. There was no vision about how a company in a quite regulated market could compete in the free market. The stock listing was harshly criticized in media. In 2000, a new CEO was appointed. He was seen, both inside and outside the company, as a saviour. He came in and initiated big changes. The cultures in both companies that constituted the merger were characterized by the bureaucracy of state owned companies, with a civil servant mentality. A lot of effort was now put on changing the culture. 'Individual initiative' was brought up as a key issue, with the aim of trying to get people to 'think out of the box' or 'run the extra mile for the company'. The seven business units were granted more responsibility – the ultimate goal was to make some of them work as independent units. One of the main strategic targets was growth. Since 2000 ICE succeeded to grow substantially, purchasing new companies in the Nordic countries and the Baltic Rim. In 2004 the two companies that were merged in 1998 were divided into two separate companies. When we entered ICE in August 2007, many change initiatives had been implemented in the structure. This included various training programs, re-structuring of the organization, new practices for performance follow-up, scanning of low-performance and change of key-persons in management teams. The first top-management meeting we attended was a two-day strategy away-day, where the goals for the next year were presented. The last meeting we attended was in January the following year, when circa 150 managers met for a two-day seminar.

In this study, we mainly rely on observation (as we mainly examine ongoing negotiations of strategic priorities during meetings), but we complement these insights with interviews and documents.

Observation: Observation data is gathered during five months in top management team meetings and in three business unit management team meetings. All in all 15 meetings that all lasted one to one-and-a-half days.

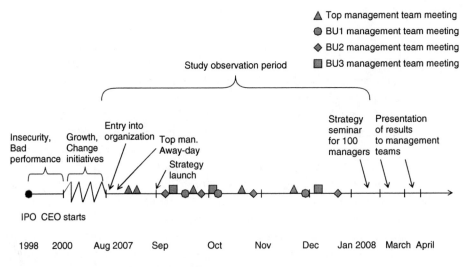

Figure 6.1 *Timeline for ICE's change initiative*

Interviews: 19 managers in top management and middle management were interviewed. Interviews took place during work hours and averaged around one hour. They were all recorded and verbatim transcribed.

Documents: This data primarily consists of public documents from ICE and newspaper articles.

We analyzed the data using a constant comparison method, moving between the data and themes to build a grounded theory (Glaser and Strauss, 1967).

How is a manager's moral agency enacted in the apparent tension between strategic aims and ethical aims?

As illustrated in figure 6.2, there are four main dimensions to the model of moral agency unfolding that emerged at ICE: (1) Managers' sensegiving of the strategic aim, (2) Managers' sensebreaking of the strategic aim, (3) Enacting moral agency and (4) Coping tactics. The strategic aim of the company was manifested in a desired future and the requirements or demands to reach that desired future. However, there were discrepancies between the organization's history and the demands, as well as between the demands and what was really done. These together lead to ambiguities and to moral agency being enacted. When the organization's strategic aims were in conflict with the persons' ethical aims, moral agency was enacted as a recourse to the feeling of self-esteem. The tension between the aims lead to coping strategies that took their forms in irony, smart compromise and conflict. The strategic aim of the company was manifested in a desired future and the requirements or demands to reach that desired future. The strategic aim to make the organization work competitively in a global market was clearly communicated and implemented. In all official statements and in the interviews, the managers were asseverating the importance and success of the change initiative. However, when we looked at the instances of when moral agency was enacted, we started to notice activity that was working against the strategic aim. The action was not purposeful, that is, it didn't presuppose a desired and clearly articulated end goal, but it was purposive, meaning that it was taken as alleviation from a negative situation. This *coping* took its forms in irony, smart compromise and conflict. In this chapter we will focus on irony as a coping device in the tension between strategic aims and ethical aims.

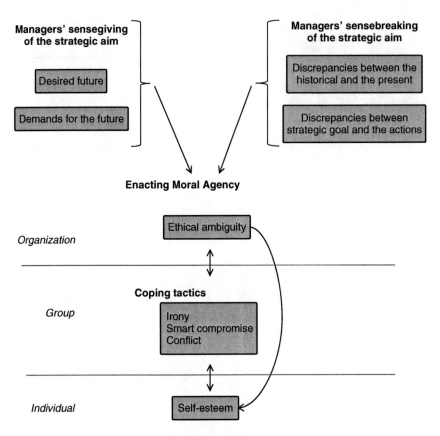

Figure 6.2 *Model of moral agency during strategic change*

Managers' sensegiving of the strategic aim

> Sensegiving at ICE was characterized by two specific themes related to the desired future and demands to achieve it. The managers' attempt to influence and the new vision and the change demands are described in more detail below.

Desired future

> The company wanted to change to become market-oriented, competitive and innovative. The 'old' culture that was characterized by the hierarchy and mind set of a state-owned company had to be changed. The current CEO started to change the culture immediately after he arrived:

You have to understand that this company has a long legacy. When I came here, all top management sat at the seventeenth floor. The CEO's room was behind three secretaries and two long corridors. My nearest colleagues called the secretaries to make a 15-minute appointment. I had been here for 4 months when I moved down to the first floor. My door is open. I am sure it has been a good idea, now I know what people talk about.

CEO in interview

However, the employees continued to be compliant and even deferential towards the CEO. ICE became more accustomed to the idea of changing to a market-driven culture, and the realization emerged that in order to survive in the culture, everyone had to change. The demand for compliance was strong and the new values of excellent performance and growth were integrated in all goals and measures. Goal compliance was measured with a strong hand and people were to change to 'think out of the box' and 'run the extra mile for the company'. Even more radical ways of changing the future were ventilated as this manager put it:

If I could, I would change 50 per cent of the personnel, but I cannot, I just have to stick to those that are here

Demands for the future

As we have seen, the CEO had an ambition to change the old culture to become more people driven, 'dynamic', open and market-oriented. One of the practices he had introduced were the so called performance reviews, where the business unit management teams met the top management team every second month and answered questions. These meetings were nothing the business units looked forward to, as two testimonies of members in a business unit management team put it:

We are all drilled for their questions; I hope they will not be too harsh.

There is a culture of fear here. The days before the performance review everyone is tense and nervous. The day of the review they are dressed up to the teeth and are drilled by their managers in order not to miss any answers.

The CEO himself was not unaware of this:

I know that people are nervous before coming to the meetings, I know they watch every expression on my face to get signals. But if they have done their homework, they have nothing to fear.

Also in the top management team, the line of talk was demanding. They had recurrent discussions about what it takes to make the organization change, and often the means were tough. This is a quotation from a top management team meeting:

> If you want a change in behaviour it has to be tougher than this. If it does not hurt, it is not good enough. If you are not bold enough nothing changes.

The demand by the CEO was strong and regulated by various control mechanisms. The strategic aim to be goal compliant and follow given instructions was thus very powerful. Strategy was given an omnipotent status. The CEO and the top-management team were aware of the big changes that were needed in order to make the people change, as this discussion at a top management team exemplifies:

> NN1: If we want to make a difference in our leadership style, now is the time!

> NN2: Do we need more control? How do we make sure they do not get fat and lazy?

The managers' view that the performance reviews were like cross-examinations was widespread. But the fear was combined with an admiration of the CEO. Among the most salient examples of this were the numerous examples where managers made reference to the domination and charisma of the CEO. He was received as very demanding, but also very generous when he was satisfied with what he saw. People were motivated to 'try harder' to get his acceptance. One of the managers described it like this:

> But you have to remember our history. The time before NN (the CEO) was insecure both in business and in leadership. It was terrible to work here. I talked to a lot of head hunters and tried to find a good exit. But then, six years ago, NN came, and I will never forget his first speech in the cantine. After that day, I decided not to talk to head hunters anymore . . . He told a story that captured everyone and showed that his heart was with him.

In getting the strategy implemented and understood in the organization, the CEO was seen as very important, but the problem with that was also acknowledged, as one of the members in the top management team said:

> NN's person and personality is very important, but it should not be the only thing. He also wants to communicate to the BU [Business Unit] heads that they need to take the issues further through their personalities.

The personality of the CEO was the most efficient driver of the change where one of the goals with the change initiative was to make people and groups to think and act independently. This was paradoxical, as the person-admiration and the culture of taking commands were legacies of the old culture that the top-management wanted to change. The dominant theme to emerge from our comparisons of ICE's historical identity with the demands for the future reflected a growing sense of identity ambiguity.

Managers' sensebreaking of the strategic aim

Two specific themes relating to the sensebreaking of the strategic aim characterized the managers' experiences; discrepancies between the historical and the present and discrepancies between the strategic aim and the actions.

Discrepancies between the historical and the present

Strategy work is clearly dominated by the strategic aim. A plan is made, either top-down or as an emerging process, and there are various methods to implement the plan and to make people motivated to follow the plan and to integrate the strategy into the practical work of every employee. At ICE, rather than recent initiatives to make people 'think out of the box' and to 'take own initiative', past experience provided the most representative reference for the attitudes of the managers who participated in my study. Many of the managers had been working for ICE for over 20 years, and it was hard to change the attitudes, as a manager described it in an interview:

> All our routines and bases for minutes for meetings have come to ICE from the two merged companies. Many people still feel that they need instructions and commands. For instance I have this brilliant guy in Sweden who is in my team, but it took him two years to understand that he was supposed to make his own job description.

Managers seemed quite sure of the strategic aim of the company, but the change from the historical culture was hard. The hierarchy and the historical power relations were still present, as this manager told in an interview:

> These companies: old utility top-down companies. 20 years ago all profitability was decided at the top, now it is at the middle management. But this leads to strategy still being interpreted as a dogma, as something we have to do precisely in the way it is said.

As we have seen, historically, power relations at ICE were hierarchical and demanding, but that also the way the new CEO implemented the change initiative was demanding. A conflict arose in the dilemma between the demanding culture and the aim to give more free rein to individuals and groups.

The HR-department had a big role in changing the company to what they called a 'people-driven' company, but after seven years there still were doubts about the success, as this HR-manager points out at a meeting:

> Based on the business agenda, what does it mean for the HR strategy? Every employee must know 'What does it mean for my work?' The 'people compass' says that we are a people-driven company that lay on our values. But I do not think we are that at the moment, we are still an engineer- and issue-driven company that does not take people into account.

The managers' sense of the strategic aim lead to an ambiguity in identity that didn't serve the strategic goals. There was a tension between the demand for change and their own sense of 'sameness' – not complying with the collective goals.

Discrepancies between the strategic goal and actions

One of the main strategic goals was to mitigate climate change. There were many guidelines to make sure that this aim was followed. However, there were conflicts between the goal and what the operational managers thought was appropriate. They laughed at what they considered unnecessary actions, like changing the light bulbs to energy saving ones, when they at the same time felt that they couldn't do their jobs properly with all the commands coming from 'upstairs'. A recurrent discussion was about a video conference system that was supposed to reduce flying. Everyone thought the conferencing system had become far too expensive and it didn't function anyway. Nobody wanted to reduce their own travelling, as they felt that customer contacts had to be established and sustained by face to face meetings.

The goal compliance and the increased demand of reporting details to the top management also led to discrepancies in aims. There was a dilemma between whether to follow the historical pattern of 'hiding' issues, or the change initiative to be open and effective. This is a discussion at a business unit meeting, where there is a discrepancy between how the members would have liked to handle the matter and how the strategic aim stated it:

> BU Head: We take global warming very seriously. Take it from that angle and make it good. We take CO_2-free as our main target.
>
> NN2: Do we want to cut emissions in the world or just in this company?
>
> BU Head: We thought we would buy this company in [another country]
>
> NN2: In that case I would not like to have the business unit-level emissions public, as we then have to explain why we do things the way we do. My proposition is that we will not publish our own figures.
>
> BU Head: We must have the figures, send everything to the corporate level they need. It is all about choices.
>
> NN2: and as a customer, what is it you want to hear. They want to hear that we have done a good job.
>
> BU Head: We have announced that we are a CO_2-free company, and we have to communicate to our people in the power plants when they get the questions. We have to have answers to the personnel when they are asked.

The demands from top management team was also questioned by the business units. The sensebreaking took its forms in discussions that protested against the hands-on management that the top-management team practiced. The conversation below is from a business unit, where the strategy given from above is questioned:

> BU Head: Do not let [the top-management team] drive this! Never give business to [the top-management team]! You are much much better to drive it, they are sitting in the wrong place to drive it.
>
> NN1: But very often [the top-management team] comes and tells us what to do, for instance in our branding team.
>
> NN2: Here in [country] you are so top driven! I am sure that also you, when you come to Poland, you say 'now I have been to the tower again'. You are so top down here!

Enacting moral agency

Moral agency was defined as the action caused by the recourse to the ethical aim when norms lead to conflict and antinomies. The ethical aim is to acknowledge the otherness within oneself and in the other person, apparent in for instance sympathy and reciprocity. Between the sensemaking of the strategic aim and the sensebreaking of the strategic aim, managers' identity work progressed through otherness, and through a sense of moral agency. Ethical ambiguity triggered a recourse to the ethical aim, that was manifested in solicitude towards the other person and ultimately in sense of self-esteem. These episodes occurred throughout the change process. We will show how this enacting of moral agency led to three coping tactics; smart compromise, conflict and irony.

Ethical ambiguity

Triggers to ethical ambiguity involved situations where the strategic aim and the ethical aim conflicted and where the managers took recourse to their sense of solicitude and self-esteem. The strategic aim was the comparison and the expectation. Ethical ambiguity was triggered by the discrepancies between the demands of the organization and the aims of the individuals and manifested in questioning the ways of doing things. The following quota is from an interview where the manager describes the ambiguity:

> ICE suffers from a systems stress among people. You feel you have a big responsibility but no rights. And if a company like this is to succeed, you need to get the responsibility and the rights in balance. This is the way of releasing the drive in people to do and to change things; we don't have that now. You need to give space and let it mean different things for different people.
>
> *Manager in interview*

Self-esteem

Self-esteem is the basis for the ethical aim in Ricoeur's terms. It is a concept that is difficult to grasp in strategy discussions, but in interviews the managers expressed their need for self-esteem in the corporate surroundings. The strive for self-esteem was mostly manifested in the way the managers hinted at an aim to *feel* something towards the other person in the group. In the model for enacting moral agency, it is the basis for the urge to treat people as ends in themselves, against the strategic aim of achieving something through or with the other person. The following three quotes are from interviews with different managers.

> In order to get people to understand, the communication needs to be passionate. And I do not mean fancy power point presentations, but real communication with other people, where the other part can see that you really believe in this. It is also about pride. Anyone in this organization should be able to tell his or her neighbour about all things Fortum has

done in order to mitigate climate change. And be proud. There needs to be a passion, and a willingness to listen.

Manager in interview

I feel for ICE, ICE has become a part of me after ten years. It would be extremely difficult for me to imagine working somewhere else. But then again, I have spent a lot of time thinking about the climate before ICE even knew the word. It is nothing new.

Manager in interview

Our way of working is that we work and work and it is fun, but we do not talk personal things. This culture of ours does that we do not talk about personal matters. There is a father or mother behind the person, but that is not visible for us here. For instance one of the managers, whom I have worked with for 20 years, suddenly started talking about his children and I told him: this is the first time we talk about personal matters. If we just had a little bit of warmth and normal communication. We have forgotten about the emotional side of people.

Manager in interview

Coping tactics

As described above, the strategic aim to make the organization work competitively in a global market was clearly communicated and implemented. In all official statements and in the interviews, the managers were asseverating the importance and success of the change initiative. However, when we looked at the instances when moral agency was enacted, we started to notice activity that was working against the strategic aim. The action was not purposeful, that is, it didn't presuppose a desired and clearly articulated end goal, but it was purposive, meaning that it was taken as alleviation from a negative situation. This *coping* took its forms in irony, smart compromise and conflict. We will present smart compromise and conflict in short, and then focus on irony as a way of coping.

Smart compromise

Smart compromise can be described as a form of practical wisdom or the ability to persuade others of the opposite nature of specific purposes and interests – but at the same time maintain conversational conditions by which others are able to express their own interest. It is rhetoric that is not external manipulation of feelings, but promoting good arguments above bad ones without any specific exploitative interests. This example is from a business management team meeting when the HR manager starts her presentation:

> I could say that we plan for the personnel, and I could tell you we are counting costs and I could tell you that we are planning for the 'people day'. But you already know this, and this is why I thought I tell you why we have a HR strategy. This is about people and inspiring people.

This can be interpreted as only smart rhetoric to persuade the others in self-interest, but what happened after this opening, was that the group started discussing how they could help inspire people by listening to their genuine desires and wishes. When practical wisdom is turned into smart compromise in a strategy setting, it is a form of coping between the strategic aim and the ethical aims. It appeals to sympathy, generosity and collective creation that is inherent in human life.

Conflict

Coping with moral agency also led to situations where managers disagreed openly. The managers did not suspending their opinions or attitudes at all. Sometimes the conflict was dissolved by smart compromise, but at other points it lead to a dead end in the discussion.

Irony

In organization studies, irony has mostly been noted in situations where traditional power structures have endured, and is therefore associated with non-liberating discourses and resistance to change (Johansson and Woodilla, 2005). Hatch (1997) showed that managers used irony to deal with ambiguities and their own emotional reactions to the cultural situation. Irony became a tool for individuals to deal with a contradictory situation, and a device to cope in that situation, rather than change it. In the episodes when moral agency was enacted, the managers coped in the contradiction between the strategic and the ethical aims through two types of irony: preservative and a destabilizing.

IRONY AS A PRESERVATIVE DEVICE

At ICE irony was used as an oppressive device in situations where the strategic aim and goal was seen as inevitable, but where the persons participating in the discourse felt uncomfortable in the situation. In the top-management team irony appeared when the strategic aim was put on the managers, but their feeling of mutuality in an ethically uncomfortable situation triggered a disruption or conflict of aims. The managers were aware that the means to change the culture were tough, and that the organization wasn't always coping well with them. That led to many ironic remarks about themselves and their behaviour. A manager saying, *'How do we make sure that they don't become fat and lazy?'* is probably talking with tongue in cheek. The managers know that their discourse is powerful and that the remark is inappropriate. As Mulkay (1988) notes, humour handles diversity and complexity much better than a serious mode, because in humour it is accepted to 'change' the reality; 'within humour, it is accepted that "reality" is constantly changing, that various contradictory "worlds" can coexist, and that it is through our active use of language that these "realities" are created and made to alter' (1988:218). Humour can handle multiple realities that may cause problems in a serious discourse. The top-managers knew that the strategic aim wasn't always ethical towards the individuals in the organization, but in their role as managers, they felt they didn't have a choice. Kirkegaard talks about the ironist as one hypocritically resisting change and making ironic tales about the world where he/she feels lost, where the world all around him does not feel real and irony seems to be the only way to handle it. In this way, irony didn't become a resistance to the strategic change *per se*, but a device to preserve the ongoing strategic change, no matter how the people in the organization felt about it.

Also the world outside the organization was a threat to the strategic aim of the top-management. One of the challenges in the company was that the top-management had got huge compensations by bonus-programmes, which had been harshly criticised in the media. The moral accusation was that they had gained at the expense of the taxpayers. This is an extract from a meeting:

NN1: We have a style, and I think we are quite open.

NN2: We also need to put in targets, like CO_2 targets.

NN1: But I would not disclose for instance markets financial targets. We could of course at some point discuss if we would disclose profitability per country. We could put as a headline 'Management well compensated' [*laughter*]; [the largest newspaper] will thank us!

This irony shows their awareness of the risks with the media publicity, but still, irony is used in a preservative manner – the outside world cannot change the way in which the strategic change is handled.

Many of the discussions at the top-management team dealt with numbers. At one point, after a lengthy conversation about one number in the performance demands for one business unit, this dialogue took place:

NN1: Should we put 20? That is an even number

NN2: 19 looks more thought through, let us put 19.

NN3: Hey hey, do not forget the fly on the wall! [*referring to me, the observer*]

NN1: I think she has seen enough not to be surprised anymore.

This is a form of irony that gives a kick towards the number-centred strategic aim, and is also an example of the Kirkegaardian ironist who hypocritically resists change and makes ironic remarks about the world where he/she feels lost. The awareness of the hypocrisy of the strategic aim to measure everything in numbers led to recourse to the ethical aim of reciprocity.

Also the strategic aim of high performance was being measured. This conversation is from a top management team meeting, where one tool for measurement – the job satisfaction survey – was discussed:

NN1: For five years we have had the same survey, we need to take the next step. We will measure the engagement, not only rational but also emotional commitment. Are the people really ready to walk the extra mile for the company?

NN2: How do you communicate the change for the staff

NN1: Reporting tools will be better and it is easier to follow action plans and structure the action. We need to market the new approach and we need to measure the direction.

NN3: And we must be careful, as this kind of surveys give things that are much tougher than the other type of survey. They go directly into your leadership style.

NN1: Or should we do as in jeopardy and have the answers first and then try to find the right questions?

The team has a tacit mutual understanding that everything cannot be measured and that 'you get what you measure'. Still, the strategic aim of conformity, goal compliance and rationality is predominant. The last ironic remark by NN1 reveals the ethical aim of self-esteem and reciprocity, and a tacit consent to the uncertainty of the strategic aim.

The three examples above show how irony was used as a preservative device by the top-management to cope with the tension between the ethical aim and the strategic aim. But irony as a preservative device was also used by the middle managers:

As noted previously, ICE had so called 'performance reviews', where the business unit management teams answered questions from the top management team. The situation could be described as a cross-examination, where the Business Unit Head stood in the middle of the room, with his management team on one side and the CEO and the top-management team on the other. Anyone from the management team could get a question at any time, so the teams were coached to answer various questions. People were nervous before these meetings, but jokes were one of the means to cope with the demands of conformity. This is an example of a discussion between two members of a management team before a performance review.

> NN1: I have put on my best shoes and combed my hair so that the head-master won't disapprove. Are you ok?

> NN2: Yes, I think so; I have a new tie and I have done my home-work.

The management team members concede to the power of the performance reviews as a part of the strategic aim to high performance and high competition. Still, they acknowledge the conflict in how they are being treated as persons, and feel that their sense of self is lowered to a school child's. The irony helps them cope in the conflicting situation.

Humour is often employed to deal with paradoxes in an organization (Painter-Morland, 2008). As such jokes are quick to betray inconsistencies between an organization's publicly stated values and its internal realities. They are also used in order to deal with disappointment, fear and desires. But as the examples above demonstrate, irony may make it easier to tolerate a subordinate position, but it does not really alter the power-structure, only helping workers to cope with it (Rodriques and Collinson, 1995). This way it could be said that ironic humour may facilitate communication and cooperation. Humour may be used to distance unpleasant aspects of work-life while maintaining required work-roles. Mary Jo Hatch's 1997 paper about the role of irony within a management team of a computer parts unit showed the complexity of the humorous remarks, and the ironic outcome of the interpretation. She reported how different remarks indicated a different and often opposite meaning from that of the actual works used. The ideal and the real organization (the one that one wasn't supposed to talk about) became united within the ironic discourse. The managers that used irony, however, didn't question the dominant reality; they merely used irony to deal with ambiguities and their own emotional reactions to the cultural situation that they felt was impossible to change. Irony therefore became a device for the individual to deal with a contradictory situation, and not a device to change but rather to preserve the situation. Also Collinson (1988) show that stereotypical shopfloor humour created distinctions between workers and managers, different departments and among workers themselves. Here irony is seen as a *preservative* rather than a destabilizing device. However, because irony is a complex trope, it can also be related to destabilizing the organizational reality.

IRONY AS A DESTABILIZING DEVICE

Irony didn't only appear as a device for coping with the prevailing strategic discourse, it was also used to destabilize it. The examples above show how irony is utilized to 'test' if things can be changed, or as Kunda (1992) exemplifies in *Engineering Culture*, irony used by engineers before their meetings was like the wet finger the sailors hold up, wanting to see which way the wind blows before setting the course.

In one of the business units, the head of the unit was not always respected by the team members. Quarrel was frequent and the members slandered the Business Unit Head between meetings. In this example the member of the business unit NN1 wants the Business Unit Head to take more responsibility, and tests the atmosphere by throwing an ironic remark.

> NN1: With the final meetings in Germany we will need to have a decision from you [*turns to BU Head*].
>
> BU Head: Auuhh . . . . ., well, you see, I cannot take the risk of signing off before something goes on. The only thing we can do is keeping up the good work.
>
> NN: Don't lose your hair; I will do it for you.

One part of the performance process was to gather the so called Extended Management Team once a month. The extended management team consisted of the top management team and all heads of the seven business units. Much of the discussion circled around pitching of business proposals that the business units had prepared. This example is from the end of one of those meetings, where all business units had presented their proposals.

> Head of BU: These were the business proposals for today.
>
> CEO: Don't invent anymore for today! [*laughter*]

The company wanted to reduce travelling in accordance to their goal to mitigate climate change. This, however, was a recurrent debate all meetings, both its applicability and its benefits. This is a discussion at a business unit management team meeting:

> BU Head: All business units have to make sure that emission from travelling is reduced. We cannot make a new system for this, corporate is tracking our travelling, but we cannot do anything about it.

> NN2: There was also this plan we were supposed to do.

> NN3: But generally we can reduce travelling, as those people who sell have to travel, but the other people can use the video conference system.

> NN4: I have used the video conference, it is not good.

> BU Head: Ok, but we cannot do like this. We cannot say: You cannot go to purchase that in Bulgaria because my quota is full. You just have to hope that you are at home when the quota is filled!

The Business Unit Head uses irony to make the others see how wrong the instructions from the corporate headquarters are. He, in fact, tries to change the norm by the irony.

The destabilizing form of irony wasn't, for obvious reasons, common in the top-management team, but the issue of climate change did trigger it, as this extract from a meetings shows:

> NN1: But before we go in, I have heard that the climate change is not really happening [*silence*] . . . but we stick to the climate researchers.

This can be interpreted as irony, as what the manager says is totally politically incorrect. He didn't get any response, but he did 'put up his finger to see from where the wind blows.'

In the four previous examples irony was used as a destabilizing device. It builds upon the complexity of meanings attached to the ironic tale, where the ironic tale-maker uses this complexity to check which way the interpretation will go, always leaving open the option to ignore the underlying meanings and return to a simple description (Johansson and Woodilla, 2005:44). The ironist hints at possible alternate realities that may either confirm or deny his/her intentions, depending on the confrontation. Irony, therefore, can have a destabilizing function, testing the possibilities of moving them to either direction. Such irony may be retracted or quickly developed into a formal position, depending on others' reactions, and thereby is constantly destabilizing the situation.

Conclusion

The purpose of this chapter has been to understand how moral agency is enacted in the context of strategic change. In other words: How can we understand managers coping with an apparent tension between strategic goal compliance and non-opportunistic sympathy and reciprocity? Drawing on Paul Ricoeur, the aims of strategy and the aims of human life are disrupted and linked intimately to otherness. The strategic aim to change the culture from a civil servant mentality to a market-oriented one, led to identities being created and recreated through processes of sensegiving and sensebreaking, because of their ethical aim of self-esteem, reciprocity and sympathy. The recourse to the ethical aim when the conflict arouse was called moral agency, which led to smart compromise, conflict and irony. Gabriel (2000) points out that compliance and resistance are not mutually exclusive. Through irony, criticism can be accommodated and a space for dissent can be created without a complete and sudden overhaul of organizational systems. Jokes will, however, always signal which values may be under threat or suspicion within the organization's tacit knowledge structures.

Through our empirical analysis, we have shown that while strategic management introduces tensions toward moral agency, managers use a range of tactics to avoid collapsing otherness into sameness. We hope to have shown moral agents fully engaged with the contingencies and dynamics of the world. Instead of an abstract cognitive exercise, ethics is all about participation, relationships and responsiveness. In ICE's radical change process where the strategic aim is demanded by means of measurement and punishment, and where goal compliance is required, ethical ambiguities connected to otherness become evident as the vagueness of self-definition emerges in contrast to the 'sameness' of the strategic aim. It initiated sensebreaking processes among those involved, serving as a trigger for moral agency. Interestingly, there are serious constraints on moral agency, as the strategic aim is so powerful. This leads to managers' coping through various behaviors, of which irony was discussed in this chapter.

Previous research in moral agency more or less agrees that serious constraints on moral agency exist in organizations, especially in what they call 'capitalist' organizations, where the short-term optimizing of shareholder value can particularly constrain opportunities for moral agency. However, within identity formation, moral identity has been described as one kind of self-regulatory mechanism that motivates moral action

(Erikson, 1964; Blasi, 1984; Hart *et al.*, 1998). Aquino and Reed (2002) suggested that, like other social identities that people embrace, moral identity can be a basis for social identification that people use to construct their self-definition. And like other identities, a person's moral identity may be associated with certain beliefs, attitudes and behaviors. This framing puts the emphasis on the actions of human beings, their narratives and the harmony of those actions with one or another ethical principle or theory. Alvesson and Willmott (2002:626) argue that 'much if not all activity involves active identity work: people are continuously engaged in forming, repairing, maintaining and strengthening or revising.' Identity is disrupted over and over again through otherness, there is no substance, and everything evolves day by day. Though a process of sensebreaking the managers are involved in fundamental questioning of who they are and their sense of self is challenged. Individuals sensed identity incongruence and began to ask questions about the relevance of the strategic aim for the purposes of self-categorization. Identities are formed through purposive action that is triggered by otherness and sensegiving served as a guide to meaning construction of others towards a preferred definition of organizational reality.

The findings suggest that the ethical task of relating to one's peers, superiors and subordinates as 'others' rather than as something that has to be made the same as us, or put to our service, is at the same time alien to strategy discourse, but can be coped with. Such coping appears in irony, as it gives the means to navigate between reciprocal sympathy and goal compliant norms. The disruption of strategic aim and ethical aim brings the ends over means rationalization in strategy into question, and perhaps even the concept of strategy insofar as it simply is about the idea of something uniform and predictable. This chapter highlights that otherness is intimate to strategy and hence ethics is intimate to strategy, but is repressed in the strategy discourse. In this view, strategy should be fundamentally reconfigured as it is an inherently moral condition that accepts rather than represses uncertainty.

References

Alvesson, M. and Willmott, H. (2002). Identity regulation as organizational control: Producing the appropriate individual. *Journal of Management Studies*, 39(5), 619–644.

Andrews, K. (1989). Ethics in practice. *Harvard Business Review*, Sep–Oct, 99–104.

Andrews, K. R. (1960). *The Concept of Corporate Strategy*. Homewood, IL: Irwin.

Ansoff, H. I. (1965). *Corporate Strategy*. New York: McGraw-Hill.

Aquino, K. and Reed, A., II. (2002). The self-importance of moral identity. *Journal of Personality and Social Psychology*, 83, 1423–1440.

Ashforth, B. E., Harrison, S. H. and Corley K. G. (2008). Identification in organizations: An examination of four fundamental questions. *Journal of Management*, 34.

Barry, D. and Elmes, M. (1997). Strategy retold: Towards a narrative view of strategic discourse. *Academy of Management Review*, 22(2), 429–452.

Bauman, Z. and Tester, K. (2001). *Conversations with Zygmunt Bauman*. Cambridge: Polity Press.

Blasi, A. (1984). Moral identity: Its role in moral functioning. In: W. M. Kurtines and J. L. Gewirtz (eds), *Morality, Moral behavior, and Moral Development*. New York: Wiley.

Burke, K. (1945). *A Grammar of Motives*. Englewood Cliffs, NJ: Prentice-Hall.

Chia, R. and Holt, R. (2006). Strategy as practical coping: A Heideggerian perspective. *Organization Studies*, 27(5), 635–655.

Chia, R. and Holt, R. (2009). *Strategy Without Design; The Silent Efficacy of Indirect Action*. Cambridge: Cambridge University Press.

Clegg, S., Kornberger, M., Rhodes, C. (2007). Business ethics as practice. *British Journal of Management*, 18, 107–122.

Collinson, D. (1988). Engineering humor: Masculinity, joking and conflict in shop-floor relations. *Organization Studies*, 9, 181–199.

Du Gay, P. (2000). *In Praise of Bureaucracy*. Weber, Organization, Ethics. London: Sage.

Durand, R. and Calori, R. (2006). Sameness, otherness? Enriching organizational change theories with philosophical considerations of the same and the other. *Academy of Management Review*, 31(1), 93–114.

Erikson, E. H. (1964). *Insight and Responsibility*. New York: Norton.

Ezzamel, M. and Willmott, H. (2004). Rethinking strategy: Contemporary perspectives and debates. *European Management Review*. 1(1), 43–48.

Gabriel, Y. (2000). *Storytelling in Organizations: Facts, Fictions, and Fantasies*. New York: Oxford University Press.

Ghoshal, S. (2005). Bad management theories are destroying good management practices. *Academy of Management Learning and Education*, 4(1), 75–91.

Gioia, D. A. and Chittipeddi, K. (1991). Sensemaking and sensegiving in strategic change initiation. *Strategic Management Journal*, 12, 433–448.

Glaser, B. G. and Strauss, A. L. (1967). *The Discovery of Grounded Theory*. Chicago: Aldine.

Hamel, G. and Prahalad, C. K. (1989). Strategic intent. *Harvard Business Review*, 67(3). 63–76.

Hamel, G. and Prahalad, C. K. (1994). *Competing for the Future*. Boston: Harvard Business School Press.

Hart, D., Atkins, R. and Ford, D. (1998). Urban America as a context for the development of moral identity in adolescence. *Journal of Social Issues*, 54, 513–530.

Hatch, M. J. (1997). Irony and the social construction of contradiction in the humor of a management team. *Organization Science*, 8(3), 275–288.

Johansson, U. and Woodilla, J. (2005). Irony – its use and potential in organization theory. In U. Johansson and J. Woodilla (eds), *Irony in Organizations; Epistemological Claims and Supporting Field Stories*. Copenhagen: Copenhagen Business School Press.

Jones, T. (1991). Ethical decision making by individuals in organizations: An issue-contingent model. *Academy of Management Review*, 28(3), 494–507.

Jones, T. (1995). Instrumental stakeholder theory: A synthesis of ethics and economics. *Academy of Management Review*, 20, 404–437.

Kjonstad, M. and Willmott, H. (1995). Business ethics: Restrictive or empowering? *Journal of Business Ethics*, 14, 445–464.

Knights, D. and Morgan, G. (1991). Corporate strategy, organizations and subjectivity: A Critique. *Organization Studies*, 12, 251–273.

Kunda, G. (1992). *Engineering Culture: Control and Commitment in a High-tech Corporation*. Philadelphia: Temple University Press.

Lovas, B. and Ghoshal, S. (2000). Strategy as guided evolution. *Strategic Management Journal*, 21, 875–896.

Mulkay, M. (1988). *On Humor: Its Nature and its Place in Modern Society*. Oxford: Basil Blackwell.

Oakes, L. S., Townley, B., Cooper, D. J. (1998). Business planning as pedagogy: Language and control in a changing institutional field. *Administrative Science Quarterly*, 42, 2.

Paine, L. (1994). Managing for organizational integrity. *Harvard Business Review*, March–April, 106–117.

Painter-Morland, M. (2008). *Business Ethics as Practice: Ethics as the Everyday Business of Business*. Cambridge: Cambridge University Press.

Porter, M. E. (1980). *Competitive Strategy: Techniques for Analyzing Industries and Competitors*. New York: Free Press.

Pratt, M. G. (2001). Social identity dynamics in modern organizations: An organizational psychology/organizational behaviour perspective. In: M. A. Hogg and D. J. Terry (eds), *Social Identity Processes in Organizational Contexts*. Philadelphia: Psychology Press.

Ricoeur, P. (1992). *Oneself as Another*. Chicago: University of Chicago Press.

Rest, J. R. (1986). *Moral Development: Advances in Research and Theory*. Minneapolis: University of Minnesota Press.

Rodriques, S. and Collinson, D. (1995). 'Having fun?': Humour as resistance in Brazil. *Organization Studies*, 16(5), 739–768.

Shrivastava, P. (1986). Is strategic management ideological? *Journal of Management*, 12(3), 363–377.

Soares, C. (2003). Corporate versus individual moral responsibility. *Journal of Business Ethics*, 46, 143–150.

Sonenshein, S. (2009). Emergence of Ethical Issues during Strategic Change Implementation. *Organization Science*, 20, 223–239.

Ten Bos, R. (1997). Business ethics and Bauman ethics. *Organization Studies*, 18, 997–1014.

Van Maanen, J. (1979). The fact of fiction in organizational ethnography. *Administrative Science Quarterly*, 24, 539–550.

Watson, T. J. (2003). Ethical choice in managerial work: The scope for moral choices in an ethically irrational world. *Human Relations*, 56, 167–185.

Weick, K. E. (1995). *Sensemaking in Organizations*. Thousand Oaks, CA: Sage.

Part III
Change leadership and ethics: success and failure

7 Incompetent or immoral leadership?

Why many managers and change leaders get it wrong

Thomas Diefenbach

Introduction

The idea, if not to say *ideology* of managing organizational change is fairly established within orthodox management (Musson and Duberley, 2007). It is so deeply embedded in organizational realities as well as organization studies that Sorge and Witteloostuijn (2004) call it an 'organizational change hype'. Managing change is predominantly portrayed in functional ways, as a technology which simply needs exact execution of 'tried-and-tested' blueprints. According to the 'managerial standard model', organizational change has to be planned, linear, top-down and management-driven.

Change management understood in such ways requires first and foremost *leadership*. When it is about organizations and organizational change, leadership and management (and, hence, leaders and managers) are regarded not only as key, but as a necessity. Moreover, managers and change leaders are portrayed as skilful and competent leaders who can change organizations, or parts of it, 'at will' (Kark and Van Dijk, 2007; Ilies *et al.*, 2006; Van Vugt, 2006; Gill, 2003). Whether transformational or transactional leadership (Masi and Cooke, 2000; Bass *et al.*, 1987; Burns, 1978), the idea of leadership is closely accompanied by rhetoric about the (necessary) skills and competences of *leaders* (Siebens, 2005). Leaders seemingly have, or at least are capable and willing to develop, all the positive leadership attributes and behaviours textbooks and proponents of orthodox leadership ideology suggest (Aronson, 2001; Masi and Cooke, 2000; Bass *et al.*, 1987; Burns, 1978).

When change goes wrong – which seems to be more the rule than the exception – possible reasons for it are usually confined to a few areas.

1. Very often, criticism focuses on *technical* aspects of the change programme, an insufficient execution of otherwise right concepts; for

example, the change message was not properly communicated, necessary changes were not implemented swiftly or thoroughly enough, or managers were not decisive enough in their decisions (Gill, 2003; Greenwood and Hinnings, 1996).

2. Alternatively, or additionally, reasons for a failure of a change initiative are regularly located on the side of employees and lower management; for example, employees were allegedly not ready for change, middle managers did not fully support the strategic change initiative, and/or their individual or collective, open or hidden resistance to change created major obstacles (Shaukat, 2004; Eagle, 1999).

3. When it is about individual social malpractices within organizations, the focus is mainly on *employees'* 'organizational misbehaviour' (Vardi and Weitz, 2004), 'workplace aggression' (Bryant and Cox, 2003), 'hostile workplace behaviour' (Keashly and Jagatic, 2003) or 'bad behaviour in organizations' (Griffin and Lopez, 2005).

In contrast, possible aspects of, and reasons for *poor* leadership are largely neglected. In most leadership, management and organization studies prevail overtly positive and undifferentiated, unrealistically flattering and naive pictures of leaders as well as simplistic concepts of leader–follower relationships and organizational change (Kark and Van Dijk, 2007; Illies *et al.*, 2006; Reicher *et al.*, 2005; Bono and Judge, 2004; Lord *et al.*, 1999). Criticism of change leaders is rare (Clegg and Walsh, 2004; Harvey, 2002). Very little work has been carried out concerning change leaders' and managers' possible poor performance, malfunction or organizational misbehaviour, their lack of skills and competences or lack of values and moral standards with regard to their actual attitudes and behaviour, decisions and actions within the organizational context (Furia, 2009; Bono and Judge, 2004; Keashly and Jagatic, 2003).

If such research of organizational misbehaviour of leaders and managers had been carried out, empirical evidence suggests that 'managerial abuse of employees' (Bassman and London, 1993), 'petty tyranny' (Ashforth, 1994), 'hierarchical abuse of power' (Vredenburgh and Brender, 1998) and 'downward workplace mobbing' (Vandekerckhove and Commers, 2003) are much more widespread than usually recognized or acknowledged. They are quite common phenomena within organizations. According to Vandekerckhove and Commers (2003:42, summarizing several empirical studies) downward workplace mobbing makes up for 81 per cent of all workplace mobbing cases in the US, 63 per cent in the UK and 57 per cent in continental Europe.

Organizational misbehaviour and managerial abuse of power can be found regularly within hierarchical organizations – and the higher up, the greater; moral violence is especially structured around leadership and forms a central part of leader–follower relationships (Diamond and Allcorn, 2004:24). In this respect it would be of particular interest not only to get a better understanding of poor leadership as such (and its consequences) but also to find out more about the possible reasons for it. For example, poor individual leadership can be due to a lack of skills or to a lack of values. This chapter, therefore, will investigate some of the possible reasons for managers' and leaders' failures and shortcomings with regard to change leadership. It will focus on two aspects – *incompetence* and *immorality*.

4. With the help of socio-psychological approaches of organizational misbehaviour of leaders and managers it shall be discussed whether 'managerial abuse of employees' (Bassman and London, 1993) or 'petty tyranny' (Ashforth, 1994) might be a result of managerial incompetence.
5. The morality or immorality of actual leadership behaviour and its manifestations in 'Machiavellianism' (Rayburn and Rayburn, 1996), 'hierarchical abuse of power' (Vredenburgh and Brender, 1998) or 'organizational psychopaths' (Boddy, 2006; Maibom, 2005) will be discussed largely with regard to the concept of (self-) interest (O'Brien and Crandall, 2005; Darke and Chaiken, 2005; Rutledge and Karim, 1999) and its stage of moral development (Kohlberg, 1976).

This research is part of theoretical and empirical enquiries into the mechanisms and consequences of organizational phenomena such as management and hierarchical relationships between superiors and subordinates. During a research project into managerial processes within a smaller department of a European higher-education institution, several incidents of organizational misbehaviour of (self-acclaimed) leaders occurred. A narrative approach has been applied in order to provide some ideas about the constituted individual identity of this type of manager or leader (Czarniawska, 1997; Boje, 1995). Some of these findings and insights are provided below in the portrait of a specific person, Zara. The name is a pseudonym, any similarity to actual persons, living or dead, is purely coincidental.

The name Zara has been chosen in reference to Nietzsche's (1885/1990) *Also sprach Zarathustra* ('Thus Spoke Zarathustra'). In this uniquely experimental and esoteric book on philosophy and morality Nietzsche portrayed a 'new' or 'different' Zarathustra to the original Persian prophet, one who turns traditional morality upside down. Zarathustra aims to become the *Übermensch* ('superhuman'). For this, his 'will to power' and ignorance of any ordinary morality is essential. Such anti-social behaviour of power-oriented egomaniacs might be seen as yet another example of the 'eternal recurrence of the always same' – another key idea of Nietzsche, although intended by him in a much more philosophical, or ideological, sense. The case will be put into context by referring to other case studies on organizational misbehaviour (Boddy, 2006; Vredenburgh and Brender, 1998; Rayburn and Rayburn, 1996; Ashforth, 1994; Bassman and London, 1993).

This small case study of an aspirational change leader and organizational psychopath will be followed by two sections that analyse whether managers' and leaders' organizational misbehaviour can be explained better by references to their (in-) competence or (im-) morality. A discussion of why identification and possible punishment of managers' and leaders' organizational misbehaviour is not as easy as it might seem will also be provided (possible reasons are ideological cover-up, hypocrisy and impression management as the un-normal normality of contemporary organizations). This will be followed up by some conclusions and ideas for future research.

Zara – the case of an aspirational change leader and organizational psychopath

Zara was a middle-aged academic, sort of lower management, but highly aspirational. When she got her first senior academic post she immediately began to do what she had been doing for many years previously; networking, pursuing her own objectives and constantly being on the lookout for opportunities to initiate something – anything, as long as it would help to raise her profile. She was particularly interested in initiating processes which would demonstrate her 'proactiveness', 'leadership' and 'business orientation', which would get her in contact with the 'right' people, would put her ideas and concerns onto the agenda of meetings and committees and would get her name into the internal newsletter. Zara was constantly busy with 'projects' and 'initiatives'. She had managed to learn 'management speak' and to give everything that she did a touch of 'strategic importance', 'transformational leadership' and 'demonstrated professionalism'. Within a comparatively short period of time she was involved in most major decision-making networks and processes and had become a power within the department no-one could ignore. Her 'will to power' made her a little Übermensch within the formal and informal hierarchies.

Zara is a typical example of the kind of modern careerist that can be found in any larger organization. Saunders (2006:14) paints a very telling picture of this new breed of careerists within higher education institutions:

> For those who are neither dedicated teachers nor keen researchers, it is as if Moses had parted the Red Sea. Managerialism has created for such academics the means whereby they might not merely survive but thrive. Their entire way of life consists of mission statements, position papers and reviews of one sort or another; committee meetings, interviews and corridor discussions; phone calls, e-mails and memoranda amongst themselves; interstate conferences with other departmental heads and deans; graduation, prize and other ceremonies. Alliances are formed, favours are asked, deals are made, debts are owed, careers are advanced.

Vickers and Kouzmin (2001:105) provide some more details about careerists' attitudes and inner state:

> The modern careerist epitomizes the 'damaged' organizational actor, who appears to say and to act as is required through a process of adaptation which is beneficial for career advancement but disastrous for emotional health. This is evidenced by the apparent promulgation of 'automatons' – colourless, dull and unimaginative individuals characterizing the quintessential 'organization man' – an essentially calculating animal pursuing the necessities of organizational life.

Modern careerists' predominant attitudes and behaviour towards others are typical examples for managers' or leaders' 'organizational misbehaviour' (Vardi and Weitz, 2004), that is, 'acts which manifest disrespect for a subordinate's dignity or provide obstacles to a subordinate's performance or deserved rewards' (Vredenburgh and Brender, 1998:1339). Organizational misbehaviour describes social actions such as deviance, aggression, antisocial behaviour, violence, abuse or incivility, without explicitly including legal dimensions or issues such as criminal negligence, discrimination, sexual harassment, theft or the like (Griffin and Lopez, 2005:989). Ashforth's description of the 'petty tyrant' (1994:756–757) is probably one of the best portraits of leaders and managers who are demonstrating such organizational misbehaviour:

> Recurring elements appear to include: close supervision, distrust and suspicion, cold and impersonal interactions, severe and public criticism of others' character and behaviour, condescending and patronizing behaviour, emotional outbursts, coercion, and boastful behaviour; they suggest an individual who emphasizes authority and status differences, is rigid and inflexible, makes arbitrary decisions, takes credit for the efforts of others and blames them for mistakes, fails to consult with others or keep

them informed, discourages informal interaction among subordinates, obstructs their development, and deters initiative and dissent. Pervasive themes in these descriptions are a tendency to overcontrol others and to treat them in an arbitrary, uncaring, and punitive manner. These themes are quite consistent with common definitions of the term 'tyrant', such as that offered by Webster's New Collegiate Dictionary: 'a ruler who exercises absolute power oppressively or brutally'. The Qualifier 'petty' has been added to underscore the theme of arbitrariness and small-mindedness that runs through the various literatures.

Boddy (2006) called people with such mindsets 'organizational psychopaths'. According to him (p. 1462) organizational psychopaths 'are employees with no conscience . . . who are willing to lie and are able to present an extrovert . . . charming facade in order to gain managerial promotion via a ruthlessly opportunistic and manipulative approach to career advancement'.

Zara was very determined to pursue her projects and initiatives – and she didn't stop until she finally got what she wanted. In the pursuit of her personal agenda and career she was manipulative as well as ruthless; with colleagues higher up the hierarchical ladder or close allies she was easy-going and portrayed an image of herself as a 'collegial', 'task-oriented' and 'professional' doer. Many others, however, were regularly treated in a very different way. Zara tried to demonstrate 'authority'. Her way of doing this was to emphasize factual or to create artificial status differences. Her body language and attitudes signalled superiority as soon as other people were around. In conversations and meetings she was patronizing. Particular colleagues who were either less determined or less capable of playing political games were bullied by her. Several members of staff admitted in confidential conversations that they felt intimidated by her – male and female colleagues alike. At the same time, Zara was desperate to be seen by all as easy-going, very likeable and even to be fun with. She wanted to be feared and liked by people at the same time. Her attitudes and behaviour (or organizational misbehaviour) had reached an almost schizophrenic level. In that sense, Zara's role-play and personality traits are not so much an example of a 'one-dimensional' petty tyrant but of a multifaceted organizational psychopath.

Organizational psychopaths can be found comparatively more often in larger organizations because these provide more sources of power, prestige and other monetary and non-monetary incentives. Moreover, they provide more opportunities for people like Zara because of their hierarchical layers, complex procedures and processes and the more time available to people who do not want to concentrate solely on work-related tasks. Whether 'careerist', 'petty tyrant' or 'organizational psychopath', cases like Zara raise the question what is behind such behaviour.

On the (in-) competence of managers and leaders

One possibility is that such misbehaviour is down to *individual incompetence*. Incompetence defines cases when someone doesn't perform or achieve the goals he or she should be able to achieve and no other reasons are responsible for this failure but his or her individual physical, psychological, cognitive or social competences and capabilities. For example, in their large-scale survey on managerial abuse of employees, Bassman and London (1993) found psycho-pathological aspects and/or sociocultural aspects were the primary reasons for individual managers' poor management and leadership attitudes towards others. According to them (p. 20) 'underlying emotional disturbance', 'personality disorder characterized by the inability to control aggressive impulses' or being 'socialized into abusive relationships' provided explanations for managers' misbehaviour and abuse of subordinates.

Ashforth (1994) found that the acquisition and use of power in particular tends to corrupt the powerholder. He or she can develop 'an exalted sense of self-worth' while at the same time devaluing the worth of others. Over time, this leads to distorted images of oneself and others and corresponding attitudes and behaviours on the part of both the powerholder and his or her subordinates. For example, the greater the power differential and the stronger and more controlling the means of influence (e.g., rewards, coercion), the more inclined the manager is to attribute subordinates' successes to managerial control rather than to the subordinates themselves, and the less inclined subordinates are to openly question the manager. Accordingly, the manager comes to believe that he or she can do no wrong, that he or she should not be bound by the same constraints as others, and that subordinates must be closely supervised. (Ashforth, 1994:763). When people with distorted personalities gain power via hierarchical positions, their insecurities and narcissism, and power-and control-orientation turn into managerial incompetence and permanent tendencies toward grandiosity (concerning themselves, their actions and ideas) and distrust (concerning others) (Maccoby, 2005:127–128). They compensate for their personal insecurity by over-controlling others, for their low self-esteem by demonstrating hyper-professionalism, for their shallowness by name-dropping and for their fears by attacking others.

Zara's greatest concerns orbited around her image and the impression she made on different people. On the one hand, she was very keen to constantly portray an image of herself as a proactive doer, competent academic leader and professional (project) manager. For this, she used the usual managerial language and strategy rhetoric. She desperately wanted to be seen as strong and energetic, convincing and successful. Zara even walked up and down the corridor faster and with larger steps than necessary in order to underline her busyness and determination. On the other hand, inside she felt deeply insecure. She had made her career largely with the help of more experienced and influential people. For the best part of her career her jobs had not been too demanding and she had been able to spend most of her time networking. Over the years she had learned the language of her profession but beyond the rhetoric her professional knowledge was shallow and underdeveloped. More crucially, she hadn't developed as a person. In this sense, most of her dominant behaviour was actually a way to compensate for her personal and professional insecurity and a deeply ingrained inferiority complex. One could argue that her bad manners and organizational misbehaviour were more the symptoms of a psychological disorder, and her poor office conduct was mostly the result of social and emotional incompetence.

However unpleasant and ridiculous, sad or occasionally even funny such behaviour might be, if individual managers' and leaders' incompetence is due to cognitive, psychological or social reasons (or an overall distorted and only partly developed personality) they can hardly be held responsible for their behaviour. What can be criticized is largely the managers' (or the organization's) insufficient attempts so far to close this 'competence gap', for example via personal training and skills development programmes or a psychological therapist.

'Interests' and the moral level of managers' and leaders' misbehaviour

However, most managers usually have sufficient experience and expertise and have received enough training and opportunities, which at least potentially enables them to carry out the tasks related to their position in professional ways. Hence, there must be many more relevant factors responsible for the widespread existence of managers' organizational misbehaviour than mere incompetence.

It is clear that managerial misbehaviour like Zara's is often not the odd 'coincidental result of circumstances', due to 'honest mistakes', 'errors of judgement' or down to a rarely admitted 'lack of skills and competences'. More often, these activities are carried out *consciously and systematically* over a longer period of time and in more or less sophisticated and intelligent ways (often with the help of powerful allies, wilful servants or skilful advisers). In this sense, organizational misbehaviour is of instrumental use for achieving personal goals. Rayburn and Rayburn (1996) called people who behave in such ways 'modern-day Machiavellians'. According to them, such an individual 'has an immoral reputation for dealing with others to accomplish his/her own objectives, and for manipulating others for his/her own purpose' (p. 1209). A 'modern-day Machiavellian employs aggressive, manipulative, exploiting, and devious moves to achieve personal or organization objectives.' (p. 1210). Rayburn and Rayburn found empirical evidence that Machiavellians are more likely to be ambitious individuals and that individuals of higher intelligence tend to indicate that they would behave less ethically. They called this 'Type A personality-orientation'. Such a behaviour is

> A life-style or general orientation to life, characterized by a high degree of ambition. These individuals are constantly striving to attain material things or achievements in the shortest period of time. Type A individuals continually feel the need to prove themselves and often channel their ambitions into an area that is important to them at the moment. (p. 1212)

Ambitious people with a one-dimensional achievement-orientation are very keen to engage in organizational politics – they do it for a reason; their actions are calculated and their organizational (mis-) behaviour is deliberate. For example, when Vredenburgh and Brender (1998) investigated managers' hierarchical abuse of power they talked about a '*decision* to abuse power' (p. 1337, italics added). A key element of their comprehensive model of the hierarchical abuse of power is powerholders' *motives*. Motives or intention arise from *interests* (or self-interest, O'Brien and Crandall, 2005; Darke and Chaiken, 2005; Rutledge and Karim, 1999). Interests, hence, could be a crucial explanation for managers' misbehaviour. It therefore might help to shed some further light on what could be the interests of organizational psychopaths, immoral managers or leaders in particular.

In a 'more' rational sense, managers' and leaders' prime interest might be towards gaining, keeping and increasing their position and power (and all that comes with it, that is, responsibilities and influence, privileges and prerogatives, material and immaterial resources). Because of their career background and organizational socialization, managers and change leaders are very power conscious (Mast *et al.*, 2010:460 called it 'power motivation'). They know that organizational developments can bring crucial changes, particularly to *their* areas of responsibility. At the same time, change initiatives, whether it is their formulation, communication or implementation, provide excellent opportunities for gaining, keeping or increasing one's influence, power and control – or for losing it. Managers' concerns and interests, therefore, orbit primarily around dominance and supremacy, status and prestige, privileges and prerogatives – whose access to resources will be enlarged or reduced, whose career will continue and whose will stall, who can stay and who has to go; when change happens there are strong personal and group interests at stake (Clegg and Walsh, 2004:230–231; Willmott, 1996:326; Zaleznik, 1989:152). Hence, managers' and leaders' first allegiance is often more to their own career than to the company (Willmott, 1997:1335) and they therefore have a very strong interest in keeping, if not increasing, what they have achieved for themselves so far.

In a 'less' rational sense, managers' and (change) leaders' interests towards power can be related to the more intangible aspects of power. For example, when they embark on a new project, change managers may have feelings of childlike excitement, a sense of their own importance and the impression that things would never move forward if they weren't around to look after everything, and everyone – to get things done. Despite what many people say, there is a lot of psychological pleasure to be had from being a manager or leader. As Henry A. Kissinger (1974, quoted in Frank, 2001:629) once said, 'Power is the ultimate aphrodisiac!'. Power can be very compromising – for male and female careerists alike.

Zara was a full-blown careerist. Literally everything she did was for a purpose, and behind her actions and initiatives were more and less rational interests. From the very first day of her appointment she focused on being or becoming formally responsible for certain areas. In a hierarchical organization formal responsibilities mean power and influence. Within a comparatively short period of time she indeed managed to be responsible for the development of key areas. Although not inheriting the highest position on the hierarchical ladder she had become the most powerful and influential member of her department. At the same time as increasing her own influence she was also quite successful in reducing other people's areas of responsibility and in taking resources and influence away from them. Most of these developments did not happen in the open as direct clashes, but via more indirect and subtle methods. Zara managed to initiate most of these processes within the formal and informal networks she was part of, or even master-minded. If she deemed it useful, she got issues on the official agenda of decision-making bodies and, in so doing, could achieve a factual alloca-tion of resources in her favour via the official channels. With her new position, Zara now had all the opportunities to live the organizational life of a modern-day Machiavellian to the full. She became the manage-rial incarnation of the power-oriented political animal. Perhaps even more worryingly, she enjoyed it. She became convinced of the impor-tance of her projects, of her managerial competence and of the necessity to get her initiatives through for the sake of the whole. She enjoyed mov-ing things forward, finding allies, bending decisions her way and limit-ing the influence of others. It was this power game that she increasingly lived for; influencing and deciding issues for the sake of being influen-tial and making decisions became her world.

Whether or not there are more or less 'rational' interests behind manag-ers' and leaders' power orientation, the problem is that career-oriented psychopaths like Zara will do (almost) everything that is good *for them* and the pursuit of *their goals* – which includes conscious organizational misbehaviour ('The end justifies the means!'). In this sense, when demon-strating organizational misbehaviour, such managers and change leaders remain at the pre-conventional level of Kohlberg's stages of moral devel-opment, that is, stage 1 – 'Obedience and punishment orientation' (How can I avoid punishment?), or stage 2 – 'Self-interest orientation' (What's in it for me?) (Krebs and Denton, 2005, Rahim *et al.*, 1999; Kohlberg, 1976). Bass and Steidlmeier (1999) called them artificial or 'pseudo-transformational leaders', Aronson 2001 (p. 253) called them 'egotistic leaders'. Their conscious concerns and deliberate actions are primarily for personal gain (under the official rhetoric of serving the greater good and demonstrated etiquette of collegiality). They 'care about their own personal power and status, often depending on conspiracies and excuses, and resorting to distortion of truth and manipulation of followers to their own ends.' (Aronson, 2001:253). The carrying out of their business and managerial responsibilities, therefore, is 'a failure of ethical leadership that derives from the pre-occupation with the self that drives individu-als to seek wealth, fame and success regardless of moral considerations'. (Knights and O'Leary, 2006:126). Seen from such a moral development-perspective, most managers' and change leaders' poor leadership might be down to some incompetence, but it is largely a direct outcome of their immoral behaviour.

Hidden actions, ideological cover-up, hypocrisy and impression-management as the un-normal normality

The unacceptable behaviour of a leader or manager is fairly obvious to those close to them – subordinates, colleagues, team or project members; many of them experience it first hand on an almost daily basis and have to bear the consequences. But beyond those directly involved, leaders' and managers' organizational misbehaviour is often difficult to detect. There are several reasons for this.

By its very nature, most organizational misbehaviour (like many other negative social actions) is carried out secretly and kept hidden. Since power- and achievement-oriented managers regard such actions as part of their political manoeuvring within the organizational context, they have an even greater interest in doing so. Most managers' organizational misbehaviour happens behind closed doors, via phone calls, in informal face-to-face meetings without witnesses or in anonymous decision-making processes where it is hard to pin down who did what. Power-oriented actors usually have the experience and skills, as well as the resources and means, to pursue their immoral behaviour in secret – and it is part of their daily performance to keep it that way.

But there are more serious than mere 'technical' reasons for the difficulties in identifying leaders' immoral behaviour. On the one hand, the egoistic and intentional pursuit of one's own objectives by almost any means corresponds with the values and ideologies of individualism and individual success, market economy and careerism (provided it appears to happen within the rules). However, at the same time they are in some tension with other ideas and images of higher-ranked positions and leadership. Aspirational members of a social system are expected to work very hard and unselfishly 'for the sake of the whole'. This is also true for many managers and change leaders within organizations. According to Willmott (1996:326), the 'privileged yet dependent positioning of managers within the industrial structure induces them to represent their work – to other employees and owners – as impartial and uncompromised by self-interest or class-interest, motivated only by seemingly universal virtues of efficiency and effectiveness.' The most common rhetoric used by leaders is the claim that they are acting in the interests of the whole – whether this is 'the country', a people or an organization (Deem and Brehony, 2005:230; Pettigrew, 1973/2002:97; Burns, 1961:260). This is the (cynical) strategy of the privileged and careerists; they claim that it is the common interest they 'serve', that their partial interests are good for the whole.

It is certainly much more noble to think of oneself as developing skills
toward the more efficient allocation and use of resources – implicitly
for the greater good of society as a whole – than to think of oneself as
engaged with other organizational participants in a political struggle over
values [and] preferences.

(Pfeffer 1981, quoted in Willmott 1996:325).

In this sense it is in the very interest of managers and leaders who primarily pursue their own interests and agendas that their decisions and actions
are *not* regarded as driven by (self-) interest. And most immoral managers
and leaders are experienced enough and successful in pursuing their own
egoistic interests for personal advancement or the fulfilment of egocentric
needs while at the same time upholding the image of a 'humble servant'
of the country, organization or any other 'greater good'. Hence, most
claims put forward by leaders or their supporters are an *ideological justification and cover-up* of individual and group interests.

This suggests that behind immoral behaviour – particularly that of people
with elevated positions within social systems – consists in good part of
mendacity and *hypocrisy*. Against better knowledge, immoral leaders and
managers often provide a very one-sighted interpretation of situations
(mendacity) while at the same time regularly fail to practise what they
preach (hypocrisy). For example, while change leaders put pressure on
colleagues and subordinates in order to get their change agenda through in
the way they deem to be necessary, at the same time they have no problem
stressing 'empowerment', 'participation', 'teamwork', 'cooperation' and
'collegiality' as key elements of the new change initiative and will use a
whole range of more or less cunning tactics to overcome resistance (Musson and Duberley, 2007; Ellis, 1998). Such contradictory, if not schizophrenic, rhetoric has become 'part of the taken-for-granted managerial
repertoire' (Musson and Duberley, 2007:144). Of course, if asked these
leaders would strongly deny such allegations. As Bolchover (2005:69)
explained:

'I hate politics' is often the cry of those who seek to divert attention
away from their own latest ruse. Telling all and sundry in the office that
you hate politics is itself an obvious act of corporate politics. The label
'political' is a handicap to the corporate career, *being* political is a great
help – one more example of workplace hypocrisy.

According to this understanding, unethical leadership is a conduct of
office where the leader or other proponents of the proposed principles do
not live up to their claims, that is, where moral integrity is missing.

In addition, organizational psychopaths are *very* successful at impression-management, particularly when it concerns their own image and the impressions others get about them. According to Boddy (2006:1461):

> A key-defining characteristic of psychopaths is that they have no conscience . . . and are incapable of experiencing the feelings of others. Their other characteristics however . . . make them appear very hireable and worthy of promotion; they are smooth, adroit at manipulating conversations to subjects they want to talk about, willing to put others down, are accomplished liars, totally ruthless and opportunistic, calculating and without remorse. Their cold-heartedness and manipulativeness are the traits that are least discernable by others.

Maibom (2005:237) portrayed them in a similar way:

> Emotionally, they are significantly impaired, incapable of feeling guilt or empathy, their fear and pain responses are abnormal, and their other emotions are shallow compared to the normal population. They are manipulative, egocentric, and impulsive.

Since such an image would not help in most cases, power-oriented careerists/organizational psychopaths put a lot of effort into their public appearance. To increase their image and the positive opinion many people might have about them while at the same time pursuing their personal goals on the basis of their distorted personality and immoral convictions can be a very successful combination for the successful participation in the internal politics of organizations.

In this sense, the immoral behaviour of careerists and organizational psychopaths is quite a common problem and a deeply embedded part of the un-normal normality of contemporary organizations. Many managers and (change) leaders demonstrate organizational misbehaviour and behave immorally, for whatever reasons, on a regular basis. Most of our organizations are run by organizational psychopaths – mainly because (only) people with this type of personality, aspirations and interests are the ones who are keen and able to make careers, progress through the hierarchical ranks and get projects or other managerial responsibilities. Since power and other prerogatives increase with position in hierarchical organizations, organizational psychopaths are generally those higher up in an organization and/or those involved in organizational decision-making processes. As Boddy (2006:1462) explained:

> They have a knack of getting employed and of climbing the organizational hierarchy because of their charm and networking skills. This implies that there are more of them at the top of organizations than there

are at the bottom. Organizational psychopaths have been argued to be more motivated and better equipped than other corporate managers to rise to high corporate positions.

And if their questionable practices become public, people are rarely very upset. Even the severe misbehaviour of a superior tends not to come as a surprise; it is perceived as quite common and typical. Observers, hence, are often of the opinion that, 'This is the way things are!', 'This has always been the case!' and 'They do what they want, anyway!' Most subordinates have been socialized and conditioned in different societal institutions and organizations over decades so they can hardly see the scope of the problem, let alone possible alternatives. In his excellent study of the 'power elite', Mills (1956:157) came to the conclusion that criticism of the powerful 'does not arouse indignation on the part of anyone in a position voluntarily to do anything about them, and much less about the corporate system in which they are firmly anchored.'

'Impression-management' was key to Zara. On the one hand, she was constantly busy walking the corridor and 'communicating' – especially with people behind closed doors. At the same time, at meetings she stressed the importance of 'open dialogue' and 'getting people more involved'. She bullied people deliberately and consciously, and had no problem praising the 'collegial atmosphere' at the department. In official documents she talked about 'collaboration' and 'empowerment', 'equality' and 'support' while nevertheless using a whole arsenal of socio-psychological intimidation and political intrigue to fight whoever did or might cross her. She talked eloquently about the need to 'think strategically', 'provide leadership', 'proactively engage with students' and further 'develop' the department and even the whole institution, and yet in reality all her concerns orbited around her own projects, the pursuit of her personal interests and the development of her career. Many people even believed what Zara said in public, since she was very compelling – or at least they could hardly say much against it since the rhetoric ticked all the political correctness boxes.

All in all, managers' and leaders' immoral behaviour is a widespread and regular phenomenon in organizations, but nonetheless difficult to detect – and to punish accordingly. This is so because of the diversionary tactics, such as hidden acting, ideological cover-up, mendacity and hypocrisy, or impression-management, carried out by achievement-oriented careerists and organizational psychopaths. But it is also because it is, or has become, the un-normal normality of organizations and society. Either way, it is further evidence of the fact that organizational misbehaviour carried out by people like Zara is not just incompetence but also very conscious and calculated, therefore immoral, behaviour.

Conclusion

As indicated in the introduction, within leadership, management and organization studies so far, very little attention has been paid to the problems of managers' and leaders' (in-) competences and (im-) morality. While there is plenty of general advice available for managers who want to improve their *technical* management skills, their *social* competences and *moral* development (or their incompetent and immoral behaviour) are addressed far less.

The case of an aspirational change leader and organizational psychopath like Zara has demonstrated that the usual *Ten Golden Rules on How to Become a Good Manager* guidebooks available in airport bookshops do not sufficiently identify the problem of managers' organizational misbehaviour, let alone offer ways to cope with it. Part of the problem is that we need to increase our knowledge and understanding of the reasons behind such behaviour at an individual level, that is, whether this misbehaviour is due to a lack of competence or a lack of moral standards. (There are many more aspects to it than the individual and ethical considerations but these need to be tackled elsewhere.) The driving forces behind superiors' poor performance in particular are still far from clear. There can be *psychological factors*, such as the urge for power and dominance, a lack of self-control, impulsiveness, or emotional immaturity (Vredenburgh and Brender, 1998:1342), suggesting that it is more the incompetence of the individual leader or manager. On the other hand, a calculative mind, egocentrism, limited concern for others, a tendency towards Machiavellianism and diversionary tactics imply that *ethical aspects* are more significant.

There was quite a mixed picture of Zara. On the one hand, she had some serious psychological issues. Much of her antisocial behaviour seemed to stem from attempts to cover deeply embedded feelings of insecurity and insufficiency in her professional knowledge, with powerful demonstrations of management-like attitudes and a pretentious form of leadership. In this sense, Zara could be hardly blamed. She was simply not up to the job because of a lack of social competences. However, there was also compelling evidence that all her political manoeuvring, bullying, cover-up and impression-management were deliberate. For her, such behaviour and actions were tools for achieving personal goals. There was intent, conscious and calculative planning, as well as a careful execution. In this sense, Zara's organizational misbehaviour was not an example of (mainly) incompetent but of (primarily) immoral leadership – or what she thought leadership should be.

'Interests' and the *intent* to behave abusively indicate that there is a moral dimension to managers' and leaders' organizational misbehaviour, and it would help if we found out more about the factors that 'might motivate individuals to engage in deviant, aggressive, antisocial, and/or violent behaviors' (Griffin and Lopez, 2005:995). Moreover, 'interests' seem to provide one of the differential criteria between incompetent and immoral leadership or conduct of office. According to Vredenburgh and Brender (1998:1340) 'The distinction between a legitimate, ineffective use and a non-legitimate, abusive use is a perceptual attribution of intent or motive.' In a more general sense, immoral behaviour (of leaders or managers) can be differentiated from incompetent behaviour by the extent that

- their organizational misbehaviour is intentional;
- serves primarily personal and/or group interests;
- is justified/covered-up by a prevailing ideology (e.g. of 'serving' the greater good);
- the individual leaders are mendacious and hypocritical.

This chapter has provided some theoretical reasons as well as empirical evidence for supporting the position that managers' and leaders' perform-ance should be much more scrutinized in a variety of ways. It would help if leadership, management and organization studies dropped the overtly positive, unrealistic and flattering pictures of managers and (change) lead-ers and instead focused more on their actual attitudes and behaviours, decisions and social actions. In this sense, there is some tension between schools of thought that assert that 'leaders *cope with* problems of organi-zations and organizational change' (orthodox management and organiza-tion studies) and that 'leaders *are part of* the problems of organizations and organizational change' (critical management studies).

By concentrating on their organizational misbehaviour and poor leader-ship performance, as well as the reasons for this, we can enhance our understanding of the great relevance of personal traits as well as moral values. Although there are clear indications of the importance of the ethi-cal dimensions of leadership and management, the problem of the moral-ity or immorality of leaders' and managers' interests and behaviour, decisions and actions is still too little addressed.

At a theoretical level there is some need to further develop concepts and frameworks that can identify the immoral and mendacious behaviour of leaders and managers, careerists and psychopaths. So far, not only have general leadership, organization and management studies been somehow strangely silent about this, topic, even business ethics do not really address it. In this respect it would also help to make clearer the differences between immorality and other social and socio-psychological phenomena, such as incompetence, perhaps via concepts such as (conscious) interests, intent and deliberate social action. The calculative mind and intent (covered up by ideological rhetoric, mendacity and hypocrisy) could be used to distinguish between incompetence and immorality. In addition, to identify and address actions as (un-) ethical or (im-) moral is not enough; even organizational psychopaths follow and act according to particular ethics and moral convictions (such as Darwinism, Utilitarianism, Machiavellianism or the like). These, like other value systems, are based on explicit and implicit assumptions and it is these propositions, rationales, implications and consequences of value systems that have to be revealed and scrutinized, critically interrogated and discussed much more than has been done in the past.

The ethical and moral dimensions of management and leadership are perhaps even more crucial *at a practical level*. The ethical principles, moral values and moral integrity of leaders and managers in particular are key factors for the success or failure of management, leadership and organizational change; 'it is the leader's moral principles and integrity that give legitimacy and credibility to the vision and sustain it.' (Mendonca, 2001:266). In this sense, researchers like Spangenberg and Theron (2005) demand 'ethical leadership'. It is important to hold people accountable and responsible, particular when they enjoy privileges and prerogatives that come with their elevated positions. Many managers and (change) leaders have to have a thorough look at how they behave, how they treat others, and how conduct their office. As Mahatma Gandhi (quoted in Aitken, 2007:17) once said, 'We must become the change we want to see in the world.'

This, finally, raises the issue of the institutional context and design of social systems in which moral or immoral behaviour takes place. Of course, poor management and leadership are not only a result of individual factors. For example, institutional settings such as hierarchical organization, societal values of strong individualism (if not egocentrism), careerism and calculative and competitive minds contribute significantly to the problem both at societal and organizational levels. Ashforth (1994:764) rightly explained that 'no individual or situational factor alone is generally sufficient to sustain ongoing organizational behaviour . . . including tyrannical behaviour. Rather, ongoing petty tyranny may be a function of certain configurations of individual and situational factors.' By making the individual, situational and contextual factors of moral and immoral behaviour more explicit, by interrogating organizational realities more thoroughly and by developing theoretical frameworks that may address such issues comprehensively, organizations would be able to design and manage working conditions in general – and change initiatives in particular – in perhaps more decent, ethical and, therfore successful, ways. We might even be able to design new forms of organization and other forms of collaboration, which would further reduce the problem of incompetent and immoral management and leadership.

References

Aitken, P. (2007). 'Walking the talk': The nature and role of leadership culture within organisation culture/s. *Journal of General Management*; (32)4, 17–37.

Aronson, E. (2001). Integrating Leadership Styles and Ethical Perspectives. *Canadian Journal of Administrative Sciences*, 18(4), 244–256.

Ashforth, B. E. (1994). Petty tyranny in organizations. *Human Relations*, 47, 755–778.

Bass, B. M. and Steidlmeier, P. (1999). Ethics, character, and authentic transformational leadership behaviour. *Leadership Quarterly*, 10(2), 181–217.

Bass, B. M., Waldman, D. A. and Avolio, B. J. (1987). Transformational leadership and the falling domino effect. *Group and Organization Studies*, 12, 73–87.

Bassman, E. and London, M. (1993). Abusive managerial behaviour. *Leadership & Organization Development Journal*, 14(2), 18–24.

Boddy, C. R. (2006) The dark side of management decisions: organisational psychopaths. *Management Decision*, 44(10), 1461–1475.

Boje, D. M. (1995). Stories of the storytelling organization: A post-modern analysis of Disney as 'Tamara-Land'. *Academy of Management Journal*, 38(4), 997–1035.

Bolchover, D. (2005). *The Living Dead – Switched off, Zoned out. The Shocking Truth About Office Life*. Chichester: Capstone.

Bono, J. E. and Judge, T. (2004). Personality and transformational and transactional leadership: A meta-analysis. *Journal of Applied Psychology*; 89(5), 901–910.

Bryant, M. and Cox, J. W. (2003). The telling of violence: Organizational change and atrocity tales. *Journal of Organizational Change Management*, 16(5), 567–583.

Burns, J. M. (1978). *Leadership*, New York: Harper & Row.

Burns, T. (1961). Micropolitics: Mechanisms of institutional change. *Administrative Science Quarterly*, 6, no. 3, 1961, 257–281.

Clegg, C. and Walsh, S. (2004). Change management: Time for a change! *European Journal of Work and Organizational Psychology*, 13(2), 2004, 217–239.

Czarniawska, B. (1997). *Narrating the Organization – Dramas of Institutional Identity*. Chicago: University of Chicago Press.

Darke, P. R. and Chaiken, S. (2005). The pursuit of self-interest: Self-interest bias in attitude judgment and persuasion. *Journal of Personality and Social Psychology*, 89(6), 864–883.

Deem, R. and Brehony, K. J. (2005). Management as ideology: The case of 'new managerialism' in higher education. *Oxford Review of Education*, 31(2), 217–235.

Diamond, M. A. and Allcorn, S. (2004). Moral violence in organizations: Hierarchic dominance and the absence of potential space. *Organisational & Social Dynamics*, 4(1), 22–45.

Eagle, M. (1999). Why don't people change? A psychoanalytic perspective. *Journal of Psychotherapy Integration*, 9(1), 3–32.

Ellis, S. (1998). A new role for the Post Office: An investigation into issues behind strategic change at Royal Mail. *Total Quality Management*, 9(2/3), 223–234.

Frank, L. R. (ed.) (2001). *Random House Webster's Quotationary*. New York: Random House.

Furia, P. A. (2009). Democratic citizenship and the hypocrisy of leaders. *Polity*, 41(1), 113–133.

Gill, R. (2003). Change management – or change leadership? *Journal of Change Management*, 3(4), 307–318.

Greenwood, R. and Hinnings (1996). Understanding radical organisational change: Bringing together the old and new institutionalism. *Academy of Management Review*, 21(4), 1022–1054.

Griffin, R. W. and Lopez, Y. P. (2005). 'Bad behavior' in organizations: A review and typology for future research. *Journal of Management*, 31(6), 988–1005.

Harvey, M. (2002). The hidden force: A critique of normative approaches to business leadership. *SAM Advanced Management Journal*, 66(4), 36.

Ilies, R., Judge, T. and Wagner, D. (2006). Making sense of motivational leadership: The trail from transformational leaders to motivated followers. *Journal of Leadership and Organizational Studies*, 13(1), 1–22.

Kark, R. and Van Dijk, D. (2007). Motivation to lead, motivation to follow: The role of the self-regulatory focus in leadership processes. *Academy of Management Review*, 32(2), 500–528.

Keashly, L. and Jagatic, K. (2003). By any other name: American perspectives on workplace bullying. In: Einarsen, S. *et al.* (eds), *Bullying and Emotional Abuse in the Workplace: International Perspectives on Research and Practice*, London: Taylor & Francis, 31–62.

Knights, D. and O'Leary, M. (2006). Leadership, ethics and responsibility to the other. *Journal of Business Ethics*, 67(2), 125–137.

Kohlberg, L. (1976). Moral stages and moralization. In *Moral Development and Behavior: Theory, Research, and Social Issues*, New York: Longman, 31–53

Krebs, D. L. and Denton, K. (2005). Toward a more pragmatic approach to morality: A critical evaluation of Kohlberg's model. *Psychological Review*, 112(3), 629–649.

Lord, R. G., Brown, D. J. and Freiberg, S. J. (1999). Understanding the dynamics of leadership: The role of follower self-concepts in the leader/follower relationship. *Organizational Behavior and Human Decision Processes*, 78, 167–203.

Maccoby, M. (2005). Narcissistic leaders: The incredible pros, the inevitable cons. In: *Harvard Business Review on The Mind of the Leader*. Harvard Business School Publishing Corporation, 123–148.

Maibom, H. L. (2005). Moral unreason: the case of psychotherapy. *Mind and Language*, 20(2), 237–257.

Masi, R. J. and Cooke, R. A. (2000). Effects of transformational leadership on subordinate motivation, empowering norms, and organizational productivity. *International Journal of Organizational Analysis*, 8(1), 16–47.

Mast, M. S., Hall, J. A. and Schmid, P. C. (2010). Wanting to be boss and wanting to be subordinate: Effects on performance motivation. *Journal of Applied Social Psychology*, 40(2), 458–472.

Mendonca, M. (2001). Preparing for ethical leadership in organizations *Canadian Journal of Administrative Sciences*, 18(4), 266.

Mills, C. W. (1956). *The Power Elite*. New York: Oxford University Press.

Musson, G. and Duberley, J. (2007). Change, change or be exchanged: The discourse of participation and the manufacture of identity. *Journal of Management Studies* 44(1), 143–164.

Nietzsche, F. (1885/1990). *Friedrich Nietzsche – Das Hauptwerk*, Band 3: *Also sprach Zarathustra, Die Geburt der Tragödie, Jenseits von Gut und Böse*. Munich: Nymphenburger.

O'Brien, L. T. and Crandall, C. S. (2005). Perceiving self-interest: Power, ideology, and maintenance of the status quo. *Social Justice Research*, 18(1), 2005, 1–24.

Pettigrew, A. M. (1973/2002). Decision-making as a political process. Reprint in: Salaman, Graeme (ed), *Decision Making for Business*. Sage Publications, The Open University 2002, 97–107.

Rahim, M. A., Buntzman, G. F. and White, D. (1999). An empirical study of the stages of moral development and conflict management styles. *The International Journal of Conflict Management*, 10(2), 154–171.

Rayburn, J. M. and Rayburn, L. G. (1996). Relationship between Machiavellianism and type A personality and ethical-orientation. *Journal of Business Ethics* 15(11), 1209–1219.

Reicher, S. D., Haslam, S. A. and Hopkins, N. (2005). Social identity and the dynamics of leadership: leaders and followers as collaborative agents in the transformation of social reality. *The Leadership Quarterly*, 16, 547–568.

Rutledge, R. W. and Karim, E. K. (1999). The influence of self-interest and ethical considerations on managers' evaluation judgments. *Accounting, Organizations and Society*, 24, 173–184.

Saunders, M. (2006). The madness and malady of managerialism. *Quadrant*, 50(3), 9–17.

Shaukat, R. (2004). Resistance to change. *International Journal of Knowledge, Culture and Change Management*, 4, 1627–1646.

Siebens, H. (2005). Facilitating leadership. *EBS Review*, 20, 9–29.

Sorge, A. and Van Witteloostuijn, A. (2004). The (non)sense of organizational change: An essai about universal management hypes, sick consultancy metaphors, and healthy organization theories. *Organization Studies* 25(7), 1205–1231.

Spangenberg, H. and Theron, C. C. (2005). Promoting ethical follower behaviour through leadership of ethics: The development of the ethical leadership inventory (ELI). *South African Journal of Business Management*, 36(2), 1–18.

Van Vugt, M. (2006). Evolutionary origins of leadership and followership. *Personality and Social Psychology Review*, 10(4), 354–371.

Vandekerckhove, W. and Commers, R. M. S. (2003). Downward Workplace Mobbing: A Sign of the Times? *Journal of Business Ethics*, 45, 41–50.

Vardi, Y. and Weitz, E. (2004). *Misbehavior in Organizations. Theory, Research, and Management*. London: Lawrence Erlbaum Associates Publishers.

Vickers, M. H. and Kouzmin, A. (2001). 'Resilience' in organizational actors and rearticulating 'voice'. *Public Management Review*, 3(1), 95–119.

Vredenburgh, D. and Brender, Y. (1998). The hierarchical abuse of power in work organizations. *Journal of Business Ethics*, 17, 1337–1347.

Willmott, H. C. (1996). A metatheory of management: omniscience or obfuscation? *British Journal of Management*, 7(4), 323–328.

Willmott, H. C. (1997). Rethinking management and managerial work: Capitalism, control and subjectivity. *Human Relations*, 50(11), 1329–1359.

Zaleznik, A. (1989). *The Managerial Mystique – Restoring Leadership in Business*. New York: Harper & Row.

8 Leadership narcissism, ethics and strategic change

Is it time to revisit our thinking about the nature of effective leadership?

Malcolm Higgs

Introduction

The changing business environment, particularly as a result of the recent Global Financial Crisis, with an increase in boardroom volatility and focus on governance, requires a review of our thinking about leadership. Indeed the high-profile collapses of a number of the worlds' largest corporations prior to the current Global Financial Crisis have led to a growing interest in how the leaders of these organizations have contributed to such failures either through their personal behaviours (including unethical practices) or their impact on the behaviours of others in their organizations (McCormick and Burch, 2005). Within this context it has been notable that dramatic failures have often been triggered by, or associated with, significant strategic change, such as major acquisitions (Higgs, 2009; Furnham, 2010a; Boddy, 2006). The collapse of organizations such as Enron, Tyco and Worldcom, and the recent Global Financial Crisis with the demise of companies such as Lehman Brothers and the nationalization of UK banks such as Northern Rock and RBS have prompted speculation about the role and impact of 'bad' leadership. In particular these high-profile examples have raised questions relating to the role of leadership in relation to both personal and organizational ethics.

This has led to a growing interest in understanding the causes of failure of CEOs and senior leaders, and the exploration of why apparently well-qualified individuals effectively 'derail' (Furnham, 2010b; McCormick and Burch, 2005; Hatch and Schultz, 2004) and often engage in unethical behaviours. This question is not only being raised in the academic world, but also in the business world. Higgs (2009) points out that business analysts increasingly tend to supplement financial and economic performance data with evaluations of leadership style and governance processes in assessing corporate organizations. Whilst some early work explored the concept of leadership derailment (McCall and Lombardo, 1983), relatively little subsequent work has explored further or built on their research. As Furnham (2010a:62) comments, 'Little has been written on the taboo subject of the charming, talented, high flying CEOs who should have done brilliantly but instead fail or go off the tracks.'

Furnham goes on to suggest that leadership derailment is not rare; he estimates that the level of this is as high as 50 per cent, taken across a wide range of organizations. Within the debate the relationship between narcissistic leadership and ethical behaviour comes into particular focus within the context of the level and frequency of strategic change. Although this area remains largely unexplored empirically, the recent work of Chatterjee and Hambrick (2007) demonstrated that organizations led by narcissistic CEOs tended to engage in more high-profile actions (e.g. mergers and acquisitions) and more frequent strategic change than those led by non-narcissistic CEOs. Furthermore, the organizations led by narcissistic CEOs experienced greater volatility in return on assets and shareholder return than those led by the non-narcissistic CEOs.

Against this background two questions arise:

1. What are the courses of damaging and/or unethical leader behaviours?; and
2. How can the consequences of such 'bad' leadership be avoided or mitigated?

This chapter sets out to offer some answers to these two questions and to propose areas for future research designed to explore them in more detail. In order to do this the first section explores the causes of 'bad' leadership. This is followed by a section that explores the extent to which the concept of narcissism may offer a possible explanation of the emergence of bad leadership and result in, amongst other things, unethical behaviour. The next two sections explore the extent to which bad leadership has been researched and the consequences of its emergence in an organization. Having discussed the issues that underpin bad leadership, the chapter closes with thoughts on how the impact of this phenomenon may be mitigated and how to avoid its emergence in an organization.

The causes of 'bad' leadership

To date, the main focus of leadership studies and research has been on 'good' or effective leadership (Aasland *et al.*, 2008; Benson and Hogan, 2008). Relatively few studies have explored the concept of 'bad' or flawed leadership (Furnham, 2010a; Benson and Hogan, 2008).

The focus on 'good' leadership may be seen to be rooted in a view that any other form of behaviour is not leadership. For example Burns (2003) comments that 'if it is unethical or immoral it is not leadership' (p. 48). The more recent examples of dramatic, unethical, and indeed sometimes illegal, corporate implosions (e.g. Enron, Lehman Brothers) have clearly raised concerns about the nature and impact of 'bad' leadership. However, preceding such dramatic events the possibility of 'bad' leadership can be seen to have emerged in the early 1980s from the work of the Centre for Creative Leadership in relation to the issue of 'leader derailment/ failure' (McCall and Lombardo, 1983). McCall and Lombardo identified that the causes of leadership failure and derailment were the result of a combination of personal flaws and performance shortfalls. In exploring this concept they identified a range of causal factors which included: skill deficiencies; burn out; being insensitive to others; being cold and aloof; arrogance; betraying trust; and being overly ambitious. They argued that the personal flaws (dysfunctional tendencies) were more important than skill deficiencies as drivers of derailment (McCall and Lombardo, 1983). This view is echoed in the emergence of more recent writing on this topic (Furnham, 2010a, 2010b; Boddy, 2006).

Within this literature there are a range of descriptions of 'bad' leadership behaviours, and there do appear to be a number of central (albeit overlapping) themes. These are:

Abuse of power. This encompasses the abuse of power to serve personal goals or achieve personal gain; the use of power to reinforce self-image and enhance perceptions of personal performance; and the abuse of power to conceal personal inadequacies (Ashforth, 1994; Benson and Hogan, 2008; Kellerman, 2004; Lipman-Blumen, 2005).

Inflicting damage on others. This focuses on the negative impact on subordinates and includes: bullying; coercion; negative impact on perceptions of subordinate self-efficacy; damage to the psychological well-being of subordinates; and inconsistent or arbitrary treatment of subordinates, as well as a range of other unethical behaviours (Tepper, 2000; Kellerman, 2004; Aasland *et al.*, 2008; Ashforth, 1994).

Over-exercise of control to satisfy personal needs. For example: obsession with detail; perfectionism and limiting subordinate initiative (Tepper, 2000; Benson and Hogan, 2008; Ashforth, 1994; 1997).

Rule breaking to serve own purposes. This is the area of behaviour in which leaders engage in corrupt, unethical and, indeed, illegal behaviours (Lipman-Blumen, 2005; Kellerman, 2004; Hogan *et al.*, 1994; Tepper, 2000; Ashforth, 1994).

The ability of leaders to engage in 'bad' behaviour is seen to arise from their positional power. This is well argued by Kets de Vries (1993) who comments that 'Leadership is the exercise of power, and the quality of leadership – good, ineffective or destructive – depends on an individual's ability to exercise power' (p. 22).

In exploring this, Kets de Vries (1993) suggests that leaders need a sense of individual potency in order to be able to exercise power. Aspects of such a sense of potency include ambition, a need to make a mark, a longing to be conspicuous, and an urge to take initiative and control. All of these he sees as legitimate needs. However, he points out that the slide to excess in pursuing these needs represents the roots of 'bad' leadership and related unethical behaviours.

Whilst there is a range of views on the nature and consequences of 'bad' leadership there is relatively little work that attempts to understand the antecedents of such behaviour. The work of Kets de Vries (1993) was one early example. Adopting a psychoanalytic approach he proposed that 'bad' leadership resulted from the leader having an 'unresolved sense of self' combined with 'an unrealistic idea of their potency'. Hogan *et al.* (1994) adopted a somewhat different view based on personality theory. From their research they proposed that personality traits that are present at extreme levels can lead to negative behaviours or personal shortcomings. For example, ambition can have positive attributes, such as taking initiative, whereas at extremes it can lead to individuals constantly competing with each other. Similarly, agreeableness can have benefits in terms of individuals being likeable, but at extremes it can result in inappropriate conflict-avoiding behaviour. Building from a distinction between the 'bright side' and 'dark side' of personality (Hogan *et al.*, 1994; Benson and Hogan, 2008) Benson and Campbell (2007) and Benson (2006) demonstrated that 'dark-side' personality dimensions predicted dysfunctional performance of leaders with consequent adverse impact on followers and the organization.

It is the exploration of the antecedents of 'bad' leadership which has led to the growing interest in the relationship between narcissism and leadership. The emergence of this area of theory and research is considered in more detail below.

Narcissism and leadership

The relative dominance of the 'heroic' theories of leadership has led to a focus on the characteristics of the most senior leaders in an organization (notably the CEOs). Indeed researchers in the field of strategic management have asserted that top executives tend to invest a great deal of themselves in their business decisions and organizations (Chatterjee and Hambrick, 2007; Finkelstein and Hambrick, 1996; Eisenhart and Schoonhoven, 2004; Hambrick and Mason, 1984). This stream of research has been generally referred to as 'Upper Echelon Theory' and has tended to focus on the CEOs of organizations or top management teams.

Within the 'heroic' school of leadership many of the assertions have been made on the basis of case study and anecdotal data drawn from either biographies of CEOs or reviews of publicly available data. Within this vein, the need to understand the causes of failure of CEOs to deliver sustainable performance or even corporate failure and unethical corporate behaviour has led to the interest in the concept of narcissistic leadership (Benson and Hogan, 2008; Maccoby, 2003). In this debate there are assertions that senior/top-level narcissistic leadership has an adverse impact on the internal climate of an organization as well as performance outcomes in the longer term (Maccoby, 2003; Higgs, 2009).

Whilst narcissism is a term widely and pejoratively employed in general usage, its relationship to leadership has only been explored in the last 15 to 20 years (Kets de Vries, 1993; Chatterjee and Hambrick, 2007). However, its roots within psychology go back to the late 1800s (Ellis, 1898) and indeed had a major impact on Freud's later thinking (Freud, 1957) in which he described the manifestations of narcissism as being:

- self-admiration;
- self-aggrandisement; and
- a tendency to see others as an extension of the self.

This psychoanalytic view of narcissism tended to be notable in the early theorizing and discussions of narcissism and leadership (Kets De Vries,

1993). In much of the psychological literature, narcissism had tended to be seen as being akin to a clinical psychological disorder (Raskin and Terry, 1988; Emmons, 1987). However, the work of Raskin and Hall (1979) and Raskin and Terry (1988) provided support for the view that narcissism was indeed a personality construct rather than a clinical disorder. Working from this perspective, Emmons (1987) identified a number of distinct elements of the narcissistic trait that are all important to our understanding of the concept. These were:

- Exploitativeness/Entitlement, which they described as being 'I demand the respect due to me';
- Leadership/Authority; 'I like to be the centre of attention';
- Superiority/Arrogance; 'I am better than others'; and
- Self-absorption/Self-admiration; 'I am preoccupied with how extraordinary I am'.

A series of studies, building on the concept of narcissism as a trait, provided evidence to indicate that narcissism is positively related to: self-esteem; biased self-enhancement; mood swings (particularly following criticism); high levels of anger and aggression in response to negative feedback; perception of little room for self-improvement; high levels of over-confidence in own abilities; and tendencies to high levels of self-assessment (Rhodewalt and Morf, 1998; Emmons, 1987; Campbell *et al.*, 2004). Whilst these studies tended to reinforce the lay negative view of narcissism as a trait, other work indicated that it was the excesses of the trait that led to potentially negative consequences (Hogan *et al.*, 1994; Benson and Hogan, 2008; Hogan and Hogan, 2001).

Within this debate there is an overlap between the concept of narcissistic leadership and corporate psychopathology (Deutschman, 2005; Boddy, 2006). Indeed some of the components tend to overlap clearly (lack of empathy, manipulative behaviour, arrogance, ego-centricity, self-enhancement, need for recognition). However, as Furnham (2010a) points out, there is a difference in that narcissistic leaders can produce some short-term organizational benefits whereas corporate psychopaths rarely do.

In reflecting on this distinction the question arises as to how such individuals rise to significant leadership positions within an organization? In attempting to answer this question it is evident that both narcissists and corporate psychopaths share a number of characteristics that are superficially attractive within organizations that view leadership within an 'heroic' perspective. These include:

- charm (Furnham, 2010a; 2010b; Boddy, 2006; Campbell and Campbell, 2009)
- extroversion (Boddy, 2006; Deutschman, 2005; Furnham, 2010a) and
- self-confidence (Campbell and Campbell, 2009; Furnham, 2010a)

It is also suggested that these apparently desirable attributes assume particular significance in times of major organizational turbulence and change (Furnham, 2010a; 2010b; Campbell and Campbell 2009; Boddy, 2006). Furthermore, it is suggested that these externally (apparently) attractive traits are frequently seen by followers as defining leadership (Campbell and Campbell, 2009). Indeed in describing the narcissistic personality, Freud (1931:218) highlights just this point, commenting that 'People of this type impress others as being "personalities"; it is on them that their fellow men are especially likely to learn; they readily assume the role of leader.'

Whilst some focus on the 'dark side' resulting from the negative impacts of over-dominance of the narcissistic trait (Benson and Hogan, 2008; Benson, 2006) others assert that this work tends to ignore the positive benefits to organizations of narcissism in senior leaders (Maccoby, 2000; Kohut, 1996; Miller, 1991). In exploring these potential benefits a number of authors have developed the concept of 'productive' and 'destructive' narcissism (Maccoby, 2000, 2003; Ronningstom, 2005). This framing leads to a view that 'productive' narcissism is both necessary and beneficial to an organization. In particular Maccoby (2000; 2003) asserts that organizations have a need for narcissistic leaders as they provide a strong sense of vision and have the courage to lead organizations in new directions. In a similar vein Conger (1997) asserts that vision becomes an integral aspect of who such leaders are. In this way Maccoby asserts a strong link between narcissistic and charismatic leadership (Doyle and Lynch, 2008). In extolling the value of productive narcissists Maccoby (2003) proposes that their lead is accepted because the potential benefits to the organization are enormous. In pursuing this view of 'productive' narcissism there is a core assumption that leaders tend to be aware of their own behavioural tendencies and consciously work to control them (Maccoby, 2000, 2003). Some argue that these leaders tend to be creative and, through this self-awareness can often laugh at their own tendencies (Doyle and Lynch, 2008; Kohut, 1996; Kets de Vries and Miller, 1997; Maccoby, 2000). Others also support this 'bright side' and 'dark side' view (Furnham, 2010a; 2010b; Hatch and Schultz, 2004).

However, the visionary significance of (productive) narcissistic behaviours is challenged by some as representing a limited and incomplete view of the visionary role of leaders (Chatterjee and Hambrick, 2007; Collins, 2005). These same authors point to the fact that realization of vision requires persistence and unwavering pursuit of goals over time – characteristics that tend to be missing from narcissistic leaders. In a similar vein, Kets de Vries (1993) points out that whilst, particularly in a crisis, a degree of narcissism in a leader can be necessary for success and the creation of cohesion in a faltering organization, the impact on, and related energy in, the organization is only temporary. Interestingly, Campbell and Campbell (2009) point out that the 'bright side' view is evident in the process of such leaders emerging in an organization when little is known about them or there is little experience of working with them. However, exposure to such emerging leaders rapidly exposes the 'dark side' view.

Whilst the benefits of productive narcissism are argued for, even the strongest advocate of such a view (Maccoby, 2000, 2003) accept that their arguments relate purely to mid-term, rather than sustainable, organizational outcomes. Indeed they acknowledge that the internal impact of such leadership is most likely to be negative. As Maccoby comments, 'Even at their best, narcissistic leaders are bound to leave damaged systems and relationships in their wake' (2003:12) because they damage the organizational climate. Thus it could be seen that, in the medium to long term, narcissistic leaders fail to create the climate necessary for achieving sustainable performance.

Research into 'bad' leadership

In much of the debate concerning narcissistic leadership there is a considerable volume of assertion argument and discussion of specific cases, but little in the way of structured empirical research in an organizational context. Furthermore, there is a significant gap in more general leadership research to date in that there has been an absence of any notable work looking specifically at the phenomenon of narcissistic leadership (Maccoby, 2000, 2003; Doyle and Lynch, 2008). In particular, given that much of the writing on narcissistic leadership focuses on the very top leaders there does appear to be a clear absence of any empirical studies that explore the phenomenon within the CEO population (Chatterjee and Hambrick, 2007). The few that do exist tend to be more case-based or use demographic variables as indicators of personality traits. The case-based approach has adopted a predominantly psychoanalytic frame (Zaleznik and Kets de Vries, 1975). The trait-based approaches have tended to focus on the relationships between traits such as high need for achievement (Miller and Droge, 1986) and tolerance of risk (Gupta and Gorindarajan, 1984) and overall organizational outcomes. However, these have failed to produce consistent or conclusive results.

In research to explore narcissistic leadership in an organizational context (particularly senior level or CEO leadership) the 'upper echelon' literature (Finkelstein and Hambrick, 1996) provides some indication of the potential ways in which narcissism may be translated into strategic actions. In particular it is argued that narcissistic CEOs will (1) tend to engage in strategic dynamism, that is to say they will initiate more changes more rapidly than their non-strategic counterparts; (2) engage in acts of grandiosity; and (3) undertake bold actions that will attract attention (e.g. engage in significant and frequent merger and acquisition activity). If the 'productive' narcissistic school is to be believed (Maccoby, 2000, 2003) such behaviours would be more likely to lead to positive organizational outcomes than encountered in those led by 'non-narcissistic' CEOs. One of the very few empirical research works designed to explore these issues at CEO level was that conducted by Chatterjee and Hambrick (2007) in their study of CEOs in 111 companies in the US computer hardware and software sector. They used unobtrusive measures of CEO narcissism (e.g. prominence of photographs in annual reports, prominence of mentions of CEO in press releases, use by CEO of personal pronouns in interviews, and relationship between CEO cash and non-cash compensation in comparison to that of the second-highest-paid executive) gathered from documents covering a 12-year period. In addition they gathered organizational performance data for these organizations for the same period. The CEO data was used to compute a 'Naricssism Index'. In analysing the data they found that:

- there was a positive relationship between CEO narcissism and strategic dynamism, grandiosity and the number and size of acquisitions;
- narcissistic CEOs tended to undertake bold moves that attracted attention and resulted in both big wins and big losses;
- there was a positive relationship between CEO narcissism and both extreme and fluctuation organizational performance; and
- the overall performance of the firms led by narcissistic CEOs was neither better nor worse than that of those led by 'non-narcissistic' CEOs.

This study provided little support for the view of Maccoby (2000, 2003) that productive narcissistic leadership is of value to organizations. It did however provide a degree of support for a number of aspects of narcissism discussed above, but did not tend to provide much in the way of evidence to support the 'dark side' debate. However, their measures were indirect and non-psychometric, which limits the strength of the findings and suggests a need for further research employing direct measures. Furthermore, as with much of the debate around narcissism, the leader impact was only assessed in terms of organizational outcomes. The internal impact on climate, individuals, commitment of others, attrition, future capability, etc. were not considered directly. Yet these aspects of an organization are critical to sustained and long-term performance (Higgs, 2003; Collins, 2005) and indeed are likely to be impacted negatively by both productive and destructive narcissistic leadership (Maccoby, 2000, 2003). In fact within an organization the negative impacts of social interaction (e.g. 'bad' leadership) have a much more significant impact than positive organizational outcomes (Baumeister *et al.*, 2001).

The consequences of 'bad' leadership

In terms of the relatively limited empirical research into 'bad' leadership there has been some evidence that it leads to dysfunctional performance within the organization (Benson, 2006; Benson and Campbell, 2007). Benson and Hogan (2008) argue that 'bad' leadership can result in short-term performance success, but will inevitably lead to long-term problems and dysfunctional performance. What is notable, however, is that the 'bad' leadership studies (unlike the conventional leadership studies) are more focused on the internal effects of leader behaviours than the external performance outcomes. For example, studies have shown consistent adverse effects on followers, subjected to 'bad' leadership, in terms of job satisfaction, affective commitment and psychological well-being (Benson, 2006; Benson and Campbell, 2007; Benson and Hogan, 2008). Each of these areas is shown in the broader organizational behaviour literature to be related to longer-term organizational performance. Thus the impact of 'bad' leadership tends to be felt in the longer term through the debilitating impact on morale and motivation of subordinates. This point is well captured by Benson and Hogan (2008) who state that, 'It is (toxic) behaviour that, over the long-term, destroys the ability of people to work together productively in an organization'

(p. 12). To an extent this further endorses the view that leaders impact on the performance of individuals, groups and the organization through the work climate that they create.

In broad terms the consequences of 'bad' leadership may be seen in terms of:

- dramatic organizational failings or crises resulting from illegal or corrupt behaviour (Boddy, 2006; Hatch and Schultz, 2004; Furnham, 2010a, 2010b; Higgs, 2009);
- damage to the overall corporate culture leading to longer-term performance problems (Higgs, 2009; Maccoby, 2003; Furnham, 2010b; Boddy, 2006);
- damage to internal relationships (Boddy, 2006; Furnham, 2010a; Higgs, 2009; Kaiser and Hogan, 2007);
- Reduction in ethical standards (Kakabadse *et al.*, 2003);
- staff attrition and the associated loss of intellectual and social capital (Furnham, 2010a, 2010b; Higgs, 2009);
- loss of business opportunities (Furnham, 2010a; Boddy, 2006; Campbell and Campbell, 2009); and
- loss of corporate reputations (Higgs, 2009).

From the above it would appear that any apparent advantage of the proposed 'productive/bright side' narcissistic leadership is, at best short term, but inevitably leads to longer-term corporate damage with increasing risks of unethical behaviour (Maccoby, 2003; Higgs, 2009; Furnham, 2010a). In addition, the research of Chatterjee and Hambrick (2007) does indicate potential performance risks for organizations in terms of the volatility of financial outcomes and the exposure associated with regular strategic change and high-profile acquisitions. The latter can be particularly problematic when faced with significant macro-economic changes. For example the high-profile acquisition of ABN/AMRO by the Royal Bank of Scotland was a major factor in the collapse of RBS in the context of a major downturn in the world's financial markets.

Actions to avoid the impact and emergence of 'bad' leadership

In the literature relating to 'bad' leadership and destructive narcissistic leadership there has been a greater focus on exploring its nature than on discussing the issues relating to identifying factors that indicate that leaders may be likely to move to the 'dark side'; and suggesting interventions which may prevent such 'derailment' (McCall and Lomardo, 1983; Maccoby, 2000; Furnham, 2010a). In avoiding such 'derailment' and the negative impacts of destructive leadership, suggestions either appear to be unrealistic (given the nature of narcissism) or could indeed entail encouraging or manipulating followers to reinforce or collude with the narcissist's self-obsession. For example Maccoby (2000) proposes that the problems of the destructive elements of narcissistic leadership may be avoided or minimized by: (1) finding a 'trusted' colleague to keep them anchored to reality. Kets de Vries (1993) uses the medieval role of the court jester as an analogy to illustrate this point; (2) persuading the leader to undertake therapy; and (3) working in a way that results in people in the organization aligning themselves with the leader's goals and beginning to think in the way that he/she does.

The first two of these suggestions tend to be relevant to the 'productive' realist who has a degree of self-awareness (Kohut, 1996; Kets de Vries and Miller, 1997). However, the efficacy of such an approach with an existing senior leader who is already in the 'destructive' mode is highly questionable. The third suggestion proposes a degree of collusion, which would be likely to reinforce the narcissistic disorder (APA, 2000) and may indeed increase the likelihood of organizational damage and potentially unethical behaviour (Kets de Vries, 1993; Padilla and Mulvey, 2008). The high-profile implosions of some organizations (e.g. Enron, Tyco, Worldcom, etc.) provide extreme examples of this.

Perhaps one way of thinking about addressing the issues associated with 'bad' leadership is to consider approaching them on both a short-term and longer-term basis.

The challenge of dealing with CEOs currently in-post who may be in danger of derailing, or guarding against the possible emergence of this, requires action at the corporate governance level. The board of the organization (and in particular the non-executive directors) need to implement actions to address these risks in order to fulfil their duty to protect the interests of stakeholders. Some of the actions they can take include:

1. ensuring the appointment of an evidentially stable and non-narcissistic 'number two' to limit the possible damage that a narcissistic CEO can inflict on the organizational culture or climate (Furnham, 2010a; 2010b). In doing this they need to ensure that the person appointed to such a position has the ear and support of the board;

2. ensuring that the board hold the chief executive accountable for all of his/her decisions and actions (Boddy, 2006);

3. ensuring that the compensation of the CEO is strictly contingent on performance in the medium to long term (Furnham, 2010a);

4. designing the role of the CEO in such a way that the extent of personal discretion is reasonably constrained (Kaiser and Hogan, 2007). However, this does present the board with the challenge of achieving a balance between over-regulation and unfettered freedom that will serve the needs of the business (Furnham, 2010a);

5. ensuring that a robust, but fair, internal 'whistle-blowing' policy is both in place and audited regularly to establish that it is being implemented appropriately. In this way the narcissist's ability to stifle any negative feedback may be limited (Furnham 2010b);

6. establishing an annual appraisal process (using a 360-degree framework) for the review of all executive members of the board (including the CEO). This process should be managed by the chair of the board and operated on a 'zero tolerance' basis (i.e. no excuses will be accepted for any member of the executive in terms of not participating in such a review). In this way the board (and in particular the non-executive directors) will be in a position to identify potential problems in its senior leadership team (Taylor *et al.*, 2008). Indeed a few boards within large (often global) organizations in the UK have already implemented such a process and the non-executives feel that they have a far better understanding of the nature and quality of the organization's senior leadership team;

7. ensuring that the board are fulfilling their governance duties by conducting an annual review of the overall performance of the board (Taylor *et al.*, 2008); and

8. ensuring that the organization has an explicit code of ethics and that its implementation is monitored regularly (Kakabadse *et al.*, 2003).

In considering a longer-term approach to the management of the risks of the emergence of narcissistic (or even psychopathic) leaders, a more systemic approach to reducing the emergence (and to an extent, relative prevalence) of 'destructive' narcissistic senior-level leadership is required. This entails reviewing the nature, processes and criteria employed in the selection of leaders and, indeed, potential leaders (Benson and Hogan, 2008; Padilla and Mulvey, 2008). Both Furnham (2010a, 2010b) and Higgs (2009) suggest that a range of policies and practices relating to the identification, selection and development of leaders and potential future leaders should be developed and managed to avoid the 'derailing' dangers. Some of these actions include:

1. recruitment and selection criteria and processes. Furnham (2010a) in particular suggests more rigorous scrutiny of candidates' 'biographies' to look for signs of potential derailment and a more forensic approach to pursuing references;
2. careful 'on-boarding' of new hires who are likely to enter the talent pool;
3. structured career planning and development;
4. regular (and mandatory) use of 360-degree feedback processes for all who are considered to be in the leadership talent pool;
5. ensuring that anyone in the leadership talent pool stays in roles they are assigned to until they have provided evidence of their ability to complete the assignment and deliver results; and
6. the provision of coaching to those at higher levels in the talent pool with no 'opt out' alternative.

Whilst the above actions may be of value in minimizing the risks of the emergence of future 'bad' leaders, Higgs (2009) emphasizes the need for these to be based on a significant movement away form the dominant 'heroic' model of leadership still influencing practice in many organizations. The underlying model should move to a more 'relational' model (Higgs, 2003; Benson and Hogan, 2008) with a greater focus on developing a strong sense of self-awareness (Kets de Vries, 1993).

Indeed it is not only the dangers of the emergence of 'bad' leaders that requires such a shift. The changing business environment, with an increasing focus on growth, volatility and complexity, is seen by many as also requiring a significant change in thinking about leadership (Hiller et al., 2006; Pearce, 2004; Gronn, 2002; Yukl, 1999; O'Toole et al., 2002; Heenan and Bennis, 1999). Even within the solo-focused 'heroic' literature there have been three emerging trends that begin to recognize the complexity of the leadership phenomenon. The first of these has been the move from a predominantly rational trait model to a more emotionally based transformational one (Yukl, 1999; Hiller et al., 2006; Hunt, 2004). The transformational model, which emphasizes emotional exchange, has indeed become the dominant model in the field (Yukl, 1999; Conger and Kanungo, 1998, 1994; Bass, 1985; House, 1977). The second trend has been a shift in focus from the top leaders in organizations ('far' leaders) to the more immediate leadership relationships ('near' leaders) experienced by individuals within any organization (e.g. Shamir, 1999; Alimo-

Metcalfe, 1995). The final trend has been to move away from studying purely the role of behaviour of leaders to considering the behaviour of followers and the study of 'followership' (Gronn, 2002; Yukl, 1999).

The increasing complexity of the work environment means that individual leaders are unable to possess all of the necessary expertise to perform all of the required leadership functions effectively (Yukl, 1999; Gronn, 2002; Pearce, 2004). Against this background there is seen to be a need to move away from the dominance of viewing leadership roles and individual leadership as synonymous constructs (Bass, 1990; Avolio *et al.*, 1996) to considering leadership as a more fluid construct (Hiller *et al.*, 2006). This thinking has led to the emergence of a model that is more appropriate to an increasingly complex environment that explores the concept of collective or shared leadership (Hiller *et al.*, 2006; Gronn, 2002).

The recognition of the value and relevance of such a model and its integration into an organization's leadership selection and development frameworks would mitigate against the emergence of potential leaders with the strong narcissistic tendencies that can result in damaging and unethical behaviour. This is not to suggest that the use of one single, dominant model of leadership should be replaced by an alternative. Rather we should think in terms of replacing simplistic models with frameworks for thinking about leadership. In exploring this idea, Avolio *et al.* (2009) suggest that leadership is a complex phenomenon that has to include considerations of contextual issues and challenges. However, it is important to consider whether or not situational models may need to include some core shared components (Higgs, 2003). Avolio *et al.* (2009) and Walumbwa *et al.* (2007) suggest that there is a need to ensure that leadership is executed in an authentic manner within any framework.

Indeed the concept of authenticity and authentic leadership has been argued to be essential to success in many situations, but importantly and notably in the context of change implementation (Rowland and Higgs, 2008). There appears to be an emerging view that the components of authentic leadership include: self awareness; self-regulation; relational transparency; and a clear moral compass (Avolio *et al.*, 2009; Walumbwa *et al.*, 2007). Certainly the components of this framework relate clearly to earlier research that points to the importance of self-awareness as a core component of effective leadership (Fletcher, 1997; Gill, 2001) and the linkages between emotional intelligence and leadership (Goleman, 1996; Higgs and Dulewicz, 2002). In more recent studies Rowland and Higgs (2008) have demonstrated the critical nature of authenticity (and in particular self-awareness) as an element necessary for the effective leadership of change. Furthermore this frame places an ethical component at the heart of leadership.

The adoption of leadership frameworks, such as those outlined above, as the basis for leadership selection and development would result in avoiding the creation of a fertile ground for the emergence of narcissistic or 'bad' leaders.

Conclusion

The examples of major corporate collapse and failure (most recently encountered within the context of the Global Financial Crisis) have focused attention on the impact of the behaviours of CEOs on their organizations and raised questions about the nature and causes of such 'bad' and often unethical leadership.

Against this background, whilst within the leadership literature the predominant paradigm has focused on 'good' leadership, there has been an emerging area of discussion of 'bad' or 'dark side' leadership. In this debate it is argued that leader traits are more significant factors in the emergence of 'bad' leadership than inadequate skills (Benson and Hogan, 2008). The discussion around the issue of 'bad' leadership has tended (more recently) to focus on the concept of narcissism, which has been clearly recognized as (and been shown to be) an individual trait (Emmons, 1987; Raskin and Terry, 1988; Furnham, 2010a; Campbell and Campbell, 2009). Whilst there are assertions that there are both productive and destructive forms of narcissism (Maccoby, 2000, 2003; Kohult, 1996; Kets de Vries and Miller, 1997; Furnham, 2010a) there is some disagreement about this (Campbell and Campbell, 2009). There is a clear view that, in the longer term, narcissistic leadership is damaging to an organization internally (in terms of culture, morale, ethical behaviour, relationships, etc.) which ultimately leads to longer-term deterioration in organizational performance (Kets de Vries, 1993; Collins, 2005: Aasland *et al.*, 2008; Benson and Hogan, 2008), corporate failure (Furnham, 2010b; Higgs, 2009; Campbell and Campbell, 2009) and unethical behaviour (Higgs, 2009; Furnham, 2010a, 2010b). The question relating to the extent to which narcissim may be a dominant cause of 'bad' leadership is not clearly answered by the current literature. Certainly, in terms of short-term outcomes there is little evidence of a negative performance effect resulting from productive narcissism. However, it does appear to have a negative impact on the internal climate and thus could well have an adverse impact on longer-term performance outcomes. This does not suggest that narcissism is the sole cause of 'bad' leadership, and there is evidently a range of other antecedents that need to be considered (e.g. organizational culture, inadequate leadership skills, etc.). However, it is clear that leadership that emerges within such a context can lead to unethical behaviour that damages both organizations and individuals within these organizations.

Whilst there has been a growth in discussion of the 'darker' aspects of leadership and the concept of narcissism, there is a limited volume of empirical research (Chatterjee and Hambrick, 2007; Maccoby, 2000; Tepper, 2000). A recent study which explores narcissistic CEOs found that, whilst they engaged in more grandiose and dramatic actions (e.g. acquisitions and strategic dynamism) and their organizations experienced dramatic performance fluctuations, in the longer term their organizations performed neither better nor worse than comparator organizations led by non-narcissistic CEOs in the longer term (Chatterjee and Hambrick, 2007). This tends to further refute the argument that narcissistic leadership at senior level is a necessity for success or that it is fundamentally damaging to short- to medium-term performance. However, it is very clear that the debate around the topic of 'dark side' and narcissistic leadership needs to be underpinned by more empirical research. In order to deepen our understanding of the nature and impact of narcissistic leadership it is important that such research explores the internal impact of such leadership as well as organizational outcomes. In addition, it might also explore leadership beyond the very top of the organization to understand the way in which the narcissistic tendencies develop and emerge throughout a leadership career. This will help to develop effective assessment processes designed to spot narcissistic tendencies early and ameliorate their impact through development interventions.

References

Aasland, M. S., Skogstad, A. and Einarsen, S. (2008). The dark side: defining destructive leadership behaviour. *Organisations and People*, 15(3) 19–26.

Alimo-Metcalfe, B. (1995). An investigation of female and male constructs of leadership. *Women in Management Reviews*, Bradford: MCB.

American Psychiatric Association (APA) (2000). Diagnostic and Statistical Manual of Mental Disorders (DSM-IV-TR).

Ashforth, B. E. (1994). Petty tyranny in organisations. *Human Relations*, 47, 755–778.

Ashforth, B. E. (1997). Petty tyranny in organisations: A preliminary examination of antecedents and consequences. *Canadian Journal of Administrative Sciences*, 14(2), 126–40.

Avolio, B. J. and Gardner, W. I. (2005). Authentic leadership development: Getting to the root of positive forms of leadership. *The Leadership Quarterly*, 16(2), 315–338.

Avolio, B. J, Jung, D. I, Murry W., and Sivasubrassian, N. (1996). Building highly developed teams; Focusing on shared leadership processes, efficiency, trust and performance. *Advances in Interdisciplinary Studies on Work Teams*, 3, 173–209.

Avolio, B. J., Walumbwa, F. O. and Weber, T. J. (2009). Leadership: Current Theories, Research and Future Directions. *Annual Review of Psycholgy*, 60, 421–449.

Bass, B. M. (1985). *Leadership and Performance Beyond Expectations*. New York: Free Press.

Bass, B. M. (1990). *Handbook of Leadership: A Survey of Theory and Research.* New York: Free Press.

Baumeister, R. F., Bratslavsky, E., Finkenauer, C. and Vohs, K. D. (2001). Bad is stronger than good. *Review of General Psychology*, 5, 323–370.

Benson, M. J. (2006). New explorations in the field of leadership research: A walk on the dark side of personality and implications for leadership (in)effectiveness. Doctoral dissertation, University of Minnesota.

Benson, M. J. and Campbell, J. P. (2007). To be or not to be linear: An expanded representation of personality and its relationship to leadership performance. *International Journal of Selection and Assessment*, 15, 232–249.

Benson, M. J. and Hogan, R. S. (2008). How dark side leadership personality destroys trust and degrades organisational effectiveness. *Organisations and People*, 15(3), 10–11.

Boddy, C. R. (2006). The dark side of management decisions organisational psychopaths. *Management Decisions*, 44(10), 1461–1475.

Burns, J. M. (2003). *Transforming Leadership: A New Pursuit of Happiness.* London: Atlantic.

Campbell, W. K. and Campbell, S. M. (2009). On the self-regulatory dynamics created by the peculiar benefits and costs of narcissism: A contextual reinforcement model and examination of leadership. *Self and Identity*, 8(2), 214–232.

Campbell, W. K., Goodie, A. S. and Foster, J. D. (2004). Narcissism, confidence and risk attitude. *Journal of Behavioural Decision Making*, 17, 297–311.

Chatterjee, A. and Hambrick, D. C. (2007). It's all about me: Narcissistic chief executives and their effects on company strategy and performance. *Administrative Science Quarterly*, 52, 351–386.

Collins, J. (2005). Level 5 leadership: The triumph of humility and fierce resolve. *Harvard Business Review*, 83, 136–146.

Conger, J. A. (1997). The dark side of leadership. In: R.P. Vecchio (ed), *Leadership: Understanding the Dynamics of Power and Influence in Organisations*. Notre Dame IN:, University of Notre Dame Press.

Conger, J. A. and Kanungo, R. N. (1994). Charismatic leadership in organisations: Perceived behavioural attributes and their measurement. *Journal of Organisational Behaviour*, 15, 439–452.

Conger, J. A. and Kanungo, R. (1998). *Charismatic Leadership in Organisations.* Thousand Oaks, CA: Sage Publications.

Deutschman, A. (2005). Is your boss a psychopath? *Fast Company*, 96, 44–52.

Doyle, N. and Lynch, P. (2008). Understanding the affect narcissistic leadership has on middle management: An exploratory case study analysis. *Irish Academy of Management Conference Proceedings*, September 2008.

Eisenhardt, K. M. and Schoonhoven, C. B. (1990). Organisational growth: Linking founding team, strategy, environment and growth among US semi-conductor ventures, 1978–1988. *Administrative Science Quarterly*, 35, 504–529.

Ellis, H. (1898). Auto-eroticism: A psychological study. *Alienist and Neurologist*, 19, 260–299.

Emmons, R. (1987). Narcissism: Theory and measurement. *Journal of Personality and Social Psychology*, 52, 11–17.

Finkelstein, S. and Hambrick, D. C. (1996). *Strategic Leadership: Top Executives and Their Effects on Organisations.* New York: West Publishing.

Fletcher, C. (1997). Self Awareness – A neglected attribute. *International Journal of Selection and Assessment*, 5(3), 183–187.

Freud, S. (1957). The history of the psychoanalytic movement. In: J. Strachey (ed), *The Standard Edition of the Complete Works of Sigmund Freud*. London: Hogarth Press.

Freud, S. (1931). Libidinal types. In: J. Strachey (ed.), *The Standard Edition of the Complete Psychological Works of Sigmund Freud*, vol. 14. London: Hogarth Press, 67–104.

Furnham, A. (2010a). *The Elephant in the Boardroom*. Basingstoke: Palgrove Macmillan.

Furnham, A. (2010b). When managers lose the plot. *Management Today*, June 2010, 62–66.

Gill, R. (2001). Towards an integrated theory of leadership. Paper presented at the EIASM leadership conference, Oxford, December 2002.

Goleman, D. (1996). *Emotional Intelligence: Why It Can Matter More than IQ*. New York: Bantam Books.

Gronn, P (2002). Distributed leadership as a unit of analysis. *The Leadership Quarterly*, 13, 423–451.

Gupta, A. K. and Govindarajan, V. (1984). Business unit strategy, managerial characteristics and business unit effectiveness at strategy implementation. *Academy of Management Journal*, 27, 25–41.

Hambrick, D. C., and Mason, P. A. (1984). Upper echelons: The organisation as a reflection of its top managers. *Academy of Management Review*, 9, 193–206.

Hatch, M. J. and Schultz, M. (2004). *Organisational Identity*. Oxford: Oxford University Press.

Heenan, D. A. and Bennis, W. (1999). *Co-leaders: The Power of Great Partnerships*. New York: Wiley.

Higgs, M. J. (2003). How can we make sense of leadership in the 21st century? Development in leadership thinking. *Leadership and Organisational Development Journal*, 24(5), 273–284.

Higgs, M. J. (2009). The good the bad and the ugly; Leadership and narcissism. *Journal of Change Management*, 9, 165–178.

Higgs, M. J. and Dulewicz, S. V. (2002). *Making Sense of Emotional Intelligence* (second edition). Windsor: NFER-Nelson.

Hiller, N. J, Day, D. V. and Vance, R.J. (2006). Collective enactment of leadership roles and team effectiveness: A field study. *The Leadership Quarterly*, 17(3), 387–397.

Hogan, R. and Hogan, J. (2001). Assessing leadership: A view from the dark side. *International Journal of Selection and Assessment*, 9, 40–51.

Hogan, R., Curphy, G. J. and Hogan, J. (1994). What we know about leadership: Effectiveness and personality. *American Psychologist*, 49, 493–504.

House, R. J. (1977). A 1976 theory of charismatic leadership. In J. G. Hunt and L. L. Larson (eds), *Leadership: The Cutting Edge*, Carbondale, IL: Southern Illinois University Press, 189–207.

Hunt, J. G. (2004). Task leadership. In G. R. Goethats, G. J. Sorenson and J. M. Burns (eds), *The Encyclopaedia of Leadership*, vol 4. Thousand Oaks, CA: Sage.

Kaiser, R. B. and Hogan, R. (2007). The dark side of discretion: Leader personality and organizational decline. In R. Hooijberg J., Hunt, J. Antonakis, K. Boal and N. Lane (eds), *Being There Even When You Are Not: Leading Through Strategy, Structures and Systems*. Amsterdam; London: Elsevier JAI.

Kakabadse, A., Korac-Kakabadse, N. and Kouzmin, A. (2003). Ethics, values and behaviours: Comparison of three case studies examining the paucity of leadership in government. *Public Administration*, 81(3), 477–508.

Kellerman, B. (2004). *Bad Leadership. What it is, How it Happens, Why it Matters*. Boston: Harvard Business School Press.

Kets de Vries, M. F. R. (1993). *Leaders, Fools and Imposters: Essays on the Psychology of Leadership*. San Francisco: Jossey-Bass.

Kets de Vries, M. F. R. and Miller, D. (1997). Narcissism and leadership: an object relations perspective. *Human Relations*, 38, 583–601.

Kohut, H. (1996). Forms and transformations of narcissism. *Journal of the American Psychoanalytic Association*, 14, 243–272.

Lipman-Blumen, J. (2005). *The Allure of Toxic Leaders. Why We Follow Destructive Bosses and Corrupt Politicians – and How We Can Survive Them*. Oxford: Oxford University Press.

Maccoby, M. (2000). Narcissistic leaders – The incredible pros; the incredible cons. *Harvard Business Review*, 78(1), 68–79.

Maccoby, M. (2003). *The Productive Narcissist: The Promise and Peril of Visionary Leadership*. New York: Broadway Books.

McCall, M. and Lombardo, M. (1983). *Off the Track: Why and How Successful Executives Get Derailed*. Greensbord, NC: Center for Creative Leadership.

McCormick, I. and Burch, G. (2005). Snakes in suits – fear and loathing in corporate clothing. *New Zealand Management*, 52 (10), 34–35.

Miller, D. (1991). Stale in the saddle: CEO tenure and the match between organisations and the environment. *Management Science*, 37, 34–52.

Miller, D. and Droge, C. (1986). Psychological and traditional determinants of structure. *Administrative Science Quarterly*, 31, 539–556.

O'Toole, J, Galbraith, J and Lawler, E. E. (2002). When two (or more) heads are better than one: The promise and pitfalls of shared leadership. Centre for effective organisations: University of Southern California.

Padilla, A. and Mulvey, P. (2008). Leadership toxicity; Sources and remedies. *Organisations and People*, 15(3), 27–37.

Pearce, C. L (2004). The future of leadership: Combining vertical and shared leadership to transform knowledge work. *Academy of Management Executive*; 18(1), 47–57.

Raskin, R. and Terry, H. (1988). A principal components analysis of the narcissistic personality inventory and further evidence of its construct validity. *Journal of Personality and Social Psychology*, 54, 890–902.

Raskin, R. N. and Hall, C. S. (1979). A narcissistic personality inventory. *Psychological Reports*, 45, 590–597.

Rhodewalt, F. and Morf, C. C. (1988). On self-aggrandizement and anger: Temporal analysis of narcissism and effective reactions to success and failure. *Journal of Personality and Social Psychology*, 74, 672–685.

Ronningstom, E. F. (2005). *Identifying and Understanding the Narcissistic Personality.* New York: Oxford University Press.

Rowland, D. and Higgs, M. J. (2008). *Sustaining Change: Leadership That Works*. Chichester: Jossey-Bass.

Shamir, B. (1992). Attribution of influence and charisma to the leader. *Journal of Applied Social Psychology*, 22(5), 386–407.

Shamir, B. (1999). Leadership in boundaryless organisations: Disposable or indispensable? *European Journal of Work and Organisational Psychology*, 8(1), 49–71.

Taylor, B., Dulewicz, V. and Gay, K. (2008). How part-time directors create exceptional value: New evidence from the non-executive director awards. *Journal of General Management*, 33(4), 53–7070.

Tepper, B. J. (2000). Consequences of abusive supervision. *Academy of Management Journal*, 43(2), 178–190.

Walumbwa, F. O., Lawler, J. J. and Avolio, B. J. (2007). Leadership, individual differences and work-related attitudes: A cross-culture investigation. *Applied Psychology: An International Review*, 56(2), 212–230.

Yukl, G, (1999). An evaluation of conceptual weaknesses in transformational and charismatic leadership theories. *The Leadership Quarterly*, 10(2), 285–305.

Zaleznik, A. and Kets de Vries, M. F. R. (1975). *Power and the Corporate Mind*. Boston: Houghton Mifflin.

Part IV
Ethical change leadership and organizational sustainability

9 Leadership for sustainable futures

Dexter Dunphy and Suzanne Benn

Introduction

The UN's successive International Panel on Climate Change Reports show the immediacy of the ecological crisis facing the planet (Flannery, 2010). Global climate change is not something that will affect future generations; it is already affecting our own generation as Arctic ice and permafrost melt, seas become more acidic, desertification intensifies and extreme weather conditions increase in number and intensity. In addition, the limitations of known oil reserves (peak oil) combined with increasing demand for oil from India, China and South-East Asia will increasingly threaten established oil-based patterns of human interaction such as cheap land and air transport as well as oil-based food production. These problems will be further exacerbated by a growing global population.

The developed economies therefore need to move from their current extreme dependence on fossil fuels (the carbon economy) and substitute energy produced from alternative energy sources (the carbon-neutral economy).

How are we doing on achieving this goal? We have recently seen at the UN's Copenhagen Climate summit that political leaders were high on rhetoric before the summit but failed to achieve effective international collaboration on actions to halt and/or reverse climate change. As a result, emissions in all nations are increasing and we face a growing world food crisis.

How are commercial leaders faring by comparison? We see an increasingly divided commercial world. The leaders of some organizations are moving rapidly to pursue sustainability goals and capitalize on the opportunities of the emerging alternative economy (Benn *et al.*, 2011). The leaders of other organizations, particularly many leaders of the 'old world economy' such as coal, oil and mining companies, are resisting and subverting political processes designed to encourage the shift to sustainability. These leaders claim legitimation in terms of the values of the old world economy – particularly preserving economic progress and maximizing shareholder wealth or applying new-economy terms to old unstainable practices ('greenwash').

On the other hand, we have leaders – particularly of organizations in those industries with a stake in the future alternative-energy and service-centered economy – who are attempting to move their organizations onto the path to a different future. The latter often act on a new ethical imperative, based on respect for preserving the global ecology and supporting social justice.

Nevertheless, there seems to have been a widespread, recent shift on the part of many of the world's corporate leaders to at least accept the legitimacy of the demands represented by the movement to create commitment to more sustainable enterprise practices. A 2009 survey of 1,500 global executives and managers conducted by the MIT Sloan Review and the Boston Consulting Group found that most corporate leaders and managers thought that sustainability would have an impact on their business. However, the majority also reported that their companies were not acting decisively enough on the issue (Berns *et al.*, 2009).

One major reason for the lack of action was reported to be that the managers had no clear idea of the specifics of what sustainability means for management and leadership. However, the survey found that those companies that were committed to sustainability and taking major initiatives were reaping substantial rewards. Clearly there are some effective sustainability change champions.

This survey indicates that we may have reached a high level of awareness amongst executives of the need to move toward corporate sustainability but that, for most, this awareness is not translating into widespread and effective action. Given the urgency and scale of the ecological and social crises, there is a need for more widespread corporate transformation than has yet occurred.

However, it is not only the environmental and social crises that are dictating the need to transform organizations. Every second year IBM surveys over 1,000 leaders of global companies. In 2008, before the Global Financial Crisis, IBM conducted a survey with the theme of 'The Enterprise of the Future' (IBM, 2008a). The CEOs of 1,130 companies were asked to suggest what the enterprise of the future would look like.

They indicated that their organizations are bombarded by change and struggling to keep up. They thought that enterprises of the future would be: 'hungry for change, innovative beyond customer imagination, globally integrated, disruptive by nature, and genuine, not generous'. The need to make rapid transformational change was widely accepted, including the need to go beyond adaption to environmental changes to actually leading them. They suggested that the enterprise of the future would be home to what the report characterizes as 'visionary challengers', that is, people who question assumptions and suggest radical alternatives. The need to make rapid transformational change was widely accepted but the majority of executives perceived that the capacity of their organizations to make that change is lagging severely behind the speed and discontinuity of environmental changes. Comparison with a similar survey in 2006 showed that the disparity between how much change was expected and perceived ability to manage it had nearly tripled over that period.

To explore this perceived change-skills gap, IBM initiated another global study *Making Change Work* (IBM, 2008b). This study consisted of interviews and surveys with 1,500 project leaders and sponsors of major organizational projects involving large-scale change in global companies. Only 41 per cent of these project managers characterized their projects as successfully meeting project objectives within planned time, budget and quality constraints. Yet the study illustrates that this was not true of all organizations – some organizations had built in the capacity to make transformational change effectively. The top 20 per cent of organizations reported an average project success rate of 80 per cent, nearly double the average and ten times better than the bottom 20 per cent. Clearly change skills can become an integral part of the culture and skills set of an organization; some organizations create high-level skills in developing effective change leaders. The transformation of organizations demanded to make the transition to a post-carbon society will involve multiplying the existing numbers of these leaders and engaging them in the task of moving their organizations toward sustainability.

This chapter explores the challenges that achieving corporate sustainability poses for the nature of organizational leadership and for the selection and development of present and future leaders. We identify the following key challenges in moving to a sustainable society:

• The urgency and scale of the environmental crisis demands leaders who can initiate and manage widespread transformational change. Recent research shows that effective transformational leaders are in short supply.

- The exponential growth in complexity of an organizational world means leaders are required to manage the sometimes conflicting goals of triple bottom-line performance – financial viability, social responsibility and ecological health. These are not simply abstract concepts but political processes represented by vocal and powerful external stakeholders who are increasingly seen as having legitimate rights to influence organizational processes and outcomes. Managing triple bottom-line performance involves not only managing inwards but also managing outwards, responding to and influencing the diverse demands of many stakeholder groups.

- Governmental requirements for sustainability (laws, regulations, incentives and penalties) vary widely across political units (nations, states, municipalities). This is a problem for all but the most localized enterprises but particularly for multinational enterprises, and greatly increases the complexity of the leadership task. Just achieving compliance with the varying requirements of these multiple constituencies is a challenge in itself.

- Particular organizations have reached differing stages along the path to corporate sustainability and, often within the same organization, differing stages have been reached by the various divisions, departments and units. For example, two organizations (or organizational sub-units) may be committed to achieving sustainability but one may be still working at achieving *compliance* to government regulations and the expectations of important community stakeholders. Another organization (or sub-unit) may have achieved this years before and be actively pursuing *strategic sustainability* through establishing new markets and developing new products. The leadership task is therefore complicated by the fact that each major phase of sustainability involves different objectives, the introduction of different operational practices, access to different knowledge bases and technical skills, and a distinctive discourse. The nature of effective leadership at each phase of corporate sustainability differs.

- Within the one enterprise, employee awareness and knowledge of sustainability issues varies widely. A particular dilemma for sustainability leaders is that rapid transformational change to create sustainable organizations requires high levels of employee engagement and commitment. This intensifies the need for leaders who can manage transformational change through employee involvement rather than through top-down command and control.

We are facing the need for a shift in the global economy at least equivalent to the historical shift from an agrarian economy to an industrial economy. We must now move from a carbon-based economy to an economy based on alternative, renewable energy sources and move from a globalizing world to a glocalizing world, that is, a world with a new combination of both centralization and decentralization of human activities. Organizations, particularly commercial organizations, are the core of the economy and therefore this shift requires creating a series of major transformations at the enterprise level. Most of the leaders who must make this shift will need new values and new kinds of knowledge and skills for the task. This chapter addresses the nature of this 'New Wave' leadership and ways in which the new leadership cadre can be selected and developed.

Managing the new complexity

Achieving enterprise sustainability requires organizations to address multiple and diverse demands such as acting to redress climate change, to develop policies and practices on social issues such as human rights and worker health and safety, and to maintain or enhance financial outcomes such as return on investment for shareholders. Sustainability champions in managerial positions face a new level of complexity with major implications for the nature of the leadership they must exercise. The first of these new levels of complexity relates to understanding the demands of stakeholders, who reflect the demands of the wider range of external elements that the modern manager faces – in particular the three triple bottom-line elements of economic, social and environmental values. We first explore this particular leadership challenge.

Once again an IBM Global Survey casts some light on this issue. The most recent IBM Global CEO Survey, *Capitalizing on Complexity* (IBM, 2010), emphasizes that the world's public and private sector leaders believe that a rapidly escalating complexity is their biggest challenge – and one that will only increase rapidly in the near future. Part of the increasing complexity faced by enterprise leaders is and will continue to be the broader task of meeting the demands of a wider range of stakeholders than the traditional organization has taken into account.

Integrating the key elements of corporate sustainability

Integrating the three key elements of corporate sustainability involves expanding and redefining the traditional notion of the commercial enterprise. It involves maintaining the requirement that the organization be financially viable and, if a public company, that it make adequate returns to investors. Moving to sustainability involves incorporating social sustainability goals, which include the corporation creating an internal developmental environment for staff and externally meeting the legitimate expectations of key stakeholder groups that the company have a positive impact on the life of the communities it affects. The ecological imperative means ensuring that the corporation meets the expectations of governments and communities by, minimally, eliminating negative impacts on the natural environment and more positively, contributing to the health of the ecology and society with which it interacts.

There are theorists who argue the business case for corporate sustainability (Salzmann, Ionescu-Somers and Steger, 2005), claiming that 'sustainability is simply good business'. The assumption is that there are automatic synergies between the three elements of sustainability and that any actions taken to pursue sustainable objectives will necessarily have a positive impact on the 'bottom line'. We do not doubt that there are often synergies between the three elements; for example, reducing water used in minerals processing can yield substantial savings – so there is a win/win for the environment and the company finances. Similarly, pursuing a strong set of corporate social responsibility policies can add to a company's reputation and attract new investors and bright young professional recruits.

But clearly there are also tensions between the three sustainability elements and the problem becomes to what extent can sustainability be applied as an integrated concept in organizations. The issue for leaders and managers wishing to implement corporate sustainability is that theoretical models that may emerge in the academic management literature are dealing with concepts that are emergent and still highly ambiguous. Absolute standards do not exist and there are major sectoral and national differences in their interpretation. Conditions of uncertainty are compounded by the complexity of the inter-relationships between the economic, social and environmental elements

Some studies focusing on environmental and economic sustainability have identified synergies between these specific elements (Russo and Fouts, 1997; Orlitzky *et al.*, 2003). Russo and Fouts' study (1997), for instance, found that environmental improvements led to financial benefit. Other evidence suggests a link between social sustainability (interpreted as workplace effectiveness and humanistic work structures in organizations) and increased productivity and profits

(Gollan, 2006; Kimmet, 2007). So for example, researchers have shown that the adoption of progressive HR practices such as promoting better environmental management system (EMS) training, feedback, employee reward, engagement and empowerment achieve higher levels of environmental performance (Bhattacharya and Sen, 2004; McWilliams *et al.*, 2006). The positive relationships between all three elements have been well documented in the so-called business case for sustainability (Kurucz *et al.*, 2008).

However, making these changes is never without costs, so there is at least an initial investment and often an ongoing one, which means that the financial viability of the actions will usually be assessed in terms of its potential return on that investment. This is made quite explicit, for example, in home furnishing company IKEA, where there is a clear policy to invest in both ecological and sustainability initiatives wherever possible but with the requirement that the investment should be at least cost-neutral over a period of seven years.

There are also other situations where taking sustainability initiatives threatens the viability of the business itself, at least in the short to medium term, rather than strengthening it. If the core business of a company, for example, is viewed as mining and selling coal or clear felling old-growth forests for woodchips (unsustainable activities in themselves) then clearly sustainability initiatives threaten the economic viability of the business. Of course, one can argue that the leaders of these organizations need to redefine their businesses if they are to survive; however they are often reluctant to do so, particularly while their businesses continue to be highly profitable and/or currently receive the benefit of government subsidies.

The problem with the triple bottom-line approach is that the trade-offs that companies make between the three elements often remain unspecified and tend to privilege the economic/financial benefits to the detriment of the other two elements (Angus-Leppan *et al.*, 2010) and the short term over the long term. The ideal relationship between these three elements is hotly debated in the literature (Margolis and Walsh, 2003; McWilliams and Siegel, 2001). In a recent debate on this between leading scholars in management studies published in the *Academy of Management Perspectives* (Siegel, 2009), Siegel argues that firms should adopt greener management only if it complements other strategies and contributes to shareholder wealth. By contrast, Marcus and Fremeth (2009) argue that greener management should be pursued regardless of whether it contributes to shareholder wealth.

Leading and influencing diverse stakeholder constituencies

A second linked problem for leaders in implementing sustainability initiatives is the wide diversity of stakeholders who preferentially support one or two particular elements. These may include various NGOs who conduct special pleading for human rights or environmental objectives, but often not both, and environmental activists, for example, who support higher employment rather than environmental mitigation. The three elements of the triple bottom line do not confront corporate leaders as abstract concepts but usually as vociferous and emotional demands from rival stakeholder groups. Balancing competing demands and ethical considerations while examining the business case is not a new challenge for executives but doing this as environmental pressures create broader definitions of corporate social and environmental responsibility has added a higher level of complexity and sophistication to decision making. Effective sustainability champions must find ways of identifying and maximizing synergies and resolving the tensions between conflicting demands.

Finally, there is another element of complexity unique to the task of the sustainability champion. Governmental action on sustainability (laws, regulations, incentives and penalties) varies widely across political units (nations, states, municipalities). This is a problem for all but the most localized enterprises but particularly for multinational enterprises, and greatly increases the complexity of the leadership task. Simply achieving compliance with the varying requirements of these multiple constituencies is a challenge in itself.

We have described major elements that contribute to the increasing complexity confronting the enterprise change champion. While this difficulty has some elements unique to sustainability, the increasing intricacy of organizational environments is a challenge for all enterprise leaders as indicated above in our discussion of the IBM global CEO study of 2010.

A move to corporate sustainability necessarily involves leaders having to manage higher levels of complexity. However this is not only a challenge for sustainability leaders but for all contemporary managers. Cherishing nostalgia for a simpler organizational past will not allow the leader of the future to take the effective action needed to survive and thrive in a highly dynamic and complex world. Inevitably leaders in senior executive positions now need to manage outward, relating to the changing expectations of powerful stakeholder groups, identifying synergies between the demands of these groups where they exist and also negotiating optimal trade-offs where demands conflict. For sustainability champions this needs to be done with integrity, respecting both the rights of stakeholder groups and personal and ethical organizational standards.

Changing leadership requirements on the journey to sustainability

Sustainability is not one particular state but rather a process which change agents frequently refer to metaphorically as a 'journey'. Elsewhere we have outlined what we see as the major phases that mark key stages on the journey (Dunphy *et al.*, 2007). Figure 9.1 reproduces the

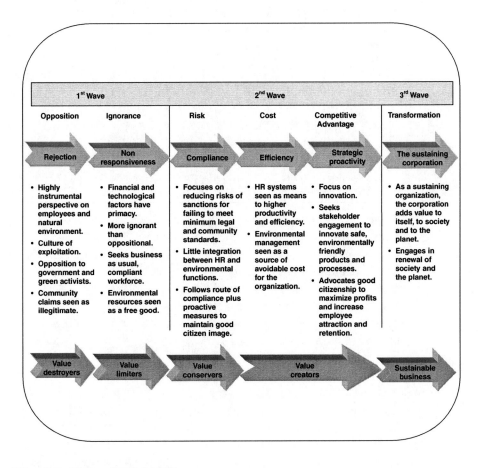

Figure 9.1   Waves of sustainability
Adapted from: Dunphy et al. (2007) p. 17.

broad outline of the six phases of sustainability categorized according to three waves.

The complete model, as shown, moves from opposition to commitment. The intentional movement toward achieving sustainability starts with Phase 3 Compliance and moves through Phases 4 and 5 to Phase 6, The Sustaining Corporation. What we have found in our research is that the sustainability goals, organizational actions and interventions and types of effective leadership vary from phase to phase. The successful sustainability leadership qualities at Phase 3 Compliance are dramatically different from, say, those that are effective at Stage 5 Strategic Proactivity. Not only do the leadership requirements vary but the prevailing discourse around the change process changes from phase to phase also; each phase has its own language, particularly around the dialogue of change toward sustainability, which shapes and is shaped by the core issues emerging in that phase.

So what are the major leadership differences that emerge in the evolution of the sustainable corporation? To answer this question we first briefly review the major theoretical orientations to leadership in the social science literature in order, and show how these theories describe important and distinctive features of leaders at each phase.

A review of current theories of leadership

- **Transactional leadership:** In transactional leadership, the leader influences others using an exchange relationship which appeals to the self-interests of others in the relationship (Bass and Steidlmeier, 1999). Transactional leaders set up reward systems for behaviours that meet their expectations and, if well designed, these reward systems help create a consistent and reliable set of rewards linked to the organization's goals. The transactional leader's interpersonal behaviour then acts as another set of rewards, reinforcing at a day-to-day level the impact of the reward systems.
- **Distributed leadership:** Some recent contributions to leadership theory debunk the 'great person' or 'heroic' theories of leadership and argue that leadership is the capacity to influence others and extends well beyond character and authority as the bases of leadership. Distributed leadership occurs within group situations and involves more than one leader. The basic idea is that within a group or organization, different individuals can exercise leadership functions at different times; no one individual dominates (Pearce and Conger, 2003).

- **Enabling leadership:** A number of scholars emphasize that modern organizations are so complex that traditional leadership notions do not do justice to the role of those in organizations who do not specifically lead themselves but who enable or guide others to do so (Marion and Uhl-Bien, 2001; Plowman *et al.*, 2007). Enabling leaders create 'structures, rules, interactions, interdependencies, tension and culture' that support the leadership actions of others who use these to further their change objectives (Marion, 2008:11).
- **Transformational leadership:** Transformational leadership is evident in leadership behaviours that demonstrably transform and have the ability to motivate others to perform their best – they go beyond their own interests for the sake of the organization as a whole (Avolio, 2009). Transformational leaders are visionary, enthusiastic and confident and the basis for identification by those they influence. Transformational leadership has been strongly identified with change agents who are responsible for organizational innovation, including sustainability innovations (for a comprehensive review see Taylor, 2010).
- **Complexity leadership:** Complexity leadership is a relatively new contribution to leadership theory that derives from recent developments in complexity theory. Leadership in complex systems is viewed as an outcome of many interactions between people in the system and emerges as people try to create order from what may be an uncontrolled and somewhat chaotic process. Complexity theory challenges linear, mechanistic views of organizational behaviour and traditional top-down models where leaders direct the behaviour of those below them in the hierarchy.

In our view, these theories of leadership each have relevance to the nature of effective leadership and have evolved to describe changes in leadership style demanded by an organizational environment of increasing complexity and speed of change. We now relate these theories of leadership to the changing nature of leadership at different phases of the sustainability journey.

A model of phase leadership

Leadership of the Compliance phase: transactional/distributed

In the Compliance phase, sustainability is defined as meeting governmental legislative and statutory requirements and the legitimate demands of stakeholders representing communities and the ecology. Once these demands are taken seriously by senior executives, transactional leadership is important because it rewards organizational members for 'keeping to the rules' and acting according to the norms rather than finding ways around them. Compliance is largely about putting in place new rules around ethical behaviour in areas such as occupational health and safety, emissions monitoring and community relations. Transactional leadership establishes basic trust in the organization and its leaders as employees feel that they are 'getting a fair go', being appropriately rewarded for observing ethical norms and that there is consistency between the values the organization espouses and what it rewards.

However to effectively achieve the institution of both explicit rules and accepted norms, that is, to create a culture of compliance, the Compliance phase also must begin the process of building in leadership capability at all levels of the organization. People at all levels must start to take initiatives in ensuring that the organization is compliant. Compliance is not just about ensuring that the rules are kept, it is also about interpreting how the rules can be applied in specific, sometimes novel, situations to ensure that the purposes for which the rules were instituted are achieved.

Leadership of the Efficiency phase: distributed/enabling

In the Efficiency phase, sustainability is interpreted as minimizing waste and maximizing use of productive resources, without necessarily redefining the strategic direction of the organization. Leaders must be planners, fostering the efficient deployment of finance and other resources internally, analysing the efficiency of day-to-day operations, and identifying and minimizing waste of plant, equipment, materials and human resources. Externally emphasis is placed on negotiating changes with those in the supply chain and delivery systems which also reduce or eliminate waste and pollution and increase efficiency.

At the Efficiency phase, leadership continues to be distributed, as increasing efficiency in the use of resources requires action at all levels of the organization. No one leader can oversee the multitude of changes that need to be introduced but reward systems which rely on transactional leadership can continue to reinforce new norms and behaviours, as long as they are modified to align with the new more efficient operational approaches.

But in addition, enabling leadership becomes increasingly important. At the Compliance phase, a traditional command and control authority-based leadership approach can be relatively effective but as organizations move beyond compliance, internal commitment becomes increasingly important and novel solutions that depart from the status quo are needed. Enabling leaders encourage this (Plowman *et al.*, 2007). They also create active networks across boundaries for information sharing and the emergence of new ideas (Ibarra and Hunter, 2007; Taylor, 2010), as well as managing the conflicts that arise around the dialogue about adopting new approaches to old ways of operating (Taylor, 2010; Uhl-Bien *et al.*, 2007). They move resources to the point in the organization where they are needed to make change happen. Through their authority, networked connections and access to organizational resources, enabling leaders can raise the power of others to achieve far more than they would otherwise be able to do by their own efforts alone.

Taylor, for instance, notes that, 'Proponents of this theory have suggested that enabling leadership suits senior leaders who are patient, comfortable with uncertainty, open to new ideas, proficient in systems thinking and have a propensity to control change' (Taylor, 2010:25).

The combination of senior enabling leaders who back up the actions of the work of other distributed leaders at various levels throughout the organization brings the Efficiency phase to a successful conclusion.

Leadership of the Strategic Proactivity phase: enabling/ transformational

In the Strategic Proactivity phase, enabling leadership continues to be important. Senior executives in particular work to maintain and expand the culture of voluntarism built at the previous phase. At the Efficiency phase, the emphasis was in finding new and improved ways of doing what the organization already does. The Strategic Proactivity phase requires a significant shift in mindset, requiring radical rethinking of the organization's strategies so as to make sustainability central. There is an emphasis on consistently pursuing the opportunities presented by emerging new industries such as alternative energy production or new products such as biodegradable plastics. This kind of radical thinking is needed throughout the organization.

But it is at the Strategic Proactivity phase that transformational leadership comes into its own. Making sustainability central to the corporation's business strategies usually requires a major strategic reorientation, including a radical rethinking of the nature of the business the enterprise is engaged in and of its product and/or service mix.

Transformational leaders work actively with organizational members and stakeholders to develop shared visions; they initiate new organizational directions, modify organizational culture, and work through inspiring and motivating others. They move organizations from one system state to another and can have a marked positive impact on organizational performance (Jones *et al.*, 2006).

Leadership of the Sustaining Corporation phase: transformational/complexity

In the Sustaining Corporation phase, the organization is not content to pursue sustainability only for its business advantages but also adopts an ethical viewpoint that sustainability is worthwhile in its own right. It goes beyond traditional views of the nature of the corporation as existing primarily to make returns for shareholders to a view which sees the corporation as an integral cell in the ecology and society as well as the economy. As such, it regards the function of the 'cell' to contribute to the health of the planet and society on which its own health depends. It therefore actively supports a wider range of activities than is customarily the case and engages with a wider range of stakeholders.

In the Sustaining Corporation, the development of a shared vision is still vital and the activities of the organization are in a process of continuous transformation so that the corporation can remain on the leading edge of change toward a sustainable world. Therefore there is still a powerful need for transformational leadership. However the organization itself and the external relationships and networks that it contributes to and relies on are increasingly complex. This requires a new kind of leadership to come to the fore – complexity leadership.

Sustainability and sustainable development are systems-based concepts and the full development of sustainability depends on recognizing the systemic context of production and consumption (OECD, 2002) (Tukker *et al.*, 2008). The natural and social environments are complex open systems of which we are part and therefore if organizations are to be truly sustainable, corporate leaders must learn to operate within that complexity and with respect for it (Montuori and Purser, 1996). Modern organizations are themselves complex adaptive systems; the move to sustainability increases their level of complexity and also complexifies the leadership task.

Leaders of sustainable organizations emphasize heterarchy rather than hierarchy and heterogeneity rather than homogeneity, ensure that knowledge is distributed across the organization rather than focused in expert and specialized areas, and recognize the need for dynamism and creativity rather than stability and predictability (Montuori and Purser, 1996). Such thinking reflects the growing influence of chaos and complexity theory on organization studies and leadership theory, which themselves are responses to the changing world characterized by these qualities.

Key skills for sustainability leaders

Apart from the distinctive leadership skills outlined above, sustainability leaders require generic organizational change-agent skills. These skills are in three major areas: (1) skills associated with managing one's own personal change, that is, self change skills, (2) skills associated with leading change in interpersonal relationships, and (3) skills of change project leadership including skills for leading organizational change interventions. We will deal with each of these briefly below.

- **Self change skills:** Effective change leaders are able to manage the process of personal change within themselves. In particular, studies of effective transformational leaders show the intimate connection between self transformation and the ability to transform organizations (Fuda, 2010). There is a strong rationale for this. The power of transformational leadership depends on role modelling – as Ghandi said: 'We must first be the change we want to bring about in others.' Recent detailed case studies of effective transformational leaders emphasize that those leaders who transformed the cultures of their organizations also went through a deep process of self transformation themselves (Fuda, 2010).
- **Interpersonal change skills:** Effective change leaders have a broad repertoire of interpersonal skills which they draw upon to influence others. They are aware of and accurately assess their personal impact on others and on the organization – a characteristic that has been labelled 'reflexivity' (Jones *et al.*, 2006). Skills of stakeholder engagement and management have been identified as those of radical transactiveness (Hart and Sharma, 2004). On this view, the ability to identify, interact with and integrate the concerns of traditionally marginalized stakeholders and non-humans, into forward-looking and highly innovative business planning and disruptive change management facilitates both business success and can deliver on social and environmental objectives.
- **Change project leadership skills:** Effective change leaders also have the skills necessary to manage change projects. Modern organizations

are less and less hierarchical structures and more and more moving networks of interrelated change projects. They are characterized less by repetitive standardized operations which continue for lengthy periods largely unchanged, and more by changing novel initiatives with differing time frames for completion.

Consequently, change leaders need to be able to understand and lead both individual change projects and manage the complex and constantly shifting interrelationships between these temporary teams. In doing this, they need to be able to work with the hot human process through influence processes to achieve high performance levels throughout the organization. Figure 9.2 summarizes in more detail the skills needed in each area.

Leadership skills for making organizational change interventions

Effective change agents also need the skills to make a range of macro change interventions at various organizational levels. These range from expertise in mentoring personal change processes to managing mergers and takeovers. Figure 9.3 shows these macroskills in more detail.

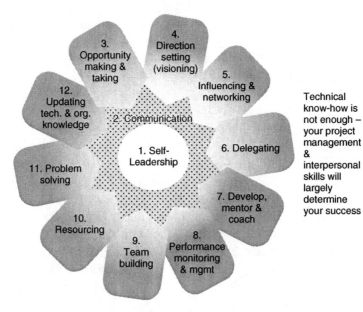

Figure 9.2 Microskills of effective change agents
Adapted from: Dunphy et al. (2007), Figure 9.1, p. 304.

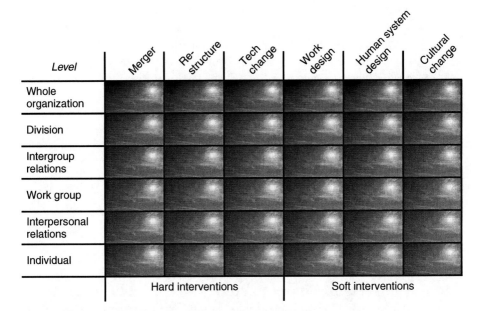

Figure 9.3 *The Dunphy intervention strategy matrix (copyright Dexter Dunphy)*

Of course, no single change leader can possess the full complement of skills we have outlined here and this is particularly true of the macroskills. What is vital for sustainability leaders is to progressively expand their skills base along these lines through experience, training and being mentored, and to understand the skills needed to operate effectively in the context where they choose to make a difference. No single leader can assemble this formidable array of skills. The array of skills needed refers to the team of distributed leaders managing the transition from one phase of sustainability to another. In some situations, particular macro intervention skills may be unnecessary, for example the skills of managing mergers when no merger is involved. But in managing the transition from the Compliance phase to the Efficiency phase, for example, it will be necessary for some change agents to have the skills associated with work redesign.

'New Wave' leadership is leadership of the kind that will take us into the post-carbon world, where transformational change will be the norm not the exception. New Wave leadership involves drawing on all facets of leadership identified by the various leadership theories we have summarized. We have argued the need for significant shifts in the dominant leadership style as an organization progresses through the phases of sustainability we have outlined. We are not, however, arguing that the types of leadership typically used at less advanced stages of sustainability are abandoned as the organization progresses through these phases but rather that some leadership styles are more salient at each stage because they are demanded by the changing sustainability goals at that stage. Transactional leadership, for example, will be part of any well-managed organization, even at the Sustaining Corporation phase.

So we argue that, as we move into the post-carbon world where rapid transformational change is the norm, New Wave leadership draws on the distinctive contributions of leadership theory as a whole not on one particular school within it. This is consistent with the spirit of Avolio and Bass's 'Full Range Leadership Model' (Avolio and Bass, 2004).

Conclusion

We have outlined the increasing complexity of the leadership task as management of commercial enterprises moves from concentrating primarily on satisfying the needs of shareholders to managing an increasingly broad range of stakeholders who are internal and external to the organization. In particular, as organizations move toward a more complete model of sustainability, their leaders must increasingly build a constructive culture of employee involvement and internalized commitment to the implementation of full sustainability. This is the main challenge of managing inward. However the greatest level of increasing complexity comes with the new demands of managing outward – identifying and negotiating with an increasingly complex set of external stakeholders.

As we have outlined above, part of this challenge is to locate important synergies between stakeholder demands and use these synergies to provide momentum for organizational change toward enhanced levels of sustainability. Leadership here involves developing a conscious consensus between the organization and its stakeholders that will provide an impetus to drive support of the organization's evolving sustainability initiatives. Just as the surfer waits for the right wave and, finding a confluence, launches their surfboard forward using the power of the wave, so also the change leader can use the momentum for change in the field surrounding the organization to amplify the organization's power to reach its sustainability objectives.

However it would be naive to imagine that such synergies will not be offset by tensions, that is, differences in ideologies and interests among the stakeholder groups and their expectations for the organization's action on sustainability. Different stakeholders will demand action on some issues and oppose others. Some with a strong investment in the old smokestack economy and maintaining privileged minorities will try to block or impede the organization's move toward a more sustainable relationship with the natural and social worlds. The task of the sustainability champion is to realistically recognize and grapple with these forces, negotiating compromises where necessary and allocating scarce resources to where they will create the greatest impetus for progression.

The complexity of this new leadership task is amplified by the increasing speed of change created in part by the rapid feedback loops that have emerged with the use of modern communication technology. Metaphorically speaking, butterflies flapping their wings on Wall Street or in Afghanistan may create unexpected discontinuities on a global scale. The challenge of discontinuous change is itself magnified by the move to a post-carbon economy, which creates both an increased need for global coordination of some activities and the radical localization of others. Consequently all organizations must be ready for strategic reorientation and have an inbuilt capacity for transformational change. Nevertheless the ultimate leadership objective is clear: to transform all our organizations so that they minimally eliminate their negative impact on the ecology of nature and on society and, better still, contribute to the ongoing health of both sectors.

We have therefore argued for New Wave leadership which is widely distributed and exemplifies across different situations aspects of all the leadership theories we have reviewed. At its highest level, New Wave leadership demonstrates an ability to lead innovative sustainability initiatives within the complexity of sometimes chaotic, rapidly changing environments that are moving into an unknown and uncertain future. Controlling such shifts is an impossible ideal but inspiring, enlisting and empowering multiple players to pursue the sustainability ideal is possible and is already happening, if not yet taking place on the scale that is needed. The challenge of the present and immediate future is to build a cadre of corporate leaders with the skills to collectively accomplish what we need for all species including our own to survive and thrive on this planet.

References

Angus-Leppan, T., Benn, S. and Young, L. (2010). A sensemaking approach to trade-offs and synergies between human and ecological elements of corporate sustainability. *Business Strategy and the Environment*, 19(3), 230–244.

Avolio, B. (2009). Leadership: Current theories, research, and future directions. *Annual Review of Psychology*, 60, 421–449.

Avolio, B. and Bass, B. (2004). *Multifactor Leadership Manual*. Menlo Park, California: Mind Garden Inc.

Bass, B. M. and Steidlmeier, P. (1999). Ethics, character, and authentic transformational leadership behaviour. *Leadership Quarterly*, 10(2), 181–217.

Benn, S., Dunphy, D. and Perrott, B. (eds) (2011). *Cases in Corporate Sustainability and Change: A Multidisciplinary Approach*. Prahhan, Victoria: Tilde University Press.

Berns, M., Townend, A., Khayat, Z., Balagopal, B., Reeves, M. and Hopkins, M. (2009). *The Business of Sustainability: Findings and insights from First Annual Business of Sustainability Survey and the Global Thought Leaders Research Project*. MIT Sloan Management Review in collaboration with BCG.

Bhattacharya, C. B. and Sen, S. (2004). Doing better at doing good: When, why, and how consumers respond to corporate social initiatives. *California Management Review*, 47(1), 9–24.

Dunphy, D., Griffiths, A. and Benn, S. (2007). *Organizational Change for Corporate Sustainability: A Guide for Leaders and Change Agents of the Future*. Abingdon, New York: Routledge.

Flannery, T. (2010). *Here on Earth – An Argument for Hope*. Melbourne: Text Publishing.

Fuda, P. (2010). Leadership transformation – what does it take for traditional managers to transform into contemporary leaders? DBA thesis, Macquarie Graduate School of Management, Sydney.

Gollan, P. (2006). High involvement management and human resource line sustainability. *Handbook of Business Strategy*, 7, 279–286.

Hart, S. L. and Sharma, S. (2004). Engaging fringe stakeholders for competitive imagination. *Academy of Management Executive*, 18(1), 7–18.

Ibarra, H. and Hunter, M. (2007). How Leaders Build and Use Networks. *Harvard Business Review*, 85(1), 40–47.

IBM (2008a). Global CEO Survey. New York.

IBM (2008b). *Making Change Work*. New York.

IBM (2010). Global CEO Survey. New York.

Jones, Q., Dunphy, D., Fishman, R., Larne, M. and Canter, C. (2006). *In Great Company: Unlocking the Secrets of Cultural Transformation*. Sydney: Human Synergistics.

Kimmet, J. (2007). Partnering for sustainability in the workplace. *International Journal of Environment, Workplace and Employment*, 3, 37–49.

Kurucz, E., Colbert, B. and Wheeler, D. (2008). The business case for corporate social responsibility. In: A. Crane, A. McWilliams, D. Matten, J. Moon and D. Seigel (eds), *The Oxford Handbook of Corporate Social Responsibility*. Oxford: Oxford University Press, 83–112.

Marcus, A. A. and Fremeth, A. R. (2009). Green Management Matters Regardless, *Academy of Management Perspectives*, 23, 17–26.

Margolis, J. D. and Walsh, J. P. (2003). Misery loves companies: Rethinking social initiatives by business. *Administrative Science Quarterly*, 48(2), 268–305.

Marion, R. (2008). Complexity theory for organizations and organizational leadership. In: M. Uhl-Bien and R. Marion (eds), *Complexity Leadership: Conceptual Foundations*, 1–17. Information Age Publishing.

Marion, R. and Uhl-Bien, M. (2001). Leadership in complex organizations. *Leadership Quarterly*, 12(4), 389.

McWilliams, A. and Siegel, D. (2001). Corporate social responsibility: a theory of the firm perspective. *Academy of Management Review*, 26(1), 117–127.

McWilliams, A., Siegel, D. and Wright, P. (2006). Corporate social responsibility: Strategic implications. *Journal of Management Studies*, 43(1), 1–18.

Montuori, A. and Purser, R. (1996). Ecological futures: Systems theory, postmodernism, and participative learning in an age of uncertainty. In: Boje, D., Gephart, D. and Joseph, T. (eds), *Postmodernism and Organization Theory*, 181–201. Newbury Park: Sage.

OECD (2002). *Towards Sustainable Household Consumption? Trends and Policies in OECD Countries Consumption? Trends and Policies in OECD Countries*. Paris.

Orlitzky, M., Schmidt, F. L. and Rynes, S. L. (2003). Corporate social and financial performance: A meta-analysis. *Organization Studies*, 24(3), 403–441.

Pearce, C. and Conger, J. (2003). All those years ago: the historical underpinnings of shared leadership. In: C. Pearce and J. Conger (eds), *Shared Leadership.* Thousand Oaks: Sage Publications.

Plowman, D. A., Solansky, S., Beck, T. E., Baker, L., Kulkarni, M. and Travis, D. V. (2007). The role of leadership in emergent, self-organization. *The Leadership Quarterly*, 18(4), 341–356.

Russo, M. and Fouts, P. (1997). A resource-based perspective on corporate environmental performance and profitability. *The Academy of Management Journal*, 40(3), 534–559.

Salzmann, O., Ionescu-Somers, A. and Steger, U. (2005). The business case for corporate sustainability: Literature review and research options. *European Management Journal*, 23(1), 27–36.

Siegel, D. S. (2009). Green management matters only if it yields more green: An economic/strategic perspective, *Academy of Management Perspectives*, 23, 5–16.

Taylor, A. (2010). Sustainable urban water management: The champion phenomenon, Ph.D thesis. Monash University, Melbourne, at arrow.monash.edu.au (accessed 7 October, 2010).

Tukker, A., Emmert, S., Charter, M., Vezzoli, C., Stø, S., Andersen, *et al.* (2008). Introduction. In: A. Tukker. *et al.* (eds), *System Innovation for Sustainability 1: Perspectives on Radical Changes to Sustainable Consumption and Production*, 1–13. Sheffield: Greenleaf Publishing.

10 Leadership for the age of sustainability

A dualities approach to organizational change

Fiona Sutherland and Aaron C. T. Smith

Introduction

Conventional approaches to managing and introducing organizational change adopt a linear, rational model, prioritizing control under the stewardship of a strong leader or 'guiding coalition'. Underlying this top-down, leader-centric approach remains the enduring assumption that organizational change follows an inexorable and universal pattern. Change operates as a finite, one-off phenomenon invoking a series of predictable, reducible steps enabling senior managers to mandate new work routines. However, in the face of unprecedented environmental turbulence and uncertainty, standard leadership approaches, conceiving change as an inconvenient distraction to be brought under control as expeditiously as possible, only lead to disappointment. Top-down leadership control in the age of sustainability is unworkable because it fails to appreciate that change occurs naturally and is intimately entwined with continuity. At a time when organizations must be capable of adapting to immense competition while maintaining new levels of environmental and ethical performance, change leadership must assume a new form. We argue in this chapter that the change–continuity continuum defines organizations. The ability to exploit and explore simultaneously comes at the price of new leadership dynamics. Sustainable leadership means accepting that organizational change has changed. Successful change no longer equates with fast change. We propose that sustainable leadership for change demands accepting a worldview where either/or choices such as flexibility or control are misleading. We argue that change and continuity do not exist as opposite sides of the leadership see-saw, but co-exist as dualities that sit side by side without compromising one another.

The sustainable leader has to be comfortable with dynamic and hostile environments. Change takes place within a context of rigid structures of accountability and due process, but also where short-term competitiveness and long-term economic performance rely upon innovation underpinned by fluidity. As organizational boundaries blur and organizations operate in global markets, responsible leaders are faced with managing 'loose/tight' relationships, establishing structures that enhance flexibility and responsiveness while bolstering performance efficiencies. Flexibility and responsiveness remain essential, but not sufficient, conditions for the achievement of sustainable competitive advantage. Consequently, in turbulent and uncertain environments, a leadership approach focussed on maintaining stability and order is constrained and inevitably becomes counterproductive. Research evidence from numerous organizational change cases (Leanne and Barry, 2000; Luscher and Lewis, 2008; Davis *et al.*, 2009) demonstrates that healthy organizations rely on an interactive mix of continuity and change. The key to long-term sustainability therefore depends on being able to manage these seemingly paradoxical dualities effectively. To cope with these concomitant imperatives, leaders must ensure that organizations remain sites of enduring change and continuity, combining flexible, innovative responses with reliable and consistent performance (Farjoun, 2010). A new leadership lens is therefore required; one that recognizes and accepts the pluralistic extremes that exist in organizations, such as: the need for strong leadership which supports empowerment; efficiency and creativity; long-term vision and short-term performance management; and cost control and quality (Cameron and Quinn, 1988; Evans, 1999; Lewis, 2000). Exploiting the push/pull tension between organizational dualities provides the stimulus for organizational renewal and sustainability.

The continuity–change dilemma represents a central organizational conundrum that has perplexed and consumed management scholars and practitioners for decades (Hedberg *et al.*, 1976; Cameron and Quinn, 1988; Farjoun, 2010). Change and continuity represent competing but complementary narratives, introducing both ambiguity and novelty to destabilize as well as validate existing organizational routines. In practice, change intimately entwines with continuity, allowing the simultaneous exploitation of strengths and the exploration of new opportunities. The challenge for leadership sustainability lies with determining how to simultaneously maximize performance efficiencies while enhancing flexibility. Managing the continuity–change duality guards against complacency and inertia, and underpins an organization's capacity both to exploit and explore for sustainable competitive success. We argue that a dualities approach to leadership provides an advantageous conceptual framework for exploring and exploiting the tensions that arise from what appear to be competing directives. Since ethical dilemmas emerge from tensions, we suggest that leadership decision-making can benefit from a dualities conception of change. Duality theory offers unique insight into the complexities, ambiguities and nuances of the change management process.

Duality theory advocates that the leadership practices behind the ostensibly contradictory efficiency–flexibility duality represent complementary tensions. Both need to exist rather than seeking to find some equitable balance. That is, the pursuit of long-term sustainability does not constrain the introduction of radical change; short-term profitability does not come at the expense of continuity. For the ethical leader, this means that the structures and practices supporting organizational change can offer both freedom and control. In the first section of this chapter, we consider the continuity–change challenge confronting organization leaders in their pursuit of performance efficiency and long-term economic sustainability. We consider the importance of adopting a dualities-aware perspective to exploit and explore what we claim are in fact fundamental interdependencies between ostensibly competing leadership directives. The second section of this chapter elaborates upon duality theory. We propose that sustainable economic growth depends on the way leaders manage the twin imperatives of continuity and change. Building on this premise, the third section introduces dualities-aware leadership and the dualities characteristics change leaders should manipulate. A framework for sustainable change leadership is presented in the penultimate section of the chapter, providing a model showing how to manage dual approaches such as control and collaboration, accountability and flexibility, and hierarchy and networks. In the final section, we suggest that sustainable change demands an acceptance of tension around ethical decision making.

Organizational dualities: the leadership challenge

The rational, top-down approach to change leadership presupposes the centrality of discipline, order and control. Change is viewed as an exception, a passing irritation to be dealt with as quickly as possible in order to return once more to a stable, steady state operating under predictable conditions. Katz and Kahn (1966:449), for example, argued that organizations seek to maintain stability through 'authority structures, reward mechanisms, and value systems'. These become embedded in an organization's psyche, and represent the subconscious taken-for-granted 'way we do things around here' that notoriously elude challenge. The possibility of leading change by simultaneously maintaining divergent dual states does not enter the frame. Leadership decision-making has therefore emphasized 'either/or' choices, or some sort of uneasy compromise between assumed opposites that define change and continuity, such as innovation and efficiency, collaboration and competition, freedom and accountability, empowerment and leadership, or economic and ethical goals. Traditional frameworks ignore the dynamic, complex and contradictory nature of organizations as well as the diverse people working in them, with their individual needs and idiosyncrasies. As a result, conventional leadership methods also sidestep ethical judgements by assuming they will lead to unfavourable economic outcomes. But economic and ethical objectives are not mutually exclusive. In fact, duality theory insists that such forces are complementary rather than contradictory. And, ironically, the intersection of stability and change (what complexity theory advocates refer to as the 'edge of chaos') delivers unique opportunities for organizational renewal. As Tsoukas and Chia (2002:568) observed, 'If change is viewed as the exception, the occasional episode in organizational life, we underestimate how pervasive change already is.' A better approach recognizes and accepts that change and continuity rely on each other in order to function effectively. Farjoun (2010:203), for example, argued that stability comprises both static and dynamic attributes; the former implies efficiency through stasis and rigidity while the latter implies building robust, long-term dynamic efficiencies that buttress against environmental downturns. A solid foundation of organizational stability therefore serves as 'both an outcome and medium of change' (Farjoun, 2010:203). It provides the solid base from which explorative, innovative ventures, critical for organizational renewal and longevity, can proceed. But, of course, in order for leadership to be sustainable, it must operate from both the top down as well as emergently.

Duality theory proposes that the tension or 'dynamic synthesis' between contradictory forces within organizations provides a catalyst for self-renewal (Pascale, 1990). To be effective as a leader requires appreciating the pluralistic extremes that exist in organizations, such as the need for strong leadership that supports empowerment, efficiency and creativity, long-term vision and short-term performance management, and cost control and quality (Cameron and Quinn, 1988; Evans, 1999; Lewis, 2000). Rational, 'either/or' thinking would try and resolve the paradoxical tension between these 'conflicting truths' by favouring one extreme (Lewis, 2000:761). However, by prioritizing the stable dimensions (e.g. control and accountability) over the less certain dimensions (e.g. flexibility and change), organizational leaders dilute the 'enlightening' potential of paradox (Lewis, 2000:763). In contrast, exploring the links between opposing dimensions and exploiting the opportunities that arise from tension provides organizational leaders with sustainable options.

We claim that when leaders recognize organizations as dynamic rather than static entities they begin to see contradictions as advantageous side-effects of complex structures. Rather than trying to resolve opposing forces, leaders should accept the tension between order and disorder (Pettigrew and Fenton, 2000) and mine the creative potential of the torsion inherent in change (Evans, 1999). The resulting shift in focus from organizational similarity to plurality infers a more nuanced, holistic way of thinking. However, by recognizing complementarity within contradiction, 'opposites cease to be opposites' (Schumacher, 1977:126). Change leaders therefore benefit when change represents an exercise in 'paradox management' through the opportunity to explore rather than suppress the dual tensions and ambiguities that abound in organizations (Lewis, 2000:764). We believe a 'dualities aware' perspective provides such an opportunity.

Conventionally organizational change theories treat dual organizational attributes such as stability and change, control and flexibility, and efficiency and creativity as independent, unrelated variables. Most theoretical perspectives privilege one pole at the expense of the other (Van de Ven and Poole, 1988). The problem remains that a unidirectional mode of thinking collapses irrevocably in the face of dynamic organizational environments characterized by paradox and contradiction (Cameron and Quinn, 1988; Clegg et al., 2002). While prescriptive logic of the kind common in change theories seeks to resolve the contradiction by selecting one extreme over another, duality thinking encompasses the notion of 'both/and' rather than 'either/or', which 'entails building constructs that accommodate contradictions' (Lewis, 2000:773). Duality theory specifies that complementarities exist within contradiction and their synergistic co-existence ensures that the qualities of both dimensions (such as freedom and accountability; short-term and long-term; integration and differentiation) are recognized and exploited. Effective change leadership means appreciating how dualistic forces can shape and enable change. By adopting a dualities-aware perspective, leaders can come to terms with the intuitive desire to resolve contradiction by instead managing the complementarities within contradictory forces. A dualities perspective encourages organizational leaders to explore continuity–change tensions instead of equilibrating opposing forces (Lewis, 2000) or prioritizing one pole over the other. And when leaders accept ambiguity as both natural and essential to organizational transformations, they take ownership of powerful forces for change.

Duality theory – originally a by-product of Giddens' (1984) structuration theory – suggests that dualism elements may be independent and conceptually distinct, rather than opposed. Thus, change theorists who employ duality theory 'maintain conceptual distinctions without being committed to a rigid antagonism or separation of the two elements being distinguished' (Jackson 1999:549). In a change leadership context within an organization, this kind of thinking implies that pairs like stability and change, order and disorder, and predictability and unpredictability operate by 'mutual specification' rather than mutual exclusivity (Ford and Backoff, 1988:100). But how do organizational leaders accommodate the dualistic tensions that accompany a commitment to either continuity ('tight' structures, control, stability, exploitative) or change ('loose' structures, flexible, responsive, explorative)? To put the issue simply, how can leaders of organizational change pursue change *and* continuity at the same time?

Our answer introduces duality theory into change leadership. We propose that a dualities-aware perspective offers organizational leaders conceptual guidance in identifying the tensions of change and their power to challenge existing ways of thinking (Graetz and Smith, 2008). A dualities-aware approach depends upon understanding how dualities work. We reveal the composition of dualities by defining their characteristics. In the following section, we begin by further discussing the concept of dualities. We next explain the form and function of five duality characteristics and their application in managing the tensions, uncertainties and ambiguities between continuity and change. Our chapter culminates in a conceptual framework of the five duality characteristics and their change management implications. Operationalizing the duality characteristics makes explicit, and forces consideration of, competing continuity–change goals. In turn, the interacting, iterative nature of duality characteristics encourages a bimodal approach, helping organizational leaders to appreciate the interplay between apparently competing continuity–change goals and how these might shape and facilitate their change interventions for both short-term competitive success and long-term sustainability.

Duality theory: context and content

Our position maintains that sustainable economic growth depends on the way leaders manage the twin imperatives of continuity and change.

How can organization leaders deal with such contradictory and complex forces? Duality theory presents at least part of the answer. It suggests that the key lies in allowing, and even deliberately encouraging, a state of tension to emerge (Lewis, 2000). A dualities lens provides a vehicle for exploring the kind of leadership where complexity and contradiction can operate in organizations, rather than be removed, micro-managed, ignored or denied. Dualities thinking compels sensitivity and receptiveness to the complexities, ambiguities and contradictions intertwined in day-to-day routines. In fact, some change leaders would likely find that a dualities approach embracing pluralism can be liberating (Johnston and Selsky, 2006). The real leadership challenge that accompanies accepting ambiguity as a 'valued asset' remains that organizations 'are not generally equipped to cope with fragmentation and high ambiguity' (Seo *et al.*, 2004:162).

Our resolution comes in the form of a 'dualities-aware perspective'. Organizational change leaders need to equip their change agents with the capacity, not to mention the authority and confidence, to work with both poles simultaneously (Graetz and Smith, 2008). In part this demands a re-conceptualization about how change works; from the assumption that change interrupts continuity and stability, to the perspective that change and continuity perpetually co-exist. In short, dualities do not offer an either/or option. Consequently, rather than seeking resolution toward one position, a dualities-aware approach encourages a constructive tension (Evans, 1999; Evans *et al.*, 2002) between extremes of adaptive and manipulative acts (Hedberg *et al.*, 1976). With this paradigmatic shift comes the need for a different kind of leadership that approaches organizational change as a sustainable activity.

A dualities-aware approach depends on understanding how dualities operate. That is, their characteristics need to be clear. Lewis (2000) confirmed the value of understanding duality characteristics by suggesting that as a framework for change, it represents a vehicle for exploring *what* sorts of tensions exist, *why* they might trigger reinforcing cycles, and *how* actors might manage paradoxes manifest in dualities as a catalyst for change and understanding. A paradox in a dualities context arises as a range of contradictory yet interrelated elements such as perspectives, feelings, messages, identities, interests or practices. As 'constructed' entities, they explain the efforts made by change managers to simplify and make sense of the complexities and uncertainties in the work environment, because it is natural to want to resolve rather than embrace contradictory elements (Lado *et al.*, 1997:112). By adopting a dualities-aware perspective, however, organization leaders may come to appreciate dualities, such as stability and change, as fundamentally interdependent and 'mutually enabling constituent' parts (Farjoun, 2010:205).

In the following section, we propose five central characteristics of duality leadership to help articulate a sustainable and ethical position for leaders faced with the need for constant change in organizations, where change is perceived as inexorably risky. Tackling the leadership duality for organizational change includes dealing with the *simultaneous* presence of competing and ostensibly contradictory change interventions. However, these competing interventions are actually *relational*, in that they are symbiotic, requiring a *minimal threshold* level of each in order to function optimally. As a consequence, the leadership duality is characterized by *dynamism,* ensuring a creative tension between continuity and change, critical to self-renewal and learning. These four characteristics illustrate that dualities evolve, interact and are shaped through the *improvisation* of a leader.

Dualities-aware leadership

We use the term 'characteristic' to describe a prominent aspect or a definable, differentiating and universal feature, trait or property (Graetz and Smith, 2008). Understanding the characteristics of dualities reveals the implications of change leadership interventions and subsequent choices. Our argument is that both continuity and change need to be encouraged, but this requires a leadership mindset where mediation works toward simultaneity and synergistic mutuality. The following discussion identifies and describes five duality characteristics: (1) Simultaneity; (2) Relational; (3) Minimal thresholds; (4) Dynamism; and (5) Improvisation. The argument presented here hinges on the importance of considering the five duality characteristics as a unit that operates in collaboration.

It helps to perceive duality characteristics as escalating. Simultaneity is the most basic property. But, the simultaneous presence of competing change and continuity goals represents a necessary but not sufficient condition for dualities to emerge. Because organizational forms and practices are interdependent and relational, minimal levels of competing forces are needed to create the benefit to be realized from both the poles of continuity and change. However, thresholds shift with contextual pressure, so for dualities to endure they must also possess a dynamic property. Ultimately, improvisation infuses dualities because the previous conditions do not arise without some form of intervention (Graetz and Smith, 2008).

1. The simultaneity advantage

Simultaneity provides the foundation duality characteristic. Dualities represent the simultaneous presence of what conventionally have been considered contradictory if not mutually exclusive elements (Cameron and Quinn, 1988; Van de Ven and Poole, 1988). Nearly 40 years ago, Lawrence and Lorsch (1967) argued that organizational sustainability would depend increasingly on leaders' abilities to manage heterogeneous environments in which dynamic parts of organizations operate simultaneously alongside stable parts. Similarly, Abernathy (1978) observed that an organization's long-term survival depends not only on its ability to increase efficiency, but also on its ability to be efficient and innovative simultaneously. The importance of dualistic simultaneity to organization leaders is further underlined by Pascale's (1990) claim that the tension or 'dynamic synthesis' between contradictory opposites provides the catalyst for long-term organizational effectiveness and self-renewal. If not paradoxical, simultaneity seems at least ironic in that there is no point in being efficient at under-performance; the 'holy grail' of change leadership comes with the achievement of innovation that can be exploited through consistent practices.

From a leadership perspective, simultaneity's 'both/and' kind of thinking opens up novel perspectives and new opportunities. Responsible leaders can challenge existing preconceptions about the organizing and structuring legacies of past, more benign and certain times. Increasing environmental turbulence has fuelled the need to manage existing revenue streams while trialling new initiatives (March, 1991; Smith and Tushman, 2005). Awareness of simultaneity encourages leaders to establish 'loose', organic operations encouraging grassroots, creative thinking and innovation to emerge, while working within a clear performance-management framework that ensures quality, accountability and consistency. Limerick and Cunnington (1993), for example, present new forms of organizing as 'loosely coupled' systems characterized by autonomy and interdependence. Simultaneity sharpens the focus on change leadership as a strategic force where differentiation and integration sit side by side. The potential for complementary 'pathways' helps leaders to question the conventional tendency to favour one over the other (Raisch et al., 2009:685).

Some compelling case evidence indicates that sustainability depends on managing the tension between exploration and exploitation (March, 1991; Sundaramurthy and Lewis, 2003; O'Reilly and Tushman, 2004; Smith and Tushman, 2005). Exploration means change in the form of innovation and the flexibility that underpins its pursuit. Exploitation means continuity by capitalizing upon success through the efficiencies that drive profit economies. If we accept the claim for tension, the role that leaders play in securing a balance between differentiation and integration becomes critical. Furthermore, simultaneity highlights that the 'relative balance' between differentiation and integration depends on the nature of the task or initiative under consideration, which is likely to alternate between explorative (long-term innovation) and exploitative (short-term efficiencies) (Smith and Tushman, 2005; Raisch *et al.*, 2009:687). Simultaneity thus provides the leadership platform for exploiting existing systems and structures that underwrite the exploration of new opportunities. In this respect, change leadership is less about finding the balance between exploration and exploitation, and more about maximizing both at the same time. As O'Reilly and Tushman (2004) argued, traditional performance structures and processes set the parameters and provide a stable base from which experimentation and exploration for new growth opportunities can occur. This suggests that the focus for organization leaders should not be on managing stability *or* change, but on managing both simultaneously, developing 'understandings and practices' (Sundaramurthy and Lewis, 2003:397) that encourage a creative tension to exist between the two. And tension comes when both are pursued aggressively, rather than when an equitable and moderate balance is negotiated.

Environmental turbulence means that leaders must be comfortable and confident with managing tension. Leadership framed by tension necessitates accepting an amalgam of 'simultaneously contradictory' forces involving conflict and compromise, control and collaboration, loose/tight relationships, social and economic goals, differentiation and integration. For example, leaders must simultaneously manage control (decisive direction and leadership) and collaboration (empowerment and support), particularly in uncertain environments. Control provides performance rigour while collaboration amplifies creative potential (Sundaramurthy and Lewis, 2003). Leaders need to drive tension to ensure enduring change and uninterrupted continuity, combining flexible, innovative responses with reliable and consistent performance (Farjoun, 2010).

Simultaneity and contradiction reveal the push/pull tension of organizational dualities, such as accountability and freedom, individuality and teamwork, action and reflection, and competition and cooperation (Evans, 1992; Evans *et al.*, 2002; Pettigrew *et al.*, 2003). While 'apparent' opposites, they operate through 'mutual specification' as complementary and interdependent activities (Ford and Backoff, 1988:102). Leaders who consider issues of strategizing and organizing from a dualities-sensitive perspective do not attempt to resolve or eliminate these inherent contradictions, but instead encourage a complementary interplay between simultaneously operating forces. The interactive, 'operational' characteristics of 'simultaneity' also highlight the relational nature of duality characteristics.

2. The relational advantage

The bimodal nature of duality-aware leadership, integral to simultaneity, also manifests in its relational, interdependent nature. The relational characteristic emphasizes mutuality. Complementary forces exist between ostensibly opposing dualities such as stability and change. The relational characteristic highlights the competing yet complementary forces leaders need to manage. The most common of these include: increasing efficiency as well as creativity; building individualistic teams; providing strong leadership while supporting empowerment; maintaining hierarchies while creating networks; controlling costs while enhancing quality; and thinking globally while acting locally (Evans, 1999; Lewis, 2000). Bidirectional relationships therefore involve not only simultaneous, but also mutual feedback: 'When these relationships are symmetrical, we are in the presence of a synthesis – a synthesis that emerges in the *relationship* between the two opposite poles rather than their merger into a schizophrenic entity' (Clegg *et al.*, 2002:494). This reciprocal relationship becomes paramount when leading through the respective logics of exploration and exploitation; where new possibilities collide with old certainties (He and Wong, 2004). Recognizing the bidirectional relationship between exploration and exploitation is critical to sustainability because it leads to a dual focus on short-term viability and long-term growth (He and Wong, 2004). From a leadership perspective, the relational characteristic works in consonance with simultaneity, dynamism and improvisation. Leaders explore the links between opposing dimensions, and exploit the tensions that arise from simultaneous modes of operation.

The relational characteristic's emphasis on mutual reinforcement shows that organizations cannot be compartmentalized. No practices exist independent of others (Graetz and Smith, 2008). Dualities may also relate to other dualities, leading to bipolar systems (Pettigrew *et al.*, 2003) or sets of dualities. Certain dualities match because they represent similar tensions leading to the formation of meta-dualities. For example, routine–novelty, redundancy–efficiency and narrowness–openness can collectively intensify the level of tension. As we argue next, the more tension the better. As a result, a dualities perspective can make 'strange notions' understandable, such as the way failure can act as a catalyst for renewal (Farjoun, 2010:216). As relational interdependence suggests, a change to one can affect all of the others as well (Graetz and Smith, 2008).

3. The minimal thresholds advantage

Dualities need a minimal threshold. Clegg *et al.* (2002) argued that the poles must be maintained at a minimum level to ensure that a centrifugal (enabling) rather than centripetal (constraining) force emerges. In other words, as Hedberg *et al.* (1976) advocated, organizations should maintain a minimal threshold of desirable attributes. For example, a minimal threshold level of exploration and exploitation are essential in order to create the kind of tensions leaders can employ to empower new opportunities while reaping the benefits of old opportunities (Graetz and Smith, 2008). In one case example, Davis *et al.* (2009:438) found that 'simple rules' and 'semi-structures' were advantageous across different environments, and most vital in unpredictable ones. Duality thinking excels under such conditions. Leaders need the confidence of formal structures with control during environmental uncertainty, but also need the responsiveness to seek solutions to new problems that future market winners will solve. A degree of ambiguity, contradiction and incoherence thus provides organization leaders with the catalyst for organizational learning, diversity and renewal.

The challenge for leaders lies in determining the desirable minimal threshold between two extremes on the organizing continuum. For example, sustainability depends on the explorative and exploitative initiatives executed by leaders (Smith and Tushman, 2005). But it is easy to fall into the trap of overzealous exploration which undermines efficiency and control by leaping into risk or even catastrophe. On the other hand, dogged exploitation can stymie organizational learning leading to inertia, conservatism and rigidity. Innovation and performance enhancing practices both need vigorous support.

According to Smith and Tushman (2005:533), leading change management means embedding strategic contradiction in 'senior team cognitions', cognitive frames in which paradox is part of the senior team psyche. Within a paradox framework, contradiction is not suspicious but rather is integral to operating a viable, dynamic organization. Paradoxical cognition enables exploitative and explorative initiatives, as well as integrating between these strategies and structures (Smith and Tushman, 2005). The characteristic 'minimal thresholds' depends upon a corresponding dynamic between the 'simultaneity' and 'relational' duality characteristics to ensure a healthy tension between two opposing poles. The purposeful, active connection between characteristics leads us to consider the role of the characteristic 'dynamism'.

4. The dynamism advantage

In discussing the simultaneous, relational nature of dualities, the dynamic and fluid quality of dualities can been seen. The duality characteristic of dynamism underlines the bimodal, interactive nature of dualities relationships by emphasizing the importance of energy and feedback (Cameron and Quinn, 1988). In this way, dynamism demonstrates how duality thinking specifies that poles represent complementary forces that provide a dynamic interaction. In essence, organizations never reach a state of balanced equilibrium (Evans and Doz, 1992), but do risk a disequilibrium where one pole dominates, or worse, where both poles operate at low levels. The ability to change the level of tension dynamically may well be central to creativity and performance (Galunic and Eisenhardt, 2001). The simultaneous presence of competing tensions invokes the motor of adaptation, which plays a role in stimulating a dynamism between continuity and change, and order and disorder (Galunic and Eisenhardt, 2001).

Working to unleash dynamism, leaders need to harness the resources that accompany stability. The key lies with building an acceptance and ease with uncertainty. Dynamism, in conjunction with the simultaneity and relational characteristics, fuels exploitation and exploration, thereby guarding against inertia and complacency, the show-stopping accoutrements of success. Connectivity between the dynamic characteristic of dualities and their relational properties also acknowledges the significance of minimal thresholds in mitigating against the danger of going to an extreme. The 'dynamism' characteristic thus works with its counterparts, simultaneity, relational and minimal thresholds, to maintain a 'constructive' tension, 'a state where there is sufficient tension to mobilize change and action, but not so much as to engender politicization or perverse, unintended consequences' (Evans, 1999:330). Of course, the first four properties demand the active engagement of leaders through improvisation.

5. The improvisation advantage

The dynamic and symbiotic properties that go along with leading change with a dualities mindset introduce the importance of improvisation (Graetz and Smith, 2008). Improvisation might be seen as the fusion of intended and emergent action which manifests as a mix of control with innovation, exploitation with exploration, and routine with non-routine (Weick, 1998). In this sense, improvisation represents a dynamic and central component of dualities, intrinsically embedded as a consequence of its emergent potential (Tsoukas and Chia, 2002). Improvisation illustrates the value of a bidirectional relationship between two opposing poles. Leaders respond in practice by employing activities that alter, revise, create and discover rather than simply shift, switch or add (Weick, 1998). The goal is a dynamic interplay between duality poles. For example, plans and action (representing continuity and change) are not separate. Rather, plans become amended through improvisation as the result of changing circumstances, both before and during their enactment (Clegg *et al.*, 2002). From a leader's perspective, improvisation provides the primary mechanism for change mediation as it reinforces how two organizing dualities can work dynamically to shape strategic decision-making. Improvisation can therefore be seen as the ongoing, iterative action which works in sync with the characteristics simultaneity, relational, minimal thresholds and dynamism to manage continuity and change. In the following section, we explore how leaders can improvise to leverage duality characteristics.

Leading change toward sustainability: managing tension

Figure 10.1 provides a framework of the five duality characteristics and typical continuity–change dualities that organization leaders must deal with daily. It defines the nature and role of each characteristic and how they operate in tandem to manage dual approaches such as control and collaboration, accountability and flexibility, and hierarchy and networks.

It also aims to depict their role in arbitrating between the competing continuity–change goals. Simultaneity, which captures the heterogeneous, qualitative nature of dualities, represents a leader's starting point for understanding and managing organizational dualities. The relational duality characteristic points to the interactive, symbiotic attributes of the dualistic tensions that arise from continuity and change. In addition, relational interdependence within these dual forms of organizing highlights the advantages that come from managing contradictions as complementarities. This in turn illustrates the importance of a 'both/and' rather than 'either/or' mindset, facilitated through a dynamic balance of minimal levels along the continuity–change continuum. The characteristic dynamism keeps the minimum thresholds in tune to ensure the organization stays poised on the competitive cusp (Deephouse, 1999) between order and disorder, and that an enabling tension is maintained between exploration and exploitation. Improvisation serves as the arbiter between the intended and the emergent by encouraging simultaneity, interdependence, minimal thresholds and dynamism. Improvisation works deliberately and extemporaneously to ensure that contradictions become complementarities.

From a leadership perspective, taking action to enable the five characteristics requires a profound, almost paradigmatic, mind-shift. It necessitates moving from ordered, linear approaches to change leadership that stress stability and control, to working confidently with paradox and ambiguity, which treat change and continuity as fundamentally interdependent, 'mutually enabling' forces. We propose that the characteristics also imply boundary principles that can be placed around change leadership to bolster the exploration of dualities. For example, simple heuristics can work effectively as guidelines around which minimal thresholds can be established more safely. That is, a high degree of flexibility can be introduced in certain areas while still maintaining high levels of control. For example, MacIntosh and MacLean (2001) have shown how pockets of innovation can be cultivated without compromising the stability that comes through performance management.

Duality boundary heuristics can also help to lead change in complex, non-linear systems where the innovation that accompanies putative 'edge of chaos' conditions can be approached without fear of degenerating into random chaos. Equally, by deliberately introducing a minimal threshold through, for example, teams, leaders can offset the chances of over-bureaucratic order. In so doing, rather than seeking to find an awkward balance between two forms of organizing, leaders can increase or decrease

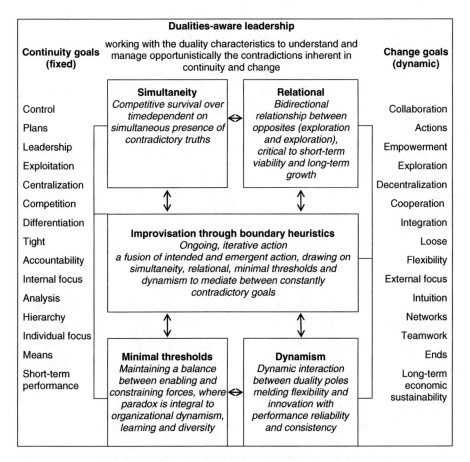

Figure 10.1 *Leading change toward sustainability: Arbitrating the continuity–change tension*

the levels of each type relative to situational contingencies. This is, of course, where the role of improvisation comes into play.

A simple example regarding the structure of office environments provides a useful illustration of how boundary heuristics can be employed. Haynes and Price (2004) showed that organizations with high levels of bureaucracy have high levels of order but low levels of connectivity between employees; a relationship underpinned by a closed, segmented and regimented office environment. On the other hand, open-plan office structures were correlated with high levels of inter-employee connectivity and low levels of order. Duality heuristics would encourage leaders to keep in mind that the best of both worlds is not necessarily a function of finding equilibrium somewhere in the middle where every employee gets an office with moveable partitions. Boundary heuristics would be used in this example by experimenting with the ideal of critical densities of each configuration. In the end, for example, Haynes and Price (2004) observed that it is desirable to find a tension between the 'frozen' order of walls and doors and the 'erratic' stimulation of interruption and distraction. Instead of a compromise with a little of each, the best approach came with the informal connectivity of both walls and interruption, encouraged by some guidelines that maintained boundaries (and precluded continuous interruption), but also allowed for emergent interaction. From the viewpoint of duality theory, office structure is 'synchronistic' in that the two conditions (solitude and interaction, or in metaphoric terms, stability and change) connect through a random factor generated as a consequence of the iteration of simple heuristics.

Boundary heuristics can provide guidance one step removed from operational activity and therefore be less likely to be obstructed by contextual variables. The practical implication is that change leaders have a deliberate tool of improvisation by manipulating boundaries. In some cases, the combination of a minimal threshold, simultaneity and dynamism means that leaders seek to introduce destabilizing influences or order-infusing mechanisms depending on the circumstances. Research in group dynamics has revealed, for example, that formal structures set around work teams prior to their formation can be particularly helpful in ensuring high levels of both creativity and focus (Okhuysen and Eisenhardt, 2002). Boundary heuristics such as these operate a little like Grint's (1998) notion of 'strange attractors', which act to pull a system back toward dynamic equilibrium. While the price for reaching the destination is uncertainty about the nature of the journey (Stacey, 1996), boundary heuristics offer a mechanism for enabling dualities to work through leadership improvisation.

Figure 10.1 highlights dualities that can be stimulated by observing the characteristics, and manipulated through improvisation around boundary heuristics. For example, consider the duality Fixed/Dynamic where the presence of a duality implies that both poles are represented, and that the opportunity to pivot around both is critical to success. When a CEO deliberately fails to provide senior management with any plans other than a broad vision in the hope that it will stimulate their own strategic imagination, he or she is providing a boundary heuristic governing several dualities including Plans/Actions and Centralization/Decentralization.

Boundary heuristics can amplify the properties of a duality. For example, a simple heuristic establishing one hierarchical relationship in an organization can also liberate all other relationships as well. To illustrate, if the CEO of a small firm is the only real 'boss' to whom performance is reported, then there are no obstructions to the evolution of cross-functional teams and networks. Similarly, rules establishing broad objectives but without clarifying specific methods or mechanisms, while contrary to conventional strategic planning wisdom, can stimulate emergent and innovative solutions. Dualities can be pursued with boundary heuristics which set strict guidelines that cannot be exceeded, but simultaneously allow many possibilities within their confines. The limitation for most leaders is that it may be easier to create new activities on one side of the dualities ledger than on the other. Goals, budgets and definitive reporting relationships are simple and uncontroversial to introduce. Fewer managers would be prepared to create project teams, informal groups and allow resources to be deployed without careful approval. If organizational innovation needs flexibility and a critical mass of connective density between responsible employees and managers, then the minimal threshold for cross-functional groups, ad-hoc meetings, task teams and other informal mechanisms that encourage unpredictability, needs to be developed.

Managers cannot control organizations the same way that an operator can control a machine made of moving but inanimate parts. This means that it might be more effective for leaders to encourage dualities and help establish boundary heuristics, but to remain less involved in operational activities. Excessive rules to help employees problem-solve can communicate that they are considered incapable of solving problems, and can lead to a workforce averse to thinking for itself and initiating innovative solutions. Equally, the complete absence of rules implicitly abandons the need for any kind of efficiency and planning toward pre-determined goals. However, dualities imply that there is greater potential for emergent creativity and innovation when they are as close to disorder as they are from order. The minimal threshold comes about in the achievement of goals within order-generating rules.

Dualities theory illustrates how tensions are managed not through definitive resolution toward one pole or the other, but through the application of boundary heuristics that establish a broad conforming imperative while opening up enabling mechanisms. The concept also reinforces the need to discard assumptions about opposing values, instead replacing them with an appreciation of complementary concepts.

The change–continuity and accountability–flexibility tensions do not need to be interpreted as unidimensional choices. Flexibility might be essential in a turbulent environment in order to find new paths to innovation, but order is also necessary to ensure that innovation is focused and relevant.

Sustainable change and ethics: a new kind of tension

We have argued that a dualities approach requires an unusual level of comfort with tension and ambiguity. In fact, the acceptance of dualities implies that avoiding decisions that decrease or resolve tension could undermine innovative, non-additive behaviour emerging from interactive networks. Controlling all the inputs does not necessarily lead to the best outputs. However, uncertainty introduces complications for managing change ethically, where conventional black and white positions about behaviour fit uncomfortably with notions of tension and ambiguity. While some behaviours will always remain unethical and unacceptable, such as deception or financial impropriety, we suggest that sustainable change also benefits from some tension around ethical decision-making. We take the view that opportunities for organizational learning can be stimulated by the ethical tensions that envelop pivotal change decisions. For example, conventional change leads to difficult choices where jobs may be lost, or employees are subjected to traumatic events. In contrast, leading change through dualities management takes a more sustainable approach because change emerges naturally from the tension, rather than being imposed from the top down.

Dualities operate between predictability and non-predictability, a position sometimes described as the 'edge of chaos'. Here, enough chaos or unpredictability ensures that definitive causality is elusive, but also enough order or predictability exists for consistent patterns to endure. The opportunity with 'edge of chaos' tension lies with undetectable variations that can lead to novel outcomes. New and unimagined properties can emerge leading to new directions. If organizations under duality tensions operate as complex systems, the devolution of ethical choices is inevitable. Employees under a dualities framework will work in 'loose/tight' structures with only general structural boundaries. Change leaders can not hope to exercise full control over the behaviour of their employees and, when they try, confronting ethical choices have to be made. In any case, the outcome will be an equilibrium point where ongoing change must overcome an entrenched inertia.

Leaders cannot control organizations that comprise people the same way that an operator can control a machine made of moving but inanimate parts. This means that it might be more effective for change leaders to define the parameters of ethical business, but remain less involved in the operational choices. Indeed, it might be dangerous for change leaders to make decisions based upon linear assumptions about what is uniformly right or wrong.

The assumption that strict governance policies lead to high levels of organizational ethics does not hold. For example, excessive rules to guide ethical problem-solving communicates that employees are considered incapable of being ethical. More rules can lead to a workforce averse to thinking independently and incapable of initiating innovative solutions. The tensions that accompany dualities encourage employees to find new ways of navigating problems that if unsolved will eventually force change leaders to make black or white decisions. Heuristics can work with ethical boundaries to allow the space for adaptive tension to resolve problems before they reach a level where a top-down, tension-breaking mandate throws the baby out with the bath water.

In some organizations tacit ethical frameworks can evolve emergently through cultural forces and lead to further unconventional networks encouraging innovation. As we have suggested, a dualities model assumes that organizations offer greater potential for emergent creativity and innovation when there is a tension between uncertainty and certainty, which only arises when both poles are pursued. Such adaptive tension transpires when a critical mass of both rules and freedom become part of a sustainable approach to change.

Duality thinking helps to sidestep causal thinking about ethical judgements during organizational change. We think that a dualities change management philosophy allows some room for experimentation and the potential emergence of genuine innovation that cannot be forced or prescribed through didactic, top-down ethical rules.

Conclusion

It is clear that traditional, positivist approaches that view organizational change as a passing irritation that can be resolved by charismatic leadership have no conception of the 'unfolding, emergent qualities' of change (Tsoukas and Chia, 2002:568), or of the complex, competing dynamics which confront organization leaders. Case analyses reveal that successful organizational change generally defies attempts at linear, prescriptive logic. It is never simple and straightforward, but rather a messy, sometimes emergent and typically uncertain process occurring within a complex and contradictory 'living' social system. Recognizing the dualistic forces that naturally exist in organizations represents *the* leadership imperative in the age of sustainability. Ironically, long-term economic sustainability starts with short-term dynamism.

We have sought to develop a dualities-sensitive framework to enhance change leaders' ease with the tensions and ambiguities that accompany the management of continuity and change. As Figure 1 illustrated, a dualities-aware perspective makes explicit competing continuity–change goals. In turn, the interacting, iterative nature of duality characteristics shows where complementarities flourish within contradictions. Paradox and ambiguity mean healthy sites for innovation and change.

Twenty-first-century leaders must confront a complex, turbulent and global environment characterized by flux but demanding constancy. The traditional, rational decision-making approach to change leadership that insists on an 'either/or' resolution, fails in the dynamic melting pot of competing demands. Organizations face contradictory directives where long-term survival relies on embracing and exploiting tension. A dualities-aware perspective helps change leaders to understand the fundamental interdependence and mutually enabling qualities of dualities. Change and continuity, innovation and efficiency, collaboration and competition, freedom and accountability, and new and old all represent dynamic tensions. Dualities also introduce the relevance of other dual forms of organizing and structuring such as top-down leadership and bottom-up empowerment, teamwork and strong individuals, centralization and decentralization, differentiation and integration. Understandably, some leaders may reject one approach for the other because they seem to represent diametrically opposed positions. However, as organizational boundaries blur and environmental turbulence becomes the norm, responsible leaders need to manage 'loose/tight' relationships by establishing structures that enhance flexibility and responsiveness within a strong risk and performance management framework. Organizational growth and long-term economic sustainability mean finding a balance between order and disorder. We believe the five duality characteristics offer change leaders a rich and powerful medium for managing organizational dualities as 'complementary contradictions' that provide the stimulus for organizational renewal in the age of sustainability.

References

Abernathy, W. J. (1978) *The Productivity Dilemma: Roadblock to Innovation in the Automobile Industry* (Baltimore: John Hopkins University Press).

Cameron, K. S. (1986) Effectiveness as paradox: Consensus and conflict in conceptions of organizational effectiveness, *Management Science*, 32(5), 539–553.

Cameron, K. S. and Quinn, R. E. (1988) Organizational paradox and transformation, in: R. E. Quinn and K. S. Cameron (eds) *Paradox and Transformation: Toward a Theory of Change in Organization and Management* (Cambridge, Massachusetts: Ballinger Publishing).

Clegg, S. R., da Cunha, J. V. and e Cunha, M. P. (2002) Management paradoxes: A relational view, *Human Relations*, 55(3), 483–503.

Davis, J. P., Eisenhardt, K. M. and Bingham, C. B. (2009) Optimal structure, market dynamism, and the strategy of simple rules, *Administrative Science Quarterly,* 54, 413–452.

Deephouse, D. L. (1999) To be different, or to be the same? It's a question (and theory) of strategic balance, *Strategic Management Journal*, 20, 147–166.

Evans, P. A. L. (1992) Balancing continuity and change: the constructive tension in individual and organizational development, in: W. Bennis, R. O. Mason and I. I. Mitroff (eds) *Executive and Organizational Continuity: Managing the Paradoxes of Stability and Change* (San Francisco: Jossey-Bass Publishers).

Evans, P. A. L. (1999) HRM on the edge: A duality perspective, *Organization*, 6(2), 325–338.

Evans, P. A. L. and Doz, Y. (1992) Dualities: A paradigm for human resource and organizational development in complex multinationals, in: Vladimir N. Pucik, N. M. Tichy and C. K. Barnett (eds), *Globalizing Management: Creating and Leading the Competetive Organization* (New York: Wiley), 85–106.

Evans, P. A. L., Pucik, V. and Barsoux, J. L. (2002) *The Global Challenge: Frameworks for International Human Resource Management* (New York: McGraw-Hill/Irwin).

Farjoun, M. (2010) Beyond dualism: Stability and change as a duality, *Academy of Management Review*, 35(2), 202–225.

Ford, J. D. and Backoff, R. W. (1988) Organizational change in and out of dualities and paradox, in: R. E. Quinn and K. S. Cameron (eds), *Paradox and Transformation: Toward a Theory of Change in Organization and Management* (Cambridge, Massachusetts: Ballinger Publishing Company).

Galunic, D. C. and Eisenhardt, K. M. (2001) Architectural innovation and modular corporate forms, *The Academy of Management Journal*, 44(6), 1229–1249.

Giddens, A. (1984) *The Constitution of Society: Outline of the Theory of Structuration* (Cambridge: Polity Press).

Graetz, F. and Smith, A. (2008) The role of dualities in arbitrating continuity and change in forms of organizing, *International Journal of Management Reviews*, 10(3), 265–280.

Grint, K. (1998) Determining the indeterminacies of change, *Management Decision*, 36(8), 503–508.

Haynes, B. and Price, I. (2004) Quantifying the complex adaptive workplace, *Facilities*, 22(1/2), 8–18.

He, Z.-L. and Wong, P.-K. (2004) Exploration vs. exploitation: An empirical test of the ambidexterity hypothesis, *Organization Science*, 15(4), 481–494.

Hedberg, B. L. T., Nystrom, P. C. and Starbuck, W. H. (1976) Camping on seesaws: Prescriptions for a self designing organization, *Administrative Science Quarterly*, 21, 41–65.

Jackson, W. A. (1999) Dualism, duality and the complexity of economic institutions, *International Journal of Social Economics*, 26(4), 545–558.

Johnston, S. and Selsky, J. W. (2006) Duality and paradox: Trust and duplicity in Japanese business practice, *Organization Studies*, 27(2), 183–205.

Katz, D. and Kahn, R. L. (1966) *The Social Psychology of Organizations* (New York: Wiley).

Lado, A. A., Boyd, N. G. and Hanlon, S. S. (1997) Competition, cooperation and the search for economic rents: A syncretic model, *Academy of Management Review*, 22(1), 110–141.

Lawrence, P. R. and Lorsch, J. W. (1967) Differentiation and integration in complex organizations, *Administrative Science Quarterly*, 1–47.

Leana, C. R. and Barry, B. (2000) Stability and change as simultaneous experiences in organizational life, *Academy of Management Review*, 25(4), 753–759.

Lewis, M. W. (2000) Exploring paradox: Toward a more comprehensive guide. *Academy of Management Review*, 25(4), 760–776.

Limerick, D. and Cunnington, B. (1993) *Managing the New Organisation* (Sydney: Business & Professional Publishing).

Luscher, L. S. and Lewis, M. E. (2008) Organizational change and managerial sensemaking: Working through paradox, *Academy of Management Journal*, 51(2), 221–240.

Macintosh, R. and Maclean, D. (2001) Conditioned emergence: Researching change and changing research, *International Journal of Operations and Production Management*, 21(10), 1343–1357.

March, J. G. (1991) Exploration and exploitation in organizational learning, *Organization Science*, 2(1), 71–87.

Okhuysen, G. A. and Eisenhardt, K. M. (2002) Integrating knowledge in groups: How formal interventions enable flexibility, *Organization Science*, 13(4), 370–386.

O'Reilly, C. A. and Tushman, M. L. (2004) The ambidextrous organization, *Harvard Business Review*, April, 74–81.

Pascale, R. T. (1990) *Managing on the Edge: How Successful Companies Use Conflict to Stay Ahead* (New York: Viking Penguin).

Pettigrew, A. M. and Fenton, E. M. (2000) Complexities and dualities in innovative forms of organizing, in: A. M. Pettigrew and E. M. Fenton (eds) *The Innovative Organization*, 279–300 (London: Sage).

Pettigrew, A. M., Whittington, R. L., Melin, L., Sanchez-Runde, C., Van Den Bosch, F. A. J., Ruigrok *et al.*, T. (2003) *Innovative Forms of Organizing* (London: Sage).

Raisch, S., Birkinshaw, J., Probst, G. and Tushman, M. L. (2009) Organizational ambidexterity: Balancing exploitation and exploration for sustained performance, *Organization Science*, 20(4), 685–695.

Schumacher, E. F. (1977) *A Guide for the Perplexed* (New York: Harper and Row).

Seo, M.-G., Putnam, L. L. and Bartunek, J. M. (2004) Dualities and tensions of planned organizational change, in: M. S. Poole and A. H. Van de Ven, (eds) *Handbook of Organizational Change and Innovation* (Oxford: Oxford University Press), 73–107.

Smith, W. K. and Tushman, M. L. (2005) Managing strategic contradictions: A top management model for managing innovation streams, *Organization Science*, 16(5), 522–536.

Stacey, R. (1996) Emerging strategies for a chaotic environment, *Long Range Planning*, 29(2), 182–189.

Sundaramurthy, C. and Lewis, M. (2003) Control and collaboration: Paradoxes of governance, *Academy of Management Review*, 28(3), 397–415.

Tsoukas, H. and Chia, R. (2002) On organizational becoming: Rethinking organizational change, *Organization Science*, 13(5), 567–582.

Van de Ven, A. H. and Poole, M. S. (1988) Paradoxical requirements for a theory of organizational change, in: R. E. Quinn and K. S. Cameron (eds) *Paradox and Transformation: Toward a Theory of Change in Organization and Management* (Cambridge, Massachusetts: Ballinger Publishing Company).

Van de Ven, A. H. and Poole, M. S. (2005) Alternative approaches for studying organizational change, *Organization Studies*, 26(9), 1377–1404.

Weick, K. E. (1998) Improvisation as a mindset for organizational analysis, *Organization Science*, 9(5), 543–555.

Part V
Conclusions

11 Looking back to move forward

Bernard Burnes

Introduction

It is a commonly accepted view that the key role of leaders is to bring about change (Bass and Riggio, 2006; Yukl, 2010). This has given credence to the transformational-charismatic approach to leadership, which in many instances appears to have offered leaders an almost free hand to change their organizations as they see fit (Barker, 2001; Bones, 2011; Storey, 2004). As the previous chapters in this book have shown, this has not always been a good thing; there has been a tendency for many leaders to put their own interests above those of other stakeholders, sometimes to disastrous effect. Consequently, as Burnes and By (2011) have recently argued, a leader's ability to achieve beneficial outcomes for all stakeholders is inextricably linked to their own ethical values. Burnes and By (2011) also argued that some approaches to change are more likely to lead to ethical outcomes than others. Certainly, over the last 20 years or so, there has been a great deal of attention paid to the use of power, politics and manipulation to gain compliance when attempting to bring about change, usually to the detriment of those who have to experience the change (Burnes, 2009b). Therefore, if the changes that leaders bring about are to benefit all stakeholders, then not only do leaders have to pursue ethical outcomes, but they also need to adopt an approach to change that is based on ethical values. After all, it is difficult to see how ethical ends can be achieved by unethical means.

Hence , what is called for is not just an ethical approach to leadership, but also an ethical approach to change. At first glance, this might appear to make the job of developing and promoting an ethical approach to leadership even more difficult. However, we would argue that rather than being more difficult, it becomes easier because an ethical approach to change already exists and has been around for over 70 years, that is, Kurt Lewin's Planned

Approach to Change. This concluding chapter will review the ethical basis of Lewin's approach and argue that in order to move forward, the debate on ethical leadership needs to look backward. The chapter begins by briefly reviewing the ethical challenge faced by organizations. It then examines the work of Lewin and shows how this relates to both ethical change and ethical leadership. Following on from this, we show how Lewin's worked formed the basis of Organization Development (OD). The chapter concludes by arguing that Lewin's work provides the basis for tackling the ethical challenges that organizations and their leaders face.

The ethical challenge

The *Oxford Dictionary of English* (2006:595) defines ethics as 'moral principles that govern a person's behaviour or the conducting of an activity'. In organizational terms, ethics are beliefs about what is right or wrong, they provide a basis for judging the appropriateness or not of behaviour and they guide people in their dealings with other individuals, groups and organizations (Jones *et al.*, 2000). Since the early 1980s, and especially after the 2008 credit crunch, there has been a growing movement to put ethics at the centre of organizational life (Gopalakrishnan *et al.*, 2008; Porter, 2008; Stiglitz, 2010). However, though often driven by financial scandals, the promotion of ethics is not just about promoting financial propriety. As Dunphy *et al.* (2007) argue, environmental sustainability – the future of the planet – requires organizations to adopt a more ethical approach to managing their businesses. In particular, they have to move from:

- doing the minimum the law requires to doing the right thing in terms of the environment;
- downplaying public concerns to identifying and addressing those concerns; and
- ignoring or fighting environmental advocates to seeking to work with them.

Whilst it is relatively easy to produce such lists of ethical behaviours, the ability of leaders to ensure such behaviours are carried out is often limited by other factors. Deresky (2000:56) points out that:

Managers today are usually quite sensitive to issues of social responsibility and ethical behavior because of pressure from the public, from interest groups, from legal and government concerns, and from media coverage. It is less clear where to draw the line between socially responsible behaviour and the corporation's other concerns, or between the conflicting expectations of ethical behaviour among different countries.

In an attempt to overcome such conflicts, some organizations have adopted the 'triple bottom line' approach, that is, they seek to measure and balance the financial, social and environmental consequences of their operations (Savitz and Weber, 2006). Whilst this approach highlights the need to take account of wider ethical considerations, it does not indicate how leaders should resolve such ethical dilemmas and conflicts. To address this point, Peale and Blanchard (2000), in their book *The Power of Ethical Management*, suggest that managers need to ask themselves three questions when making decisions:

- **Is it legal?** In other words, will you be breaking a law or company policies by engaging in this activity?
- **Is it balanced?** Is it fair to all parties concerned both in the short term as well as the long term?
- **Is it right?** How does this decision make you feel about yourself? Are you proud of yourself for making this decision? Would you like others to know you made the decision you did?

However, whilst this approach is valuable when an individual is faced with an ethical decision which they recognize as such and have the power and inclination to influence, this may not always or even often be the case in organizations. Regardless of an individual's propensity to act in a particular way, once they are a member of an organization, they are also heavily influenced by the norms and values of that organization, which may push them in a different direction to which their conscience might dictate (Burnes and James, 1995; Burnes and Jackson, 2011; Kotter and Heskett, 1992).

These values form the core, the foundation, of an organization's culture (Schein, 1985; Cummings and Worley, 2005). Consequently, an organization's ethics are embedded in its culture and its culture is reflected in its ethics. Therefore, expecting to change the norms of behaviour in an organization by adopting new policies or asking individuals to address three questions, powerful though they are, seems somewhat over-optimistic (Amis *et al.*, 2002; Fox-Wolfgramm *et al.*, 1998; Kabanoff *et al.*, 1995; Scott, 2002). If we could change the behaviour of individuals, groups and organizations by adopting new rules or appealing to their common decency, motorists would not speed, companies would not exploit child labour and Bernard Madoff's clients would not be wondering where their money went.

As Lewin (1943a and b) showed, the behaviour of individuals in organizations tends to be determined by the values of the primary group to which they are a member and, therefore, if one seeks to promote ethical behaviour, it is group rather than individual values that need to be changed. Lewin and many others have also shown that for behaviour change to be successful, those concerned have to be able to adopt the changes of their own volition (Bruch and Ghoshal, 2004; Burnes, 2009a; Kegan and Lahey, 2001; Lewin, 1947a; Schein, 1996; Sniehotta *et al.*, 2005). Unfortunately, since the early 1980s, governments and international bodies have attempted to get organizations to behave more ethically through compulsion in the form of increased regulations which by themselves, as successive financial scandals have shown, do not seem to have been particularly successful (Stiglitz, 2010). In the same period, the management of change in organizations has become focused on approaches that emphasize the deployment of power and politics in order to force compliance (Burnes, 2011; Collins, 1998; Hendry, 1996). As a result, it is not perhaps surprising that attempts to promote ethical behaviour in organizations seem to have failed in many cases. Instead of attempting to change behaviour by imposition and coercion, what is required is an approach to change that promotes ethical behaviour and allows those concerned to change of their own free will. This is, of course, what Kurt Lewin's Planned Approach to Change was designed to do.

Kurt Lewin: ethics, leadership and change

As Edgar Schein (1988:239) commented, 'There is little question that the intellectual father of contemporary theories of applied behavioural science, action research and planned change is Kurt Lewin.' Lewin's seminal work on leadership and planned change, which took place in the 1930s and 1940s, has been a dominant force in the study and practice of organizational change ever since (Boje *et al.*, 2011; Burnes, 2007). However, Lewin's primary interest was not in organizational change per se, but in resolving social conflict and promoting ethical leadership through behavioural change, whether within organizations or in the wider society. Underpinning Lewin's work was a strong ethical belief in the importance of democratic institutions and democratic participation and values in society. Lewin was a Jew who left Germany in 1933 to escape the rise of Hitler. Tragically, many of his family, including his mother, were not so lucky and died in the holocaust (Burnes, 2004b; Marrow, 1969). Lewin believed that only by strengthening democratic participation in all aspects of life and being able to resolve social conflicts could the scourge of despotism, authoritarianism and racism be effectively countered.

Two events in 1939 laid the basis of Lewin's Planned Approach to Change: the publication of Lewin's work on the impact of different leadership styles on children's behaviour; and the beginning of his involvement with the Harwood Manufacturing Corporation (Burnes, 2009a).

The first of these, Lewin's leadership research, was based on classic laboratory experiments. Three groups of teenagers were exposed to three different styles of leadership: autocratic, laissez faire and democratic. The results showed that the two groups that operated under autocratic and laissez faire leadership behaved in a dysfunctional manner. However, the group that operated under democratic leadership behaved in a co-operative and effective manner (Lewin *et al.*, 1939). This confirmed Lewin's belief that democratic leadership – participative management – was the most effective way of managing groups and changing group behaviour (Lewin, 1943a and b). It also showed that before leaders attempted to change other people's behaviour, they needed to consider the appropriateness of their own behaviour. As Zimmerman (1978) pointed out, modern concepts of participative management stem from Lewin's work.

The second event, the beginning of Lewin's work with the Harwood Manufacturing Corporation, allowed Lewin to move from the laboratory to the workplace and to show that participative leadership could be applied and succeed in the real world (Burnes, 2007). The importance of the Harwood studies was noted by Dent (2002:272):

> Although this comprehensive effort is much less well-known than the Hawthorne studies, the research which came out of it has perhaps had a greater impact on group decision-making processes, self-management, leadership development, meeting management, stereotyping and resistance to change, among others.

Burnes's (2007) review of Lewin's work at Harwood supports Dent's claim that it constitutes a milestone in the practice of organizational change. Harwood became the arena where Lewin developed, tested and proved Planned Change, and as such laid the foundations of Organization Development (OD). Though the origins of modern industrial-organizational society can be traced to the British Industrial Revolution of the late eighteenth century, it was only in the 1940s through the work of Kurt Lewin and his Planned Approach that a fully fledged change theory emerged (Burnes, 2004b).

Planned change comprises four elements:

- **Field theory:** Lewin maintained that for group behaviour to change, it was necessary to 'unfreeze' the forces restraining change, such as personal defences or group norms (Weick and Quinn, 1999). Field Theory is an approach to understanding group behaviour by identifying and mapping the totality and complexity of the field in which the behaviour takes place (Back, 1992).
- **Group dynamics:** Lewin was the first psychologist to write about 'group dynamics' and the importance of the group in shaping the behaviour of its members (Allport, 1948; Bargal *et al.*, 1992). Group Dynamics stresses that group behaviour, rather than that of individuals, should be the main focus of change (Bernstein, 1968; Dent and Goldberg, 1999). Lewin (1947b) maintained that it is fruitless to concentrate on changing the behaviour of individuals because the individual in isolation is constrained by group pressures to conform. Consequently, the focus of change must be at the group level and should concentrate on factors such as group norms, roles, interactions and socialization processes to create 'disequilibrium' and change (Schein, 1988).
- **Action research:** Lewin conceived of Action Research as a two-pronged process which, firstly, emphasizes that change requires action, and is directed at achieving this, and secondly, it recognizes that successful action is based on everyone involved analysing the situation correctly, identifying all the possible alternative solutions and choosing the one most appropriate to the situation at hand (Bennett, 1983).
- **Three-step model:** This is often cited as Lewin's key contribution to organizational change. The three steps in the model are:

  o *Unfreezing*: Lewin believed that the stability of human behaviour was based on a quasi-stationary equilibrium supported by a complex field of driving and restraining forces, hence his development of Field Theory. Lewin argued that the equilibrium (the forces of inertia) needs to be destabilized (unfrozen) before old behaviour can be discarded (unlearnt) and new behaviour successfully adopted.
  o *Moving*: As Schein (1996:32) notes, unfreezing is not an end in itself; it '. . . creates motivation to learn but does not necessarily control or predict the direction of learning.' This echoes Lewin's view that any attempt to predict or identify a specific outcome from Planned Change is very difficult because of the complexity of the forces concerned. Instead, one should seek to take into account all the forces

at work and identify and evaluate, on a trial and error basis, all the available options (Lewin, 1947a). This is, of course, the learning approach promoted by Action Research.

o *Refreezing*: This is the final step in the Three-Step Model. Refreezing seeks to stabilize the group at a new quasi-stationary equilibrium in order to ensure that the new behaviours are relatively safe from regression.

It needs to be recognized that when he developed the Three-Step Model, Lewin intended it to be used separately from the other three elements that comprise Planned Change (i.e. Field Theory, Group Dynamics and Action Research). Rather, Lewin saw the four concepts as forming an integrated approach to analysing, understanding and bringing about change, whether it be in organizations or in society at large.

Lewin argued that for change to be successful, though, there has to be a 'felt-need' (Alavi and Henderson, 1981). Felt-need is an individual's inner realization that change is necessary. If felt-need is low, introducing change becomes problematic. Felt-need can only arise if individuals and groups are given the opportunity to reflect on and learn about their own situation, and change of their own volition (Burnes, 2004b: Lewin, 1947a). Lewin did not believe that people could be tricked or coerced into change. Instead, he advocated a participative, open and ethical change process. His approach was greatly influenced by the work of the Gestalt-Field theorists, who believe that successful change requires a process of learning (Lewin, 1942; Rock and Palmer, 1990). This allows those involved to gain or change insights, outlooks, expectations and thought patterns. This approach seeks to provide change adopters with an opportunity to 'reason out' their situation and develop their own solutions (Bigge, 1982). Therefore, for Lewin, the change process is fundamentally a learning process. It is an iterative, cyclical, process involving diagnosis, action and evaluation, and further action and evaluation. It recognizes that once change has taken place, it must be self-sustaining (i.e. safe from regression).

Though Lewin's original purpose was to develop an approach to change capable of resolving social conflict in society, he also saw the benefits it could bring to organizations (Burnes, 2007). In organizational terms, the focus of the Planned Approach is on improving the effectiveness of the human side of the organization. Central to the approach is the emphasis placed on the collaborative nature of the change effort: the organization, both leaders and recipients of change, and the change agent jointly diagnose the organization's problems, and jointly plan and design the specific changes required. Underpinning Planned Change is a strong humanist and democratic orientation based on Lewin's own personal beliefs and his work on participative management (Lewin *et al.*, 1939). Marching hand in hand with this humanist and democratic orientation was the development of a host of tried and tested tools and techniques for promoting group participation and change.

From planned change to organization development

After Lewin's death in 1947, his work was further developed and provided the inspiration and core approaches for the OD movement, which emerged in the 1950s (Cummings and Worley, 2005; French, 1982). The crucial link between the two was Lewin's work with the Connecticut Interracial Commission, who in 1946 asked him to organize a training workshop for community leaders to enable them to deal more effectively with racial and religious prejudice (Marrow, 1969). Lewin saw this as an opportunity to put his democratic-humanist values into practice and also to conduct field research on group dynamics (Bradford, 1967).

The resultant workshop, which took place in New Britain, Connecticut, has become famous in the annals of behavioural science and can claim to have laid the foundations for OD (Burnes, forthcoming; Highhouse, 2007; Rogers, 1970). It was led by Kurt Lewin, Kenneth Benne, Leland Bradford and Ronald Lippitt (French, 1982). Benne (1976:28) described it as 'a project in cooperative action research' which was based on Lewin's previous research. What emerged from New Britain was both an approach to change – T-groups, and an organization for promoting that approach – the National Training Laboratories Institute (NTL) (Freedman, 1999).

The original T-groups were unstructured, agendaless groups of strangers who, working with trained facilitators, would learn from their own interactions and the evolving dynamics of the group (French, 1982). The original idea was to use such groups to explore the feelings and attitudes of the participants in order for them to understand and reflect on their behaviour in the 'here and now' and so improve their interpersonal skills in order to bring about change in their 'back home' situations (Bradford *et al.*, 1964). T-groups emerged from the New Britain workshop when the group members, almost accidentally, started to provide feedback to each other on their attitudes and behaviours (Benne, 1964; French and Bell, 1990). This evolved into a method by which individuals could gain personal insight into themselves and how their behaviour impacted on others (French, 1982). In essence, this was an extension of Lewin's earlier work, which showed that leaders often needed to change their behaviour before they could change other people's behaviour. In passing, we can also note that it shows some remarkable similarities with the modern concept of emotional intelligence (Sosik and Megerian, 1999).

Though T-groups dominated the practice of OD up to the end of the 1960s, the other two core aspects of OD were also growing in popularity, that is, Planned Change/Action Research and participative management. All three stemmed from Lewin's work. However, Lewin's influence on OD went beyond providing its core practices; he also provided the humanistic values that underpin it (Burnes, 2004b, 2007; French and Bell, 1995). These values have been articulated by many writers over the years (Conner, 1977; French and Bell, 1999; Gellerman *et al.*, 1990; Warwick and Thompson, 1980). One of the earliest attempts was by French and Bell (1973), who identified four core values of OD:

- The belief that the needs and aspirations of human beings provide the prime reasons for the existence of organizations within society.
- Change agents believe that organizational prioritization is a legitimate part of organizational culture.
- Change agents are committed to increased organizational effectiveness.
- OD places a high value on the democratization of organizations through power equalization.

In a later survey of OD practitioners, Hurley *et al.* (1992) found these values were clearly reflected in the five main approaches they used in their work:

- Empowering employees to act.
- Creating openness in communications.
- Facilitating ownership of the change process and its outcomes.
- The promotion of a culture of collaboration.
- The promotion of continuous learning.

In the years since its creation, OD has broadened out its focus from group behaviour change to more organization-wide transformational approaches (Cummings and Worley, 1997; French and Bell, 1995) However, as Wooten and White (1999) argued, the core values of OD – equality, empowerment, consensus-building and horizontal relationships – are ones that are still relevant to the needs of contemporary organizations, especially in terms of their ethical implications.

Conclusion

From the 1980s onward, successive American administrations have attempted to clean up Wall Street and have palpably failed (Partnoy, 2003; Stiglitz, 2010). It is true that a few high-profile figures such as Michael Milken, Ivan Boesky, Jeffrey Skilling and Bernard Madoff have been jailed, and new ethical codes and financial regulations have been introduced. Nevertheless, as the events of 2008 showed, these did nothing to deter fraud on a truly gigantic scale (Porter, 2008; Tett, 2010). This confirms something that we have known for many years – threats and deterrents are by themselves inadequate methods for changing behaviour.

Lewin's approach to behavioural change is based on co-operation not coercion, and on democratic and open leadership rather imposition, manipulation and secrecy. He believed and demonstrated that successful behavioural change could be achieved, but only through a participative learning process where people changed of their own volition rather than by coercion or manipulation (Lewin, 1947a; Burnes, 2007; Wheeler, 2008). As others have shown subsequently, free will is enormously important in achieving change and this is unlikely to be present if those concerned feel that they have been tricked or forced to change (Festinger, 1957; Bennett, 1983; Schein, 1996; Elrod and Tippett, 2002; Makin and Cox, 2004). Central to Lewin's approach is its ability to explore and reveal the agendas, objectives and ethics of those involved. This open scrutiny ensures that individuals cannot seek to pursue their own interests to the detriment of other stakeholders. Therefore, rather than accepting organizations and society as they are, or seeing power concentration and unethical behaviours as immutable, Lewin's approach was designed to allow those concerned to meet as equals and bring such behaviours out into the open in order to challenge and change them. He believed and demonstrated that changing human behaviour, especially in its more unacceptable forms, such as racism, could be achieved. Consequently, Lewin offers us an optimistic view of human nature and the ability of human beings to create better organizations and build a better world. Furthermore, there is much evidence of the success of Lewin's approach in achieving sustained behavioural change (Burnes, 2007; Gallos, 2006; Macy and Izumi, 1993; Marrow, 1969; Robertson et al., 1993; Woodman et al., 2008).

Though it may surprise Lewin's critics, some of the newer and more radical perspectives on organizations and change appear to offer support to his view of democratic participation and organizational change (Burnes, forthcoming). For example, there are those in the postmodern-social constructionist camp who argue that a more open and democratic approach to change is both preferable and achievable. As Hatch (1997: 367–368) observed:

> In a socially constructed world, responsibility for environmental conditions lies with those who do the constructing. . . . This suggests at least two competing scenarios for organizational change. First, organization change can be a vehicle of domination for those who conspire to enact the world for others. . . . An alternative use of social constructionism is to create a democracy of enactment in which the process is made open and available to all. . . . such that we create opportunities for freedom and innovation rather than simply for further domination.

Similarly, Wooten and White (1999) argue that the core values of OD – equality, empowerment, consensus-building and horizontal relationships – are ones that are particularly relevant to the post-modern organization. From the complexity perspective there is an even more emphatic call for greater democracy and power equalization in all aspects of organizational life (Burnes, 2004a, 2005; Kiel, 1994; Bechtold, 1997; Jenner, 1998).

The world is changing and organizations must also change if they are to have a sustainable future. However, in seeking to replace unethical behaviour with ethical behaviour, governments, pressure groups and organizations may be condemning themselves to failure unless they also seek to promote an ethical approach to change. As argued in this chapter, Lewin developed such an approach – Planned Change – and it has a successful track record stretching back to the 1940s. Therefore, in order to move forward, organizations will need to look to the past and embrace the democratic-participatory leadership and change methods promoted by Lewin.

References

Alavi, M. and Henderson, J. (1981) An evolutionary strategy for implementing a decision support system. *Management Science*, 27 (11), 1309–1323.

Allport, G. W. (1948) Foreword. In: G. W. Lewin (ed): *Resolving Social Conflict.* London: Harper & Row.

Amis, J., Slack, T. and Hinings, C. R. (2002) Values and organizational change. *The Journal of Applied Behavioral Science*, 38 (4), 436–465.

Back, K. W. (1992) This business of topology. *Journal of Social Issues*, 48 (2), 51–66.

Bargal, D., Gold, M. and Lewin, M. (1992) Introduction. In: The heritage of Kurt Lewin. *Journal of Social Issues*, 48 (2), 3–13.

Barker, R. A. (2001) The nature of leadership. *Human Relations*, 54 (4), 469–494.

Bass, B. M. and Riggio, R. E. (2006) *Transformational Leadership*. Lawrence Mahwah, NJ: Erlbaum Associates.

Bechtold, B. L. (1997) Chaos theory as a model for strategy development. *Empowerment in Organizations*, 5 (4), 193–201.

Bemstein, L. (1968) *Management Development*. London: Business Books.

Benne, K. D. (1976) The process of re-education: An assessment of Kurt Lewin's views. *Group & Organization Management*, 1 (1), 26–42.

Bennett, R. (1983) Management research. *Management Development Series, 20*. Geneva: International Labour Office.

Bigge, L. M. (1982) *Learning Theories for Teachers*. Aldershot: Gower.

Boje, D., Burnes, B., and Hassard, J. (2011) *The Routledge Companion to Organizational Change*. London: Routledge.

Bones, C. (2011) *The Cult of the Leader: A Manifesto for More Authentic Business*. New York: Wiley.

Bradford, L. P. (1967) Biography of an institution. *Journal of Applied Behavioral Sciences*, 3 (2), 127–143.

Bradford, L. P., Gibb, J. R. and Benne, K. D. (1964) *T-Group Theory and Laboratory Method*. New York: Wiley.

Bruch, H. and Ghoshal, S. (2004) *A Bias for Action: How Effective Managers Harness Their Willpower, Achieve Results, and Stop Wasting Time*. Boston, MA: Harvard Business School Press.

Burnes, B. (2004a) Kurt Lewin and complexity theories: Back to the future? *Journal of Change Management*, 4 (4), 309–325.

Burnes, B. (2004b) Kurt Lewin and the planned approach to change: A re-appraisal. *Journal of Management Studies*, 41 (6), 977–1002.

Burnes, B. (2005) Complexity theories and organisational change. *International Journal of Management Reviews*, 7 (2), 73–90.

Burnes, B. (2007) Kurt Lewin and the Harwood studies: The foundations of OD. *Journal of Applied Behavioral Science*, 43 (2), 213–231.

Burnes, B. (2009a) *Managing Change* (fifth edition). London: FT/Prentice Hall.

Burnes, B. (2009b) Reflections: Ethics and organisational change – time for a return to Lewinian values. *Journal of Change Management*, 9 (4), 359–381.

Burnes, B. (2011) Understanding the emergent approach to change. In: D. Boje, B. Burnes and J. Hassard (eds), *The Routledge Companion to Organizational Change*. London: Routledge.

Burnes, B. (forthcoming) A critical review of organization development. In: S. Leonard, R. Lewis, A. Freedman and J. Passmore (eds), *The Wiley-Blackwell Handbook of the Psychology of Organizational Development and Leadership*. New York: Wiley-Blackwell.

Burnes, B. and By, R. T. (2011) Leadership and change: The case for greater ethical clarity. *Journal of Business Ethics* (published online 2 November 2011, DOI 10.1007/s10551–011–1088–2).

Burnes, B. and Jackson, P. (2011) Success and failure in organisational change: An exploration of values. *Journal of Change Management*, 11 (2), 133–162.

Burnes, B. and James, H. (1995) Culture, cognitive dissonance and the management of change. *International Journal of Operations and Production Management*, 15 (8), 14–33.

Collins, D. (1998) *Organizational Change*. London: Routledge.

Collins, D. (2008) Has Tom Peters lost the plot? A timely review of a celebrated management guru. *Journal of Organizational Change Management*, 21 (3), 315–334.

Conner, P. E. (1977) A critical enquiry into some assumptions and values characterizing OD. *Academy of Management Review*, 2 (1), 635–44.

Cummings, T. G. and Worley, C. G. (1997) *Organization Development and Change* (sixth edition). Cincinnati, OH: South-Western College Publishing.

Cummings, T. G. and Worley, C. G. (2005) *Organization Development and Change* (eighth edition). Cincinnati, OH: South-Western College Publishing.

Dent, E. B. (2002) The messy history of OB&D: How three strands came to be seen as one rope. *Management Decision*, 40, 266–280.

Dent, E. B. and Goldberg, S. G. (1999) Challenging resistance to change. *Journal of Applied Behavioral Science*, 35 (1), 25–41.

Deresky, H. (2000) *International Management: Managing Across Borders and Cultures* (third edition). Upper Saddle River, NY: Prentice Hall.

Dunphy, D., Griffiths, A. and Benn, S. (2007) *Organizational Change for Corporate Sustainability* (second edition). London: Routledge.

Elrod II, P. D. and Tippett, D. D. (2002) The 'Death Valley' of change. *Journal of Organizational Change Management*, 15 (3), 273–91.

Festinger, L. (1957) *The Theory of Cognitive Dissonance*. Stanford, CA: Stanford University Press.

Fox-Wolfgramm, S. J., Boal, K. B. and Hunt, J. G. (1998) Organizational adaptation to institutional change: A comparative study of first-order change in prospector and defender banks. *Administrative Science Quarterly*, 43, 87–126.

Freedman, A. (1999) The history of organization development and the NTL institute: What we have learned, forgotten and rewritten. *The Psychologist–Manager Journal*, 3 (2), 125–141.

French, W. L. (1982) The emergence and early history of organization development: With reference to influences on and interaction among some of the key actors. *Group & Organization Studies*, 7 (3), 261–278.

French, W. L. and Bell, C. H. (1973) *Organization Development*. Englewood Cliffs, NJ: Prentice Hall.

French, W. L. and Bell, C. H. (1990) *Organization Development* (fourth edition). Englewood Cliffs, NJ: Prentice Hall.

French, W. L. and Bell, C. H. (1995) *Organization Development* (fifth edition). Englewood Cliffs, NJ: Prentice Hall.

French, W. L. and Bell, C. H. (1999) *Organization Development* (sixth edition). Upper Saddle River, NJ: Prentice-Hall.

Gallos, J. V. (2006) (ed) *Organization Development: A Jossey-Bass Reader*. San Francisco: Jossey-Bass.

Gellerman, W., Frankel, M. S. and Ladenson, R. F. (1990) *Values and Ethics in*

Organizational and Human Systems Development: Responding to Dilemmas in Professional Life. San Francisco: Jossey-Bass.

Gopalakrishnan, S., Mangaliso, M. P. and Butterfield, D. A. (2008) Managing ethically in times of transformation challenges and opportunities. *Group & Organization Management*, 33 (6), 756–759.

Hatch, M. J. (1997) *Organization Theory: Modem, Symbolic and Postmodern Perspectives*. Oxford: Oxford University Press.

Hendry, C. (1996) Understanding and creating whole organizational change through learning theory. *Human Relations*, 49 (5), 621–41.

Highhouse, S. (2007) Applications of organizational psychology: Learning through failure or failure to learn? In: L. L. Koppes (Ed.), *Historical Perspectives in Industrial and Organizational Psychology*. Mahwah, NJ: Lawrence Erlbaum.

Hurley, R. F., Church, A., Burke, W. W. and Van Eynde, D. F. (1992) Tension, change and values in OD. *OD Practitioner*, 29, 1–5.

Jenner, R. A. (1998) Dissipative enterprises, chaos, and the principles of lean organizations. *Omega: International Journal of Management Science*, 26 (3), 397–407.

Jones, G. R., George, J. M. and Hill, C. W. L. (2000) *Contemporary Management* (second edition). Boston, MA: McGraw-Hill.

Kabanoff, B., Waldersee, R. and Cohen, M. (1995) Espoused values and organizational change themes. *Academy of Management Journal*, 38, 1075–1104.

Kegan, R. and Lahey, L. L. (2001) The real reason people won't change. *Harvard Business Review*, November, 85–92.

Kiel, L. D. (1994) *Managing Chaos and Complexity in Government*. San Francisco: Jossey-Bass.

Kotter, J. P. and Heskett, J. L. (1992) *Corporate Culture and Performance*. New York: Free Press.

Lewin, K. (1942) Field theory and learning. In: D. Cartwright (ed) (1952), *Field Theory in Social Science: Selected Theoretical Papers by Kurt Lewin*. London: Social Science Paperbacks.

Lewin, K. (1943a) Psychological ecology. In: D. Cartwright (ed) (1952), *Field Theory in Social Science: Selected Theoretical Papers by Kurt Lewin*. London: Social Science Paperbacks.

Lewin, K. (1943b) The special case of Germany. In: G. W. Lewin and G. W. Allport (eds) (1948), *Resolving Social Conflict*. London: Harper & Row.

Lewin, K. (1947a) Frontiers in group dynamics. In: D. Cartwright (ed) (1952), *Field Theory in Social Science: Selected Theoretical Papers by Kurt Lewin*. London: Social Science Paperbacks.

Lewin, K. (1947b) Group decisions and social change. In: T M Newcomb and E. L. Hartley (eds) (1959), *Readings in Social Psychology*. New York: Henry Holt.

Lewin, K., Lippitt, R. and White, R. (1939) Patterns of aggressive behavior in experimentally created 'social climates'. *Journal of Social Psychology*, 10, 271–299.

Macy, B. A. and Izumi, H. (1993) Organizational change, design, and work innovation: A meta-analysis of 131 North American field studies 1961–1991. In: R. W. Woodman and W. A. Pasmore (eds), *Research in Organizational Change and Development*, 7, 235–313. Thousand Oaks, CA: Sage.

Makin, P. and Cox, C. (2004) *Changing Behaviour at Work: A Practical Guide*. London: Routledge.

Marrow, A. J. (1969) *The Practical Theorist: The life and Work of Kurt Lewin*. New York: Teachers College Press.

Oxford Dictionary of English (second edition) (2006) Oxford: Oxford University Press.

Peale, N. V. and Blanchard, K. (2000) *The Power of Ethical Management*. London: Vermilion.

Partnoy, F. (2003) When greed is fact and control is fiction. *The Guardian,* 14 February. Available at www.guardian.co.uk.

Porter, H. (2008) How did so many smart people get suckered by Bernard Madoff? *The Observer,* 21 December. Available at www.guardian.co.uk.

Robertson, P. J., Roberts, D. R. and Porras, J. I. (1993) Dynamics of planned organizational change: Assessing empirical support for a theoretical model. *The Academy of Management Journal*, 36 (3), 619–634.

Rock, I. and Palmer, S. (1990) The legacy of gestalt psychology. *Scientific American*, December, 48–61.

Rogers, C. R. (1970) *On Encounter Groups*. New York: Harper & Row.

Savitz, A. W. and Weber, K. (2006) *The Triple Bottom Line: How Today's Best-Run Companies Are Achieving Economic, Social and Environmental Success – and How You Can Too.* San Francisco: Jossey-Bass.

Schein, E. H. (1985) *Organizational Culture and Leadership: A Dynamic View*. San Francisco: Jossey-Bass.

Schein, E. H. (1988) *Organizational Psychology* (third edition). Englewood Cliffs, NJ: Prentice Hall.

Schein, E. H. (1996) Kurt Lewin's change theory in the field and in the classroom: notes towards a model of management learning. *Systems Practice*, 9 (1), 27–47.

Scott, E. D. (2002) Organizational moral values. *Business Ethics Quarterly*, 12 (1), 33–55.

Sniehotta, F. F., Scholz, U. and Schwarzer, R. (2005) Bridging the intention–behaviour gap: planning, self-efficacy, and action control in the adoption and maintenance of physical exercise. *Psychology and Health*, 20 (2), 143–160.

Sosik, J. J. and Megerian, L. E. (1999) Understanding leader emotional intelligence and performance: the role of self–other agreement in transformational leadership perceptions. *Group and Organization Management*, 24 (3), 367–90.

Stiglitz, J. (2010) *Freefall: Free Markets and the Sinking of the Global Economy*. London: Allen Lane.

Storey, J. (2004) Signs of change: 'Damned Rascals' and beyond. In: J. Storey (ed): *Leadership in Organizations: Current Issues and Key Trends*. London: Routledge.

Tett, G. (2010) *Fool's Gold: How Unrestrained Greed Corrupted a Dream, Shattered Global Markets and Unleashed a Catastrophe*. London: Abacus.

Warwick, D. P. and Thompson, J. T. (1980) Still crazy after all these years. *Training and Development Journal*, 34 (2), 16–22.

Weick, K. E. and Quinn, R. E. (1999) Organizational change and development. *Annual Review of Psychology*, 50, 361–386.

Wheeler, L. (2008) Kurt Lewin. *Social and Personality Psychology Compass*, 2 (4), 1638–1650.

Woodman, R. W., Bingham, J. B. and Yuan, F. (2008) Assessing organization development and change interventions. In: T. G. Cummings (ed): *Handbook of Organization Development*,. Thousand Oaks, CA: Sage, 187–215.

Wooten, K. C. and White, L. P. (1999) Linking OD's philosophy with justice theory: Postmodern implications. *Journal of Organizational Change Management*, 12 (1), 7–20.

Yukl, G. (2010) *Leadership in Organizations* (seventh edition). Upper Saddle River, NJ: Prentice Hall.

Zimmerman, K. D. (1978) Participative management: A reexamination of the classics. *Academy of Management Review*, 3, 896–901.

 **Index**